Gun Owner's Book of Care, Repair and Improvement

Gun Owner's Book of Care, Repair and Improvement

ROY DUNLAP

**WITH ILLUSTRATIONS
BY JIM CARMICHEL AND THE AUTHOR**

EDITORIAL SUPERVISION: WILLIAM B. SILL

Outdoor Life

Harper & Row
New York, Evanston, San Francisco, London

Library of Congress Catalog Number: 73-92404

Second Printing, 1974

Designed by: Howard S. Leiderman

Manufactured in the United States of America

Contents

PART II
Advanced Alterations and Repairs

Introduction

Why another book on gun care and repair, and why emphasis on the gun owner doing it? As the writer sees it, there exist today several genuine reasons, and tomorrow there will be more. Therefore, we will endeavor to cover in a practical and useful manner, the subjects of general care, normal maintenance, minor repair and general gunsmithing for all types of sporting firearms.

Every arms enthusiast soon finds himself doing or wanting to do more than just use his equipment, even if it is only refinishing a rifle stock, putting a lace-on pad to lengthen the pull on his shotgun or just screwing on a pair of big grips on the butt of his handgun. Something wants his personal touch, makes him want to improve, and no feeling is as good as the one of doing something yourself and having it prove out.

No one is completely immune from the do-it-yourself disease. Whether your name is Cabot or Cohen, whether you're a bookkeeper or a banker, you need to use your fingers for some accomplishment beyond your daily job. Those who refuse to acknowledge this need themselves sometimes end up with a doctor prescribing a ceramics class or the old basket-weaving bit. The growth of hobbies and do-it-yourself supply stores in the past decade hasn't been mass therapy, however, but rather a natural extension of what I call the manual urge.

Gun owners have always been ready to get their hands dirty, but the under-thirty-five generation does not have too much to start with, really. The new arms just don't need much alteration or work. The older man started with an ex-military rifle or clumsy shotgun, and almost any change he made was an improvement. So, he shortly found lots of work and discovered that working on his equipment as absorbing as using it. Usually he had a corner or a room or a basement that became a shop. What he couldn't pay a gunsmith to do he learned to do for himself. One young man sat on the bed of a rented room in Chicago using a pocketknife and a file to make a .22 rifle stock. Today, after making a thousand rifles and several thousand stocks, he's writing this book. He just didn't know when to stop!

The gun fancier of the future, and those in many localities today, faces a situation new to his world: a growing shortage of operating, competent, professional gunsmiths. To put it simply, the gunsmith is being forced out of business by the inflationary spiral. The small-shop man simply cannot make a livable year-around wage with normal gun work coming over the counter. Many have already been forced to quit, and almost no young man can afford to set up a shop and start in the profession, even though he may be well qualified.

The average layman has little idea of the costs of tools and tooling. My largest milling-machine *vise* alone now costs over $400, and $200 worth of carbide end-mills, needed to cut hardened or tough alloy steels, can be held easily in the palm of one hand. Equipping a professional shop requires at the minimum around $10,000 for complete tooling to do general all-around gunsmithing. And very little of this equipment can be had on time payments.

Let's say a man can make a start and get a shop and business going. If he makes $50 a day on his labor, works six days a week, takes no vacation and only three holidays off, he takes in $15,500 per year. Just about one-third of this will go for taxes and insurance; 15 percent—or more—of the remainder go for the light bill, the water bill, supply maintenance—cutting oil, tool replacements, sandpaper, etc.—all the miscellaneous dollar-users that are inevitable. He charged you nine dollars to put on a pair of target-scope bases? Did he mention that a bottoming tap broke in one hole? Three dollars gone, plus thirty minutes time. Or that when he tightened the scope mount to check fitting, the too-sharply cut detent in one base flaked off, and he had to put on another base? Two dollars more, wholesale, in the scrap box. Loss jobs like these occur often in busy shops. Our theoretical gunsmith ends up with perhaps $8,000 for a yearly income to live on, pay rent or a mortgage. You figure it out. With no paper work at night and fewer responsibilities, he can make a better living as a flagman on a construction site, and the only equipment he needs is a hardhat. Using his skills as a machinist or cabinetmaker, he's even further ahead of the game.

Gun repairmen will continue to exist, both professional and semiprofessional ex-smiths doing spare-time work apart from their now-steady jobs. Small-town and semirural men having low overhead and limited needs can continue gun work, but, if they expand to take in work from outside the immediate area by advertising and mail order, they fall to the system, too, unless they can charge prices high enough to make a profit.

The neighbor's boy was a whiz in his shop courses in high school, wants to stay at home and will work for $100 a week. That's $5,200 yearly. The little shop is paying twenty-five percent clear profit so he's hired. Now, the annual gross must instantly increase $20,000 per year just to pay the boy's salary. Will it go beyond that and make the expansion pay? Not often. Specialists, the barrelmakers and stockmakers, will stay with us, as will expensive custom arms firms, but only for those who can afford their services. Gunsmithing is already inflated; prices today are literally double what they were less than ten years ago.

The small and large city shops you can drop into and talk over a new rifle barrel or shotgun stock or handgun accurizing job will be fewer and fewer, and the prices will be higher and higher. The sporting-goods stores may have a clerk who can screw on scope bases without tearing screw slots, but they may have no one who can reblue a gun or put on a recoil pad.

The multi-gun owner, unless well off financially, able to spend $1,000 or more a year on his arms upkeep and general alteration, willing to risk loss or damage in shipment hither and yon to far-away gunsmiths, will be facing a wall. The way out is in learning to do much of his own work, just as ninety percent of the professionals started out. The gun owner's care and repair needs just may make the hobby a necessary duty. Naturally, he must carefully assess all of the possibilities and limitations. In the great majority of cases he must settle for hand tools, perhaps a couple of small electric ones, and do only the work they permit.

Many, if not most, people believe that the ability to use the hands is an inherent talent, but any surgeon, machinist or mechanic will admit that manual dexterity is an acquirable ability and rather easily attained. It is governed more by the brain than the arm muscles! Repetition will make an act almost automatic, requiring little conscious thinking, as in typing. You can learn to write left-handed in two hours if you try! The use of screwdrivers, pin-punches, files and such tools is elementary, and common sense should tell you which size and type the job calls for and how much physical effort can be exerted without damaging either the tool or the work.

Luckily, the amateur gunsmith almost always recognizes limitations and seldom gets himself in real trouble or inadvertently damages his arms badly. The gun owner respects his arms and their requirements too much to go out on a limb. Even those with some equipment and experience seldom think of risking such professional jobs as blueing, welding or barrel-fitting. When he does consider these, he prepares himself.

Such a person learns how first. High schools and junior colleges in almost every locality offer night courses for adults, at very low cost, in many trades and vocations; machine-shop and wood-shop courses are universal. A few nights a week for a winter will teach metals and how to work them, how to operate lathe, milling machines, drill presses, etc. For wood shop build a gun cabinet or a workbench or a loading-table–cabinet. Most teachers are delighted to have students suggest projects. Instructors are happy to help with barrel-threading and fitting, making a gun part or spraying a stock with a new finish. Equipment is available that would be far out of reach financially even if you had a place to put it. And even if you can afford it, there isn't much point in getting something like a welding outfit that might be used twice a year, some years!

To keep peace in the family, take your wife along. She can be learning anything from photography to sculpture while you're learning to grind the right angle on a tool. Night classes are a wonderful help in many ways, indeed.

Mutual aid can be a fine thing. If you don't belong to a gun or sportsman's club, join one or start one. A group can supply skills, equipment and knowledge that can greatly help individual members. It doesn't have to be necessary to lay back or discard a gun because it is damaged or has a broken part that the factory doesn't supply any more, and there's no gun shop to fix it. Hold a caucus, answer the questions and start working.

Safety

And when you start working with guns, the very first thought must *always* be of safety: Always. I am constantly irritated to read of someone shooting himself with a gun he didn't know was loaded, because he really didn't know it was *unloaded*—and there's a difference! Constant vigilance must be observed. I know personally half a dozen professional gunsmiths who have managed to injure themselves through careless gun-handling, familiarity dulling their vigilance. More than one accident has occurred because of a man loading a gun by reflex, thinking of something else and entirely unconscious of what his hands were doing of their own accord. Probably ninety-nine percent of all gun "accidents" are due to lack of care in gun-pointing, failure to thoroughly check the "unloaded" arm or making a sudden move to bring on a dangerous situation or condition.

A young acquaintance of mine recently shot himself, seriously but not fatally, with a loaded revolver in an open holster. He made a fast sideways stoop or dip to pick up something he'd dropped. The gun fell from the holster and fired when it landed. He made two mistakes: First, the open holster; and second, he didn't hold the gun in with one hand and reach down with the other.

When working with guns, the very first thought must *always* be safety. Here a shooter discusses and demonstrates the need for gun safety with a young shooter.

A loaded P-38 was brought in to a gunsmith, jammed. The customer told him that there was a loaded cartridge in the chamber and the magazine was in the butt. The gunsmith put his left hand over the muzzle and pushed back. Result: four bullets through his palm. Stupidity. The gunsmith didn't remove the magazine and he put his hand over the muzzle of a loaded gun. Theoretically, it couldn't fire if the recoil system was pushed out of full lock. *Theoretically.*

The next example sounds like a pure accident. A fellow was on a rifle range shooting by himself. Having finished shooting a target, he reloaded his single-action revolver and placed it on a table. He then walked out to inspect his target; a gust of wind shook the table, the gun fell off, fired on hitting the ground and produced an excellent flesh wound in one buttock at twenty-five yards! Why did he reload before he was ready to shoot?

However, just as many or more accidents happen indoors as out— usually the "cleaning the gun" situation, and most often due to an overlooked cartridge remaining in the "unloaded" arm. The majority of such cases involve rifles or shotguns with tubular magazines where a cartridge or shell can hang up in the tube even while the action is operated by hand several times, then feed and chamber after the owner is sure it is empty. To avoid such an accident: with the muzzle pointing in a safe direction, work the lever or slide and inspect with the action open to make sure you can see the end of the magazine follower and that there is no cartridge or shell in the lifter ready to feed into the chamber. If it is a takedown model, keep the muzzle pointed in a safe direction while you take it down. This, of course, applies to all types of firearms. Check and recheck for a cartridge remaining in the arm you handle indoors, and keep all live ammunition off the top of your workbench.

Bolt-action rifles, aside from tubular-magazine .22's, are more easily made safe. All clips or detachable box magazines should always be removed before the rifle is brought indoors and, if loaded, kept in a separate place until you go out again. In any event, a glance at a magazine tells if a loaded cartridge is there. Of course, with .22's, you can see the chamber with the bolt open; with large bolt actions you can see both the magazine and the cartridge if you look, though it is easier to just run your little finger into the receiver ring and into the end of the chamber. And do the same with autoloaders where you can't readily see the chamber and tell if it is clear or not.

Breaking—opening—of single and double-barrel arms naturally reveals the chamber and whether or not it is empty. Again, don't give

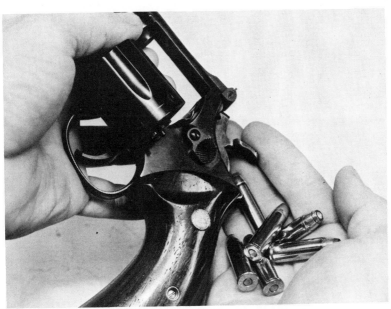

Before any kind of gun handling or gun cleaning is done, it is absolutely necessary to unload. Check and recheck for a cartridge in the arm you handle indoors, and keep all live ammunition off your workbench.

yourself the opportunity to absentmindedly load the gun—move the ammunition away and out of reach; put it in a storage box or drawer the first thing you do when you come in from the field.

Handguns are more dangerous to handle only because they are short and easy to point in the wrong direction. While the autos have one cartridge chambered when the magazine is removed—and forgetting to jack the slide and eject this live round has been the cause of countless accidental discharges—I believe more revolvers have figured in unexpected and unpleasant firings. It's probably because people like to play with them, become absentminded when handling them and suddenly surprise themselves. *Never* point a muzzle at anyone, and *never* play with a handgun—or any gun.

I know of a case where a young fellow came home, flipped open his revolver, worked the ejector rod, flipped the cylinder shut and said, "Look, Russian roulette." He put the gun against his head and pulled the trigger. You guessed it. One cartridge had hung in the ejector and rechambered. Our playboy was very dead. *Look at everything you do when you handle any firearm,* and make yourself *see* everything.

In the case of black-powder arms, practically everyone involved with them is very safety-conscious because of the flammability of the powder. These arms are never loaded, or capped or primed before the minute of firing. However, occasionally an antique gun turns up loaded. And some of them have fired charges loaded 200 years ago! Handle any old firearm with care. Never put a cap on a nipple or snap a flintlock unless you've run a rod all the way down to the breechplug first.

The curiosity of children accounts for many home gun accidents every year. Every child is interested in guns, and with all the TV programs, even a five-year-old knows how to cock, load, operate levers, open revolver cylinders, etc. Between playing with toy guns and watching actors firing blanks indiscriminately, real guns usually aren't real to children, and they'll point at each other and pull triggers happily. The cure is education.

Keep no secrets from your son. Show him your guns, explain them, let him handle them, above all let him see what a bullet can do, so that he can appreciate the force and damage that results when a bullet hits. Kids aren't stupid, and they don't impress easily. But they are very much realists.

I was in a difficult position myself—my son was born when I was operating a thriving gun business. My shop was connected to my home, with dozens of all types of arms reachable at all times, thousands of rounds of ammunition on hand and no way possible to isolate a child from them. So I decided to use the sense of possessiveness small children have. I bought him toy guns that were all his. So he had his arms, and every other one was mine and not to be touched. This worked pretty well, especially after he showed an interest in a real gun and I dug out an immense .45 Colt revolver that he couldn't lift in both hands. At six, I bought him a Ruger "Bearcat" .22, a miniature single-action revolver, took him out and let him shoot into a dirt bank at four feet: the flying dirt, report and the holes shot in a tin can made him instantly aware—and very sober, too—of the force created by just a .22. Often, thereafter, I heard him lecturing other kids not to point cap guns at each other! He himself immediately lost almost all interest in his toy guns. He knew what it was all about. It is easy to impress safety on boys with regard to guns—easier than on most adults. Ask any hunter-safety course instructor whether the kids or their fathers are most to be trusted!

Once a person, either sex, any age, is brought to an understanding of firearms, curiosity and preconceptions satisfied, safety is well on the road to achievement. No gun can discharge without ammunition. And if the muzzle never points at a person, no person will be shot. These are the thoughts to keep in mind. The only problem is in remembering them.

PART I

Basic Maintenance and Repairs

1

A Place to Work; Storage and Security

The arms owner needs some facilities for even minor care: a place to store cleaning equipment and materials, dusting and wiping cloths, plus the few tools that accumulate even when you aren't planning any specific work: screwdrivers, a bore-reflector, odd screws, brushes, a file that looked useful somewhere.

Where and how you live can determine your work area. Apartments come in all sizes, shapes and degrees of roominess. Usually from none to minimum. I know at least two cliff dwellers who had lathes set up in their living rooms, but this is a little far out for most of us. Few wives really care for such furniture. The ultralimited man seldom wants such equipment and will best serve himself by having a carpenter make him a put-away work-corner assembly. A waist-high wooden cabinet 2 feet or so square with a thick door that unhinges to affix on top to form a bench, take a clamp-on vise or Versa-Vise base, and containing shelves and drawers to hold tools and materials does well for this purpose. (I'm assuming that he can't make this himself, with no facilities to begin with.) A dollar will buy a huge plastic painter's drop-cloth that can be cut to fit around the base closely and cover the surrounding floor to

1

One man's workshop: A small add-on building, self-built. It is 8 feet square, of simple wood construction.

catch any shavings, drops of oil or other debris produced, thereby saving the rug and much clean-up work. Finished to match the room decor and put to rest with a scarf and table lamp on top, it can't be very objectionable when not in use, can it? Such a setup will allow cleaning, assembly, disassembly, work on stocks or small parts, do to hold a press if you're a handloader and in general serve one-hundred-percent better than the kitchenette table.

Most of the nation's private homes of any age at all, even the smaller ones, have basements, and in self-defense the householder has had to build himself a workbench and assemble a few tools. About all he needs is a good light and he's ready. More recently built domiciles have connecting garages or carports with service rooms attached. These can be extended or rearranged to provide a space anywhere from 4 by 6 feet upward. Some dedicated do-it-yourselfers exile the car and take over the whole garage or close in the carport.

The ranch-housed surburbanite may find no usable room at all under his roof, large though it may be. So, if he can afford the house, he can finance the now-common "yard" or "storage building" made of sheet metal with no windows and padlockable doors. With a heavy plywood or homelaid cement floor, the larger sizes will cost less than $150. Hot in summer and cold in winter maybe, and perhaps more subject to vandalism and burglary than the house, these structures are a solution to the problem of where to put a workbench and a few tools. Sizes come large enough to allow doing almost anything one might want to try. A long extension cord for light and power and a buried bell wire for any homemade or purchased alarm system makes it pretty practical.

The basic shop of the amateur gunsmith starts with a waist-high bench and "as large a swivel-base machinist's vise as one can afford." From then on it's a matter of adding the appropriate tools to do the jobs, and arranging storage space for them.

For any work and any work area, the first item to be considered is the bench. You need a minimum top area 2 feet wide and 3 feet long. Bigger is better. You can buy a bench or make one to plans in any woodworking booklet, or just prowl the nearest second-hand furniture stores or those handling new unpainted low-cost pieces and pick up a belt-high, or a little higher, chest of drawers. (Nearly all gun work will be done standing.) Cover the top with an overhanging piece of ¾-inch or heavier plywood. Cover this in turn with Masonite, and you're in business. You won't even have to make drawers to keep your equipment in. Tool racks, jar racks, wallboard with hangers, shelves—you put them up as you need them.

Get as large a swivel-base machinist's vise as you can afford and mount it out on the edge of the top so that work can be held vertically, down past the bench top edge. An alternative is the widely distributed Versa-Vise which takes a vertical column-base screwed to the bench top and can be instantly switched from vertical to horizontal mounting. These are ideal for stock work when used with wood and leather jaws to protect the stocks against marring and are a wonderful aid in holding long guns for cleaning. However, they are not rigid enough for much precision work. If used, get an additional small standard vise for metalwork.

The first power tool to be considered isn't a drill as you might think, but a bench grinder. A small, light one is adequate for tool sharpening, reshaping screwdriver blades, etc. There are several that are priced around twenty dollars or so—even one under the Toastmaster brand!

From here on, tooling is a question of what the individual wants to do and what his individual requirements are. He should learn where the surplus and second-hand tool stores are and visit them periodically to learn what can be had and at what cost. Then when he finds a need for a specific tap or punch or chisel, he knows where he can or can't find it. He'll find rawhide and rubber mallets, useful for pounding on stocks without marking them, little brass hammers that look more useful than they prove to be, and occasionally a lead hammer that can be very useful if not too big. A selection of files can be gathered at reasonable cost, over some time. Don't buy used or reconditioned files. Get a few shapes in the coarsest cut for use on wood. Often first-class files of all types can be found in the cut-rate or "surplus" places, and occasionally at the clearance tables in mill-supply houses. The latter are tool and shop-supply stores catering to machine shops and industrial firms, perhaps better known today as "industrial supply" and so listed in telephone directories. They can supply or obtain almost anything in tools, supplies and equipment. But these stores usually deal only in the best, and prices are high. A new top-brand file in any shape can cost three or four dollars each. You may have no intention of filing any of your guns or stocks, but you're going to need files anyway. Perhaps you'll only use them to remove burrs from a cleaning rod or tip, but as soon as you show the slightest indication of being able to do anything, you're going to be elected "Mr. Fixit." Where did all those sticking cabinet catches, loose panhandles and stiff doorknobs come from all of a sudden?

Industrial-supply houses won't be found in towns under 30,000 as a rule, but in such places there is always one regular hardware store that has expanded its stock to fill local needs, carrying much more than is usual in selection and quality of shop supplies.

It is to be expected that the gun owner will gradually acquire what he needs as he needs it, but finding out where to acquire it is not often easy since most, not a few, gun-working supplies are somewhat special. Should you need to sand an unfinished stock, you don't buy a housewife's little packet of assorted sandpaper at the variety store. It won't do. Garnet papers and best-grade abrasive types down to the finest grits, can be had at any well-stocked paint store or artist's supply store. You might even find the scarce open-coat types once in a while.

These stores will also have 4/0 (0000) steel wool—I'm not sure that anything finer is still being manufactured. This is an indispensable item for any gun owner, useful for working on a filled stock before final finish, helping a remover take off an old finish, cleaning metal without scratching, winding around old brushes to remove leading from shotguns and lead-bullet arms. It is vital to learn sources of supply. There are gunsmith-supply firms who catalog the really hard-to-locate special items at very fair prices—ebony blocks to make fore-end tips, taps and dies for gun-screw threads, trap buttplates for stock customizing, etc.

For example, if you should find that the threads of one of the holes in your new rifle's receiver are damaged when you try to install a scope mount and want a tap to clear them—the tap you'll need is a 6-48, a special. The hardware-store clerk may tell you that there isn't any such thread; the industrial-supply man will consult his vast catalog shelf and say he can order one special, for six dollars. You need to go to a gunsmith supplier. Get their catalogs and pay the small charge asked. You don't need one every year. They advertise in most firearms magazines, and you've probably read their ads many times.

Supply sources are always a problem even to gun shops on dozens of mailing lists. Where to buy a tang sight for the old single-shot rifle

5

you found; who makes what varieties of buttplates, makes parts for obsolete guns, supplies rare woods—the list is endless. When looking for an arms-related item, it is helpful to know if you can get it from a normal industrial source. For example, for a steel rod to make a long one-piece gun-cleaning rod you'd go to the warehouse of a steel or metals supplier and ask to look over the scrap racks around the cutting saws. Don't phone and ask, go. If you order anything specific, it'll be cut to size, and you'll pay a cutting charge higher than the cost of the rod! For fiberglass or epoxy for stocks or other uses, find the nearest boat yard or marine-supply firm. They can tell you how to use it, too. The neighborhood druggist can surprise you with his knowledge and supply of chemicals should you want to try making up a browning solution or cleaning solvent to a formula you may have. The best screwdrivers, such as you may see advertised as "special for guns," are really not sold in stores, but are primarily an automotive service item and sold directly to garages and service stations by traveling routemen. Ask your service-station dealer to buy you one each of the first four sizes, medium or short lengths, but not stubbies, when the "Mac Tool" man comes around next. Cost: a few dollars at most for all of them. Start a list or card file to record advertisements you see of items or materials that could be of future interest.

Avoid the tendency to buy things that appeal but aren't really necessary, or you'll find yourself running out of storage room. Assess your needs and fill them without going overboard. If you're just going to refinish one old stock, you don't need to buy one-hundred sheet packages of fine-grit papers, do you? A set of needle files is fascinating, but it's ten to one you'll ever have need for any but the round and triangular ones, if any need at all. The man who has room for equipment and a love of tools will accumulate them whether he needs them or not, and enjoy them whether he uses them or not. But I'm thinking of the man who owns a gun or two and wishes to maintain them under conditions that are limited by time, space or funds. In this book we will progress from simply cleaning arms after shooting to advanced jobs such as assembling a complete arm. You do what you want to and can do, as far as you care to go, and equip yourself accordingly.

Storage and Security

Now is a good time to discuss the allied fields of storage and security, today of utmost importance. The theft of firearms has become a minor industry in the United States. Few stolen guns are ever recovered, and those that are usually aren't in the best condition. Insure everything worthwhile and have the serial numbers listed on the policy. The registration of serial numbers with police is not an effective deterrent to theft—nor will it get your guns back should they be stolen. Automobiles are much larger than firearms, and have numbers all over them, inside and out. Yet three-quarters of a million cars are stolen every year, and only those abandoned deliberately by thieves are usually recovered.

It is impossible to protect yourself completely against theft, but a sensible gun owner can do a few things that will help. The first is not to

A vibrating tool is used to identify a handgun by engraving an area on the frame. When the grips are replaced, it will not show.

invite burglary. Only a few years ago glass-fronted gun cabinets of fine style were popular and desirable, and made good furniture for a living room or den. Now? Not so good, if they can be seen through a window or by door-to-door salesmen, service pickup men, the man who comes to shampoo the rugs or even your wife's bridge club. They talk. "So and so has a lot of nice guns." To be overheard by someone who wants a lot of nice guns.

Inconvenient though it may be, think of hiding places. The thinking isn't inconvenient—the places may be. Hide guns under furniture,

When identifying rifles with a vibrating tool, it is a good idea to mark them on the inside of the floorplate.

hang them inside old garments in a closet, slip them in an old rolled-up rug in the attic, a boxed handgun in the linen closet covered by a mass of towels. And don't keep them all in one place: thieves are always hurried. Also, the rear half of a shotgun, or a revolver without a cylinder are of no value to them, and they seldom have time to find everything. The bolt of a rifle takes up little space and can be hidden pretty securely against quick search in almost any room—and thieves don't usually take incomplete or inoperable items of any kind.

Booby traps are illegal, but hidden cameras aren't. In a cluttered room one can be set and probably miss detection if you're interested in after-the-theft evidence. The best insurance is the low profile—you won't be raided by a gun thief if he doesn't know you have guns. So keep them out of sight.

2

Modern
Guns and How
They Work

The firearm was the world's first and simplest internal-combustion engine and remains so today, although construction of many isn't so simple. A charge of propellant, gunpowder or nitrocellulose, is confined in a cartridge case, cylinder or barrel by a projectile—a ball, bullet or charge of shot—and when fired by a spark, it converts to a rapidly-expanding gas that forces the projectile out of the barrel with speed and force.

For 500 years men have elaborated, developed and refined this basic process. I believe far more human effort has been exerted in this field than in any other concerning a single product. Countless thousands of designs and models and manufacturing breakthroughs lie behind the millions upon millions of firearms that have been produced. Much of our modern technological development stems directly from firearms developments of the past two centuries. Precision measuring tools and gauges resulted in the production of uniform—interchangeable—parts and led to the assembly line, first by the gunmakers. Arms makers led the industrial revolution in machine-tool and metallurgical advances. Nitrocellulose powder development by Du Pont led to plastics and a new world of chemistry. Dr. Appel invented a machine to iron rifling into machine-gun barrels—and rifle barrels—for Hitler's armies. Guess what Detroit's using to make some of the gears and parts for your new car?

And arms continue to develop. While basic principles have changed little for generations in the sporting-arms arms field, modification of designs and improvement of materials never stops changing. Even the resurgent muzzle-loading black-powder arms boast modern steels and utilize the latest manufacturing methods.

Moving up in order, returning single-shot rifles and pistols duplicate their ancestors in stronger stuff. The single-shot cartridge-type arm consists of a chambered barrel hinging or fixed in a frame containing the breechblock and firing system and, of course, providing for attachment of stock and fore-end for handling. The breechblock locks the cartridge in the chamber for firing and may slide vertically, at a slight angle, or tilt or revolve to unlock and allow loading and extraction of the cartridge or casing.

In the case of ordinary single-barrel shotguns, the solid frame of the action forms a fixed breech, while the barrel hinges to allow opening and closing. The firing mechanism in most single-shot arms is the common swinging hammer whose spring forces it against a firing pin in the frame or breechblock when released by the trigger. Or it may be a more modern system of straight-line spring-loaded firing pin released directly by trigger action or through a connecting sear—first used by Sharps in 1878. Most single-shot rifles and shotguns were first operated by an underlever.

The urge for repeating arms had men studying these underlever systems. Since there had to be some manual means of making the repeater function, lever-action repeating rifles and shotguns logically developed. The lever opened a necessarily long sliding breech-bolt, and through cams and internal levers it actuated parts to lock and unlock the bolt as well as feed cartridges from magazine tubes positioned under the barrel or through the buttstock. The functioning could be achieved with a slide-handle around or under the barrel, but it was soon found that this system, which depended solely on the shooter's arm strength for extraction of fired casings, was impractical for rifle cartridges of any power. It was eminently suited for small-cartridge and shotshell use, however, and was and is fast and reliable. Thus it has survived.

However, since the underlever repeaters proved unsuitable for cartridges of ever-increasing pressures, the bolt action took over the high-power field. The bolt simulates a conventional threaded bolt, that screws into a nut—the receiver—to lock against the cartridge in the barrel, which is fixed to or is a continuation of the receiver. The locking "lugs" are the threads. The firing pin and spring are contained in the bolt with a lug on the pin projecting to contact the sear system connected to the trigger. Since the bolt has to be withdrawn quite a distance to allow loading and extraction–ejection, magazines holding a small number of cartridges are incorporated in most rifles directly under the bolt and thus provide easy and fast repeating fire. Because of its fewer parts and more solid construction the bolt-action rifle is capable of higher accuracy than either the lever or slide action, but has an edge on the falling-block single-shot only because of its one-piece stock, which allows use without tension on the barrel. Having great strength, it is almost universally used for the largest, most modern cartridges as well as all from the .22 rimfire on up.

A variation of the bolt action is the straight-pull, employing a bolt having a turning-to-lock section or incorporating locking blocks that move to lock into the receiver when the bolt is closed. A bolt handle that moves straight back without any turning or lifting first unlocks these parts and then continues back to extract, eject and then reload and cock on the forward motion. These are very fast to operate. Browning's T-bolt .22 is the only commercial arm now made of this type, but many surplus Swiss military rifles are in use in the U. S., remodeled to varying degrees by their owners for hunting use. There are also a few of the old Steyr–Mannlicher straight-pulls in use. The Ross straight-pulls, used by Canadian forces early in World War I, are now seldom seen. Though unsatisfactory for military service, they were suitable for sporting use, but received much unfavorable publicity by assorted unskilled authorities and so have a poor reputation.

The autoloading sporting rifle or shotgun, usually referred to incorrectly as "automatic," utilizes part of the power of the fired cartridge to operate the arm—extract and eject mechanically and reload through movement of the breechblock or bolt initiated by gas or recoil against strong springs. With gas operation, a small hole in the barrel allows powder gas to escape—just a small amount of it—after the bullet or shot charge has passed; this gas pushes a piston that moves a rod which in turn unlocks the breechbolt or block. The latter flies free to the rear, carrying the fired casing by an extractor until it hits the ejector, which knocks it out the ejection-loading port in the receiver. The firing pin is caught by the sear mechanism and held, "cocked." The spring tension raises a fresh cartridge to a position where the breechbolt, having compressed its recoil spring and being forced forward again, picks it up and chambers it, the locking parts camming up to again lock the breech tight.

In recoil operation, recoil and inertia combine in effecting gun operation. The barrel is locked to the breechbolt at firing, when both may recoil together a short distance before contacting a part or parts in the heavier receiver-stock assembly which has resisted rapid rearward movement. This unlocks them, arrests barrel movement but allows the bolt to continue its backward travel against springs and complete the same cycle as the gas-operated arm. This is called the "short-recoil" system. "Long recoil," now seldom seen, involves the barrel assembly moving the length of the cartridge or shell to cycle the gun. With both types a handle or finger catch extending through the receiver is used to load and cock the arm for the first shot. These may be a sliding-type free from the bolt in forward movement, fixed, in which case it moves back and forth as the arm fires, or even folding one way, the idea being to hurt less when your hand gets in the way for the first shot. (It won't be there for the second!)

The simplest autoloader is the blow-back, where there is no locked breech at all, only a heavy bolt or block and a strong spring to resist the back thrust of the firing cartridge. The barrel is fixed in the frame or receiver. This system is practical only for low-power cartridges. All .22 autoloading rifles and pistols, and .25, .32 and .380 pistols use it. Most, if not all, of the military submachine guns now being made are of this type, some incorporating delay parts to slow down the rate of fire. The blow-back is really the simplest form of modern arm, having very few essential parts. When the first shot is fired, the empty cartridge case literally blows itself back out of the chamber, slamming the breechblock back at lightning speed. As in the other types, the fired case is ejected, the mainspring forces the block or bolt forward to pick up a fresh cartridge directly from the magazine and the arm is ready to fire again.

If the sear-trigger system fails to engage the firing pin or jars out of contact when the bolt slams to stop in forward movement, the arm can continue to fire until the magazine is empty. This full-automatic fire is called "Maximing," after Colonel Maxim, who invented the first true machine gun. In military machine pistols or machine carbines (both called submachine guns in the U.S.), often there is no separate firing pin at all, just a fixed pin tip machined into the face of the breechbolt so that every time the bolt goes forward, it chambers and fires a cartridge from the magazine. The bolt has to be locked back—open— and no cartridge can be in the chamber in order to fire the first round. Such arms are said to fire from an open bolt. When a separate firing pin and sear assembly are incorporated and the bolt closes completely on a cartridge before the firing pin is actuated, it is firing from "closed bolt." No, I'm not going astray: my reason for mentioning these details is that several U. S.-made .22 rimfire autoloading rifles have been made in the past on the open-bolt with fixed firing-pin system, and they have to be kept clean inside and properly oiled or they'll Maxim and go full auto, which is highly disconcerting, dangerous and illegal.

The revolver was invented before the breech-loading single-shot rifle, and the percussion-type revolver easily adapted to cartridges. Necessarily rather large, early revolvers were supplemented by small self-defense weapons. Single-, double- and even three- and four-barreled pistols of this type were made, their mechanisms really similar to those of the single-shot rifles. Long-barreled single-shot pistols were developed for target shooting. Even today the modern international free pistol is of this type, actually a one-hand miniature rifle with great accuracy. Precise and ultra-sensitive trigger mechanisms can be used that cannot be adapted to revolvers or autoloading pistols. As with the single-shot rifle, the single-shot pistol has its adherents, and modern arms are being made for them. A replica of the Remington that was used as an ultra-rugged and easy-to-care-for arm by the U. S. Navy almost a century ago, the all-new Thompson pistol offered in almost any caliber desired, and several more-or-less custom jobs, besides the imported Stevens replicas are currently available.

The revolver employs a ratchet system that revolves a cylinder of several cartridge chambers, lining up each in turn with the barrel for firing. As the hammer is cocked either manually or by double-action pull on the trigger, a lever or "hand" moves a cylinder chamber into alignment and a spring catch holds it for firing, releasing when the hammer and hand are moved again. Revolvers come in several variations. There is the solid-frame type, in which the cylinder must be removed from the frame for cleaning and reloading, these have a pin under the barrel that must be slid forward or totally removed. Solid-frame rod-ejection revolvers are the "western" types having a spring rod housed along the barrel and a loading–ejection gate on the side. Rotated by hand, each chamber of the cylinder comes in line for the rod to push out the fired case and allow insertion of a loaded round. The solid-frame swing-out revolver has a catch on the frame that releases to allow the cylinder to swing out on a pivoting yoke (or crane) for simultaneous ejection of fired cases and subsequent reloading.

Last is the top-break arm, which has the frame hinged to allow barrel and cylinder to pivot clear of the breech to permit case insertion and removal.

The single-action revolver must have the hammer cocked by hand for each shot; the double action has an internal slip-over part that, when the trigger is pulled, forces the hammer back to a point and then disengages to let it fall. Nearly all double-action arms will also permit single-action use. They are used this way most of the time since the trigger pull can be very easy for single action but necessarily must be heavy for double.

"Automatic"—autoloading—pistols are more numerous than revolvers currently, that is, more variations and makes are available. There have been foreign-made fully-automatic military and pocket pistols, but these were almost totally worthless at full auto—their rate of fire was too fast: one touch on the trigger and the magazine was empty and the mark missed with all but the first round. These are illegal and can be identified by a change lever on the grip or frame, like an extra manual safety. The last autoloading pistol I know of that might be in any U. S. hands is a Mexican-made .22 that was discontinued in 1969 (that is, aside from old military models in collections).

Up to the 9mm Luger Parabellum, most pistols are straight blowbacks, using the slide or a heavy spring-loaded bolt as a breechblock. At this caliber, the recoil requires such a heavy slide and strong spring as to make the blow-back pistol unwieldy. Although Europeans have tried for sixty years, no really satisfactory 9mm Parabellum—or more powerful—blow-back pistol has been successful. "Parabellum" is the European term for the full-power Luger cartridge. There have been pistols made for the same size cartridge underloaded and given other names—the Glisenti, for one.

Therefore, the big pistols are recoil-operated, using a barrel joined to the frame by a toggle link as in the Colt .45 military pistol; or a camming block as in the Walther P-38; or a ramp–cam unlock as in the Luger. The barrel and slide (or bolt) move to the rear on firing for only a short distance. Then the barrel is stopped and the locking system is pulled out, leaving the slide or bolt free to continue back and complete the extraction–ejection–cocking–loading–closing cycle.

The autoloading pistol may have a hammer similar to a revolver, a spur hammer (no thumb tang, just a rounded top, so it won't catch on clothing) a concealed hammer, that is, one inside the slide and cocked by pulling the slide back, or a straight-line spring-loaded firing pin. Most .22 sport pistols have barrels fixed in frames and use only a short slide to abut the barrel breech since the small cartridge does not require a heavy slide to resist its recoil in full blow-back operation.

Maintenance and preservation of all firearms demand that they be cleaned after firing, checked for any damage that may be occurring during shooting and preserved against rust and dust.

3

Cleaning Firearms

Cleaning firearms after shooting and for preservation has only in recent years again become very important. It is necessary not only for best performance but also for maintaining correct mechanical functioning in many arms. Twenty years ago it was not particularly important to shooters other than those in coastal or damp regions or those firing muzzle-loading arms. Whether you care to blame cost accounting, product engineering by advertising departments, or whatever, several recent ammunition developments represent progress to the rear in some aspects.

For .22 rimfire arms, the lead bullets may have no grease or wax coating so they won't pick up lint and debris if carried in a pouch or pocket. The problem is that your barrel will pick up lead fouling, so you'd better clean with a solvent and brass brush and then oil before laying the gun away for even a few days. A bit of the 4/0 steel wool wound about a patch is even better than the brush unless you have a rough barrel that really leads up.

Handguns? Everybody's loading or buying super-velocity ammunition and fouling barrels with lead and copper from half-jacketed bul-

AMMONIA BORE TREATMENT

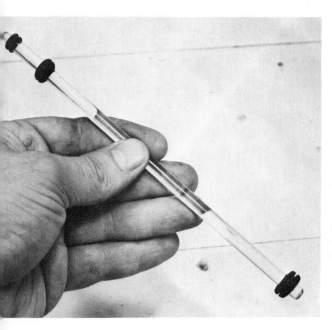

A handy tool for the 28% ammonia bore treatment is a glass
or plastic rod such as this, with
rubber grommets of various
sizes fitted to it. This makes an
excellent bore plug.

A detail of the tool in use in the gun's chamber.

Here, for the sake of additional clarity, is a barrel which has been removed from the receiver showing how the rubber grommets fit in the chamber and seal it up quite effectively.

A handy funnel is a short length of rubber tubing slipped over the rifle's muzzle when pouring the 28% ammonia solution into the bore.

The bore is being swabbed out from the breech end after the ammonia treatment.

lets that are not lubricated at all. Brush and solvent work every time. Competitive target shooters often clean guns every fifty rounds; that includes both the pistol people and the .22 riflemen.

Center-fire rifles are problem children. Back in dad's day bullet diameters were held to quite rigid standards in each caliber, as were rifle bores, commercial or custom, and bullet jackets were nearly all hard gilding-metal or bronze alloys. Thus there was little metal-fouling. Today, barrel dimensions and bullet diameters vary considerably, and bullet jackets in the main are soft—ninety-five-percent copper. And everyone wants high velocity, so they shoot a soft-jacketed bullet, probably undersize, too fast for the barrel to handle properly and perhaps with a powder that rapidly deposits a hard lacquer-type fouling. There are some combinations that require barrel cleaning almost every ten shots to maintain accuracy!

Cleaning is a very necessary chore, but many men aren't even conscious of their metal-fouled barrels. They go through them with patches and commercial solvent, or even use a brass or bronze brush first and wipe dry so the bore looks shiny and clean. Until you study closely with a good light through the bore and find the tops of lands bearing little smooth lumps and streaks that break up their sharp profile. More brushwork with solvent, leaving wet with solvent overnight, etc., is necessary. You can spend two weeks trying to get a barrel perfectly clean! The active agent to cut copper fouling is ammonia. Make up your own solution to P. O. Ackley's formula:

1 oz. ammonium persulphate
200 grains ammonium carbonate
4 oz. water (rain or distilled)
6 oz. strong ammonia, from drugstore.

Mix in glass jar outdoors, then put in small bottles for use as needed.

Cork the breech of the arm tightly, and using a small funnel such as one made or altered for reloading .22 center-fire cartridges, pour the solution in from the muzzle, being careful not to run over, of course. Let the solution stand in the barrel twenty to thirty minutes and pour it out and discard.

Then pull out the breech plug and run through a half-dozen clean patches dipped in hot water. Now dry it and see if you have a clean barrel. If not, give it another brass-brush and solvent treatment and then repeat the solvent stage. It should be clean eventually.

Should the rifling be rough, metal may build on firmly and resist all solutions at first try. You may need to use a cloth-covered jag tip smeared with one of the mild abrasive pastes now being made for just this purpose. Used with discretion, you need not fear enlarging or damaging the rifle bore.

Should you be plagued with a barrel that persists in fouling badly, try an old trick if possible: when you finish shooting, fire a couple of extra cartridges that have only half-charges of fast-burning powder behind the bullets. With some barrels, a low-velocity load will push out or loosen metal fouling left by the high-velocity cartridges. As I say, it works with *some* barrels. Under no circumstances should you ever try half-loads of slow-burning powders, such as 4350 or 4831.

The wax-impregnated cardboard shotgun shell was quite weatherproof and functioned well, but the introduction of the plastic shell has eliminated it. The waxed case left a coating of wax in the chamber, resulting in both protecting the chamber against rust and lubricating it sufficiently to make extraction easy. The unwaxed plastic case not only gives the chamber nothing but the pressure and heat of firing, but it also removes any protective coat the chamber may have at the beginning of shooting. Result: a bone-dry chamber that is very possibly powder-fouled and very prone to rust in just a few hours in any damp environment.

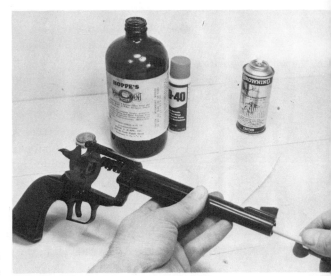

A wire bristle brush and solvent are the best prescription for cleaning a revolver barrel.

Since pump and autoloading arms do not allow easy chamber inspection, quite often the owner is unaware of anything wrong until the chamber pits and extraction begin to fail.

When this happens, the chamber has to be polished smooth and made a little oversize, which can be annoying if reloaded ammunition is to be used. Many good shotguns have been damaged and some have been ruined through the neglect of chamber-cleaning to prevent this situation by owners switching from cardboard shells to the new plastic ones and not realizing what the switch meant. The chambers should be cleaned with brass brushes, just as the bores are when leading is indicated. By going one gauge larger, you can get a brush that'll take care of your chamber, but don't go so big you can't get it back out! Special chamber brushes are appearing now. The English have always used them, having to clean and oil well to avoid rust in their climate.

The tools and mechanics of cleaning are pretty much the same for all cartridge arms, including shotguns. First, always try to have the arm horizontal, if possible clamped in some sort of vise. I even prefer to clean handguns and autos this way, the latter upside down. It's also good for single-shot rifles. The horizontal position prevents excess solvent pressed from the brush or patch from running down into the open frame, trigger system, etc. Solvents and oils do not help stocks at all, so don't let them run down and into the wood. A box of cleaning tissue can be very handy indeed for mopping up. Many of the solvents will damage plastic or varnished wood finishes if allowed to contact them for more than a few seconds. (And if they won't, they can't be very potent solvents!)

Single-shot rifles and pistols and single- and double-barrel shotguns can be lumped together for general care and maintenance procedures. All of them can be opened at the breeches, and their barrels can be easily cleaned and inspected from the breech end, allowing good visibility of the chambers and throats or forcing cones. Bits of patch held in tweezers allows cleaning down in hammer recesses, etc.

Bolt-action rifles are easy to clean if you take the trouble to make a simple tool or two. Wood or aluminum cleaning guides—bolt-length tubes to replace the bolt, with a center hole a little larger than the bore so that brushes and rod tips with patches pass through freely—keep excess solvent from flooding receiver recesses and prevent banging tips against the mouth of the chamber, or the lead of the rifling. And you can shape a piece of dowel to simulate a chamber, slot it with a saw so you can hold a patch and then clean the chambers easily. A slot in the other end can be cut to hold a rolled-up or folded patch to clean the lug

The revolver cylinders being cleaned with a bristle brush.

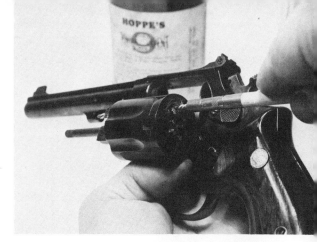

For a really thorough cleaning job with the bristle brush, remove the cylinder from the revolver and work on it.

This is the handy setup for cleaning a rifle. Place pads in the vise, of course, to protect the barrel.

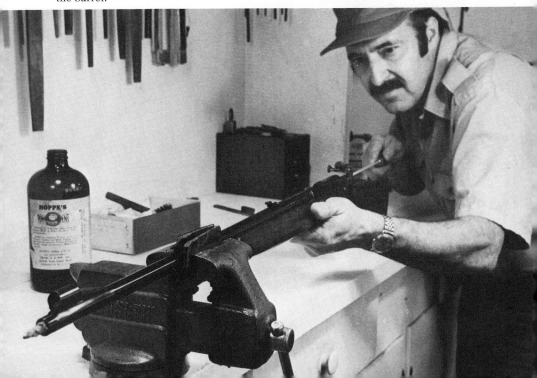

recesses in receiver ring. And don't forget the magazine: wipe it out with cleaning tissue every time you clean the rifle. Why let a cartridge carry a coat of dust into your clean chamber? Every now and then, at least once a year, take the bolt completely apart, change the grease and polish any areas that show friction marks. Clean the face and tip of the firing pin with solvent and then oil after every shoot.

Pump, lever and autoloading arms are much more difficult to clean and keep clean because many of the recesses and parts in the actions are hard to get at without complete disassembly. Of course, the takedown types allow cleaning from the breech and usually some accessibility to action parts. The cleaning of most moving parts should be done completely once a year for all arms that see much use, and their condition should be checked every time barrel-cleaning is done. Nearly

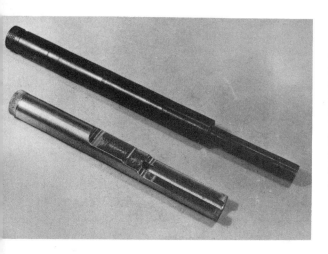

A detail of two cleaning rod guides which protect the chamber section of the barrel. In the foreground is a cleaning rod guide from a Model 52 Winchester target rifle. The big-bore model above fits almost all bolt-action center-fire rifles and protects the chamber quite effectively.

all designs require well-lubricated parts for reliable functioning, and anything well lubricated is a magnet for dirt, dust, lint and other foreign material. You'll find weed seeds inside your shotgun action after every bird season. Practically all lubricants thicken and gum up as a result of time and the absorbing of dust and so should be periodically removed and replaced.

Parts that lift out or recesses large enough to be cleaned with tweezers and patches present no problems, but there are always nooks and crannies that are hard to get at and spring-loaded parts you don't wish to disturb. Here, modern design comes to the rescue in the form of aerosol cans of chemical solvents under pressure that can be equipped

A rod guide fitted and ready for use.

with a long, thin plastic "straw" to direct the grease and dirt-cutting liquid almost anywhere needed and flush out the trash. Called "Gun Scrubber" and "Degreaser," these can be very useful, but they can damage wood finishes, so don't spray the stocks.

Since solvents evaporate and leave metal bare, you must re-oil, which may not be easy without missing some hidden point. I don't recommend the spray-can oilers, as they usually put out too much oil. All over. One way around this is to put a few drops here and there, and use a reversed-flow vacuum cleaner to blow the oil back into the action. For points of heavy pressure and friction, no oil will really do: you need a grease, and the only type to consider is a moly type—molybdenum disulphide, which is a powder that looks like graphite but isn't. In a light, highly refined grease carrier, it is far ahead of any other lubricant. Any product with "moly" in its trade name somewhere has it.

For cleaning parts removed from an arm, ordinary lacquer thinner from the paint store is better than gasoline or petroleum solvent, and the fumes are no worse. Just don't lean over the container and inhale too long! A wide-mouthed jar with a screw top, or even a pound coffee can with a press-on lid will keep it from evaporating too fast.

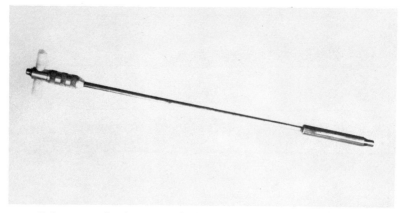

Bolt-action rifle-cleaning tool. Slotted chamber end takes normal patches or cotton cloth as needed to fill chamber, other end takes rolled-up patch of sufficient length to clean locking-lug recesses in receiver. Tool can be made from a 15-cent birch dowel.

This will take off caked oil, etc., and evaporate to leave parts dry and clean. Acetone will serve the same purposes, but it evaporates even faster and costs more. Both, and most spray-can products as well, are highly inflammable, so don't smoke around an open container of them or use them in a small, enclosed space without ventilation.

A valuable cleaning solvent that is not flammable can be obtained fairly easily: perchlorate ethylene, the standard dry-cleaning solvent today. Your dry cleaner has it, though he may not be too willing to sell to you since it is poisonous—to drink, but not to touch. It has no petroleum base, looks like water and has a mild, inoffensive smell. It will probably cost you three dollars a gallon, which is a lifetime supply. It can be used straight for general cleaning (it, too, has a high evaporation speed) or, with about three-quarters of an ounce of silicone oil mixed in, as a bore-cleaning solvent for all arms, though it has no special virtues for center-fire rifles. It is perhaps the best you can use for .22's, shotguns, revolvers, etc., where you have much powder-fouling, sludge and leading. It won't burn at all and doesn't attack wood finishes or plastics, as will lacquer thinner or acetone. However, be sure that any small brushes you use in cleaning have natural bristles, not synthetic.

Silicone oil hard to find? Not the spray cans of silicone lubricant. Get one at the nearest hardware store, clean up a tin can or small jar, go outside, hold the container right at the spray nozzle and press the button. The spray will turn to oil immediately. Why the silicone oil? The

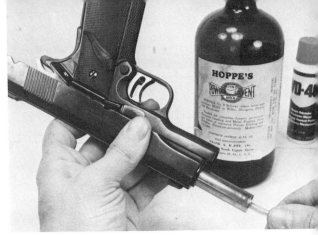

Colt .45 automatic being cleaned in the upside-down position so that the cleaning solution will not run down into the mechanism.

Tweezers are used to swab out the tang recesses in a receiver.

A needle-point oiler such as this is handy for getting into tight and cramped areas.

An aerosol gun solvent is useful for cleaning in the difficult areas of gun mechanism.

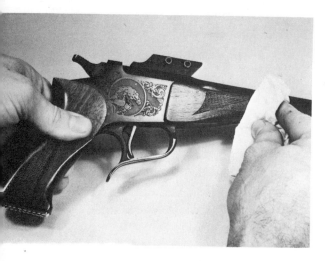

A piece of paper towel being used to clean a pistol stock.

A good coat of wax improves the appearance of handgun grips as well as rifle stocks and is also somewhat protective.

Here a solution of dishwashing detergent is used to clean a stock, as described in the text on the opposite page.

solvent evaporates fast, but there's a layer of silicone molecules left on the metal—rust protection. If, for example, you're shooting a .22 once a week, just run a patch or two wet with the solution after shooting and put the gun away. No oiling needed. No need to wipe it out before shooting again. I wouldn't trust it for long-time protection, but then I don't trust anything for long-time rust prevention. For arms not in use, "RIG" grease is the best I know for this purpose, and I renew it every few months.

For stocks and fore-ends, normal cleaning almost has to involve water because they get dirty from dirt and sweat, and only water really works. A little dishwashing liquid detergent won't hurt. Use small pieces of cloth and wash a portion of the stock at a time, rubbing dry with the cleansing tissue as you go.

Handguns are easy to clean since they're small. For a complete job, more than one fellow has discovered that he can take the grips off, put the gun in a pan of water with detergent and boil it clean! Rinsed in boiling water, the gun is hot enough to dry itself in a minute or two without rusting, after which you judiciously oil here and there and blow into the corners with the reverse-vacuum-cleaner process.

This water system, to a degree, is a must for the muzzle-loading shooter. Black-powder fouling yields to practically any solvent, but water is cheap, convenient and traditional. Much more so than "perk." As most muzzle loader shooting is done with greased-patch round-ball loading, leading is seldom a factor and simply swabbing out barrels with water and drying well serves for interior cleaning. Patent-breech rifles and shotguns are most often taken down—barrel or barrels unhooked from gun—the nipple or nipples unscrewed, the breech immersed in a can of water and ramrod with patch used as a pump to thoroughly clean barrels, the nipples being cleaned separately.

Percussion revolvers are cleaned by swabbing, though I feel the best way to clean cylinders is to boil them a little, with or without nipples, and dry them thoroughly before oiling and laying away.

On the long arms, flashholes, nipples, bolsters, etc., must be well cleaned and oiled, flintlock parts inspected, a new edge put on the flint or the flint replaced and the stock wiped down. It is important that oil or solvent not be allowed to soak in around lockplates and breeches. We'll go into more detail on really cleaning and caring for these arms in the chapters on muzzle-loading firearms.

In barrel-cleaning, the actual tools and techniques aren't known to most firearms owners. The proper tips are important—rod tips, that is. Spear, loop or jag tips to hold patches for cleaning and oiling can be

CLEANING A HANDGUN BY BOILING

1. A stripped-down revolver frame being boiled in water with detergent to completely clean it. Rinse in boiling water. This is a Ruger black-powder pistol.

2. The reverse air blast from a vacuum cleaner is used to dry out the cylinder after boiling.

3. The boiled and dried cylinder is then treated with a rust preventative spray.

The Ruger frame is then sprayed with WD-40 after being boiled and dried.

Small parts can be cleaned by soaking in a wide-mouthed jar of lacquer thinner.

easily introduced into the breech or chamber end of barrels and aren't too difficult to get into a muzzle, but a button tip is strictly rear entry. The button is ideal for breech entry in single-shot open-breech arms, or double barrels since the patch can be well centered. Where it is necessary to introduce the patch through a long receiver, as in a bolt action, the button is a poor choice, and the spear tip—a button with a point—is best. Stick the patch on the point, and it is held and centered until it enters the bore. With either the button or spear tip, you get a side benefit: you can't pull the patch back through the barrel.

Cleaning rod tips, from left: slotted, removable for replacement with brush; button, end drilled and tapped for brush; Belding & Mull tip section, removable for brush tip section; true jag for use with patch or strip wrapped on it full length; and author's spear-button tip, a modified B&M type easily made.

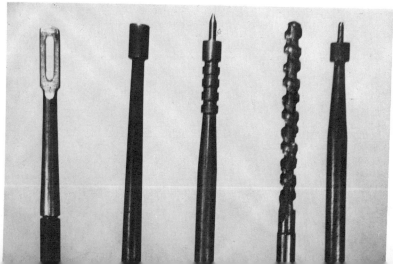

A center-fire bolt being disassembled for cleaning.

It doesn't matter much with shotguns, but with rifled arms, particularly those of high accuracy, cleaning should always be a one-way
deal—from the breech *out* the muzzle. You don't pull brush, patch or
jag back through *from* the muzzle, because in time you'll wear the rifling at the crown, which is most important to accuracy. Yes, it *is* annoying to push a brush through, unscrew it to take the rod back through the
barrel and then screw it on for the next stroke, but this is the best way
to do it.

The long jag tip is used with patch or patch material wrapped
around it to form a tight fit in the bore. This makes for much more
patch contact than the others and is ideal for scrubbing out mild metal
fouling and leading. For removing leading from shotgun barrels and revolvers, fine steel wool wound around an old brass brush or even a patch
or shotgun oiling mop dipped in solvent is most efficient. For revolvers,
you do want to pass the brush back and forth through the barrel and
chambers, and you can use the loop or slotted rod tips to advantage. For
rifles, the slotted tip is for oiling only, with an undersize patch.

The center-fire bolt on a Winchester Model 70 disassembled.

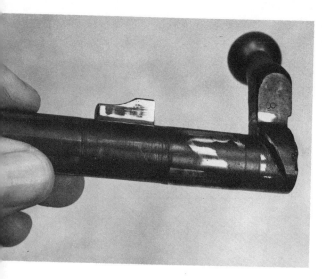

This Springfield Model 1903 bolt shows bright areas which have been stoned with Arkansas stone to reduce friction.

In the event you are fighting a case of metal-fouling in a rifle barrel by using a jag tip with patch carrying solvent or cleaning pastes, you push up to the muzzle and then pull it back. The best makes of cleaning rods advertise "stops," little collars that lock on the rod to limit the rod travel as desired. They are easily made, too, of soft metal, wood or a piece of old rubber heel positioned by a tube over the rod and cut to the correct length.

Working on a bolt with an Arkansas stone. The object here is to remove burrs or rough spots and not reduce size of the part.

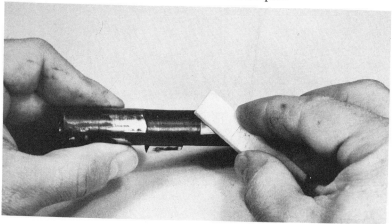

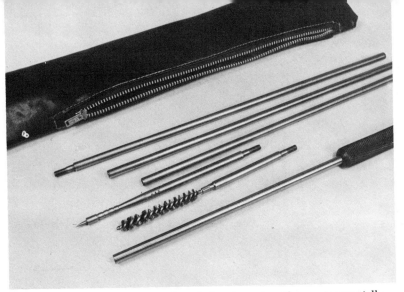

The Belding & Mull jointed steel cleaning rod, with case, is especially handy on hunting trips.

The normal tip for cleaning muzzle-loaders is called a jag, but it is more truly a modified button, having rings machined into it to hold the patch for travel both ways. The "worm" is like a double corkscrew so that it can be used to pull out charges you don't want to fire. On a non-rotating rod, it will hook into patches, wads, etc., and hold them so they may be pulled back up the barrel. For removal of round balls, a tip similar to a sharp wood screw is turned into the ball until it grips firmly enough to hold it for withdrawal. Cleaning rods for muzzle-loading arms may be either wood or metal, the same as normal shotgun rods.

Modern arms—rifles and handguns—need metal rods, and the metal should be steel. The aluminum-jointed rods commonly sold are better than none at all, but not much. Brass isn't much better either, but it is a little stronger. A cleaning rod has to take pressure: if a patch or brush enters easily, it's too small to clean the grooves in the barrel. One that bends anywhere easily won't do. A long, one-piece steel rod should be bought or made for home use. A jointed steel rod will do for use in the field or on trips. Polish the joints so that only smooth surfaces contact the barrel, and always wipe off any rod before putting it into a barrel. I don't recommend soft-metal or soft-surfaced rods at all. The principle of lapping—grinding a metal surface smooth—is based on a soft metal and a hard metal, with an abrasive between: the abrasive sticks to the soft and cuts the hard. Understand now? So, if you have a rod softer than your barrel, be sure it is kept clean. Any gritty dust that is on it will scratch the bore of the gun.

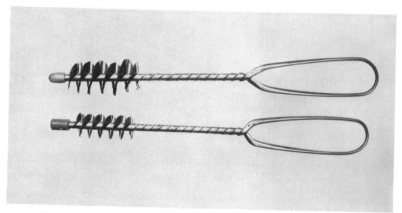

These are 20- and 12-gauge chamber-cleaning brass brushes, from Parker-Hale, Ltd., England. The twisted bronze handles can be bent to permit use in repeating shotguns.

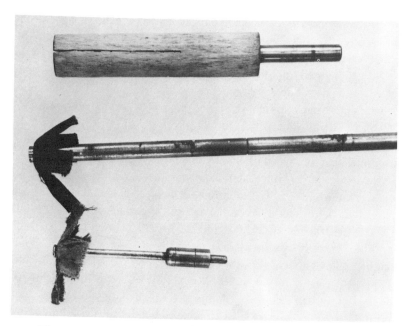

These mandrels are used to hold abrasive cloths for polishing inside bolts, chambers, and other parts.

4

Tools

The following four chapters should prove of more value to more readers than any other section of this book. They are intended to help the individual who wants to do or is forced to do his own general minor gunsmithing. The tools listed will serve to do all of the operations and work described in these chapters, and of course many other similar undertakings. Few are needed for any single job so obtain what you need as you need it.

A bench and vise setup of some sort is naturally the first consideration, and the little bench grinder the first power tool. Be sure it has tool rests and eye shields. Both are necessary.

Hand tools needed include screwdrivers, files, a couple of small pin punches, a rawhide mallet and a small hammer—the handiest is the "riveting" type, a miniature of the blacksmith's forging hammer. One of Russell's Arkansas stone sets, the "Sportsmen's Set" will be useful for a lifetime. You'll also need a hand drill and good bits, look for the sizes you need at the surplus-tool stores. Complete sets are nice but expensive. Also get abrasive finishing paper 4/0, 6/0 and 8/0, if possible, and metal cutting cloth 240, 320 and 400 grits—a couple of sheets of each. You shouldn't need coarse stuff.

This is a small but neat and convenient home workshop. A small area such as this can be used to accomplish a good bit of surprisingly sophisticated work by the amateur gun hobbiest. A good vise is essential. Note electrical outlets in bench for quick plug-in of power tools.

The oft-mentioned Versa-Vise, with wooden false jaws joined by thick leather pad glued to wood. It's invaluable for cleaning arms and stock work.

A power drill can often be very handy, but the ordinary portable hand types sold at very low prices aren't too useful. They run too fast and are hard to control. Variable-speed drills, however, can be useful. A regular drill press, if you have the room for it, can do a lot of things besides drill holes—use it with sanding drums up to 3 inches in diameter, as a press to push tight fits together without damage, do minor routing, etc. They aren't found on bargain counters, but they do crop up fairly often in the for-sale columns in newspapers.

A hand grinder, one of the little hobby-shop outfits with a kit of stones, etc., is almost a necessity. While seldom needed for actual grinding work, it will be invaluable for polishing operations with the ⅜-inch diameter sanding drums, rubber-abrasive tips and assorted mandrels. You'll also need a fine-cut type whetstone, to be used with oil.

One of the transparent face masks sold by industrial-supply houses and welding-equipment firms should be worn while using any power tool. If you wear glasses, it will protect them; if you don't, it will protect your eyes. Should you plan stock work involving much sanding, get a few of the little disposable dust masks of the type illustrated. Any wood dust will irritate nasal passages and sinus, and some varieties are real provokers of allergic attacks.

Safety is the first step of working on gun parts. Here protective eye goggles and a nose mask are being used during a grinding operation.

A few basic tools for the gun hobbyist's shop. At left, hammer, pin punches, a nylon punch. Center, a small file, a pin vise, a small parts vise, and a variety of files. Left rear, a set of needle files, and at the right a set of punches.

Wood tools? Recommendations are difficult. For stock work you can justify few or many, but many tools usually means simply that you'll save more time. On the short side, get ¼-inch and ½-inch straight chisels. (the Swedish birch-handled pro types if at all possible) and a small and a large (¼ inch and ½ inch across curve) outside-bevel straight gouges. These will get you by a lot better than any little wood-carving tool set.

Also useful is a regular hacksaw with a tubing blade (fine-tooth, 32 per inch, for cutting pins, thin metal), a standard blade for general use and a course blade for wood.

The above mentioned tools, together with your oils, solvents, patches, wiping cloths and tissue, make for a pretty well-equipped shop and take up little room.

The "punch tool" described in the text on page 49.

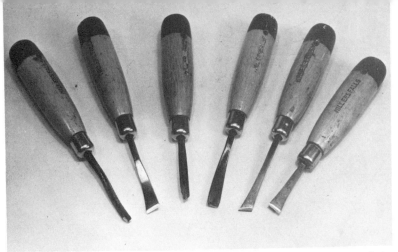

A set of inexpensive small chisels such as this can be used to accomplish some surprisingly fine stockwork. Sets like this usually cost less than $10.

For the more advanced stockmaker here is a set of special chisels. These carving tools are sufficient to handle all phases of stockmaking.

Here is a selection of sharpening tools. At the rear is a large hard Arkansas stone. At left is a contoured stone for shaping different shapes of chisels and gouges. Next is an India chisel sharpener and the others are an assortment of hard Arkansas stones.

39

A set of carbon scrapers used for inletting. They do not cut, but rather scrape away the wood, a small amount at a time.

A sharp, short-bladed but large-handled knife is handy. They used to be advertised and sold as "bench knives," but I haven't seen any listings lately. Large handles on all hand tools should be emphasized. A small handle makes a tool harder to control.

Sanding blocks should be made up in several sizes. Never try to sand a surface having any straight on it without a block backing the paper, or you'll destroy the straight. The only places you can sand freehand on any stock are around the grip and the tip of fore-end. Of course, for final finishing with very fine papers you must sand freehand, but all you're really doing is removing the scratches left by the coarser paper that did the shaping.

A close-up detail of one of the scraping tools.

Maintenance and adjustment of tools starts before using them. Screwdrivers come first since they are used first—you have to take a gun apart to do anything to it. And they are far more important than commonly thought. Here's why: screws on arms and accessories such as sights and telescopic-sight mountings must be close-tolerance types and tight. Screw heads will break if hard and tear the slot if soft. However, soft screws tend to resist loosening up better than others, so many screws used in arms and mounts are soft. To avoid damaging slots, the screwdriver tip shouldn't be just a good fit—it must be perfect. It should fit the slot in width and depth all the way and fill up the slot. This is why gunsmiths always seem to have so many beat-up looking screw-

A rack full of different screwdriver shapes in a home gun repair enthusiast's workshop. The gunsmith, either amateur or professional, cannot have too many screwdrivers.

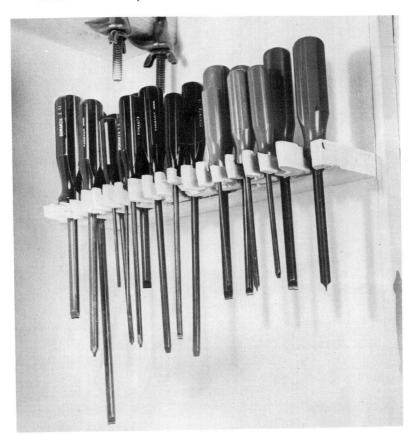

drivers lying around—they are constantly filing and grinding tips to fit particular screws. And to remove very tight screws, the tip must bottom in the slot without wedging in its top so that the screwdriver handle can be tapped gently with a hammer to vibrate it. This breaks the thread hold so that the screw can be turned out. Much pressure is often needed to hold the screwdriver tight against bottom of slot when a screw is tight or being tightened—if the tip has a wedge form it will tend to pivot up out of the slot and tear the edges, thus lessening the tip contact. So screwdrivers must be reshaped so the tip cross section would resemble a tiny square bar. This is usually done by hollow-grinding since

More tools for the amateur gunsmith's shop. From left: pliers, a small hacksaw blade and frame, a series of center punches and cabinet maker's punches, a rawhide mallet and a thread gauge. In the background is a set of tweezers.

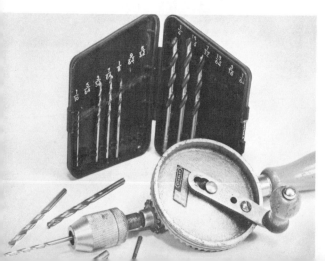

A hand drill and set of good quality drill bits.

it is almost impossible to file a tip without rounding off the sharp bottom edges, which defeats the purpose.

Wood chisels must also be hollow-ground for ease in maintaining a sharp edge, and they're worthless unless kept sharp enough to shave hair off your forearm. Hollow-grinding is easy with a bench grinder that has a tool rest. A right-handed person merely grips the tool with his left hand 3 inches or whatever distance from the tip that gives the desired angle of grind, and never lets go of this grip until the job is done. The left forefinger or its knuckle are brought into contact with the tool rest, and the right hand is used to bring the tool in contact with the wheel.

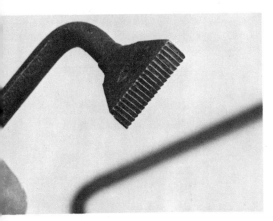

This small rasplike tool is called a "bottoming" tool and is used for inletting.

An assortment of files and rasps such as will be needed by the stockmaker. In the center foreground is a barrel-channel inletting tool.

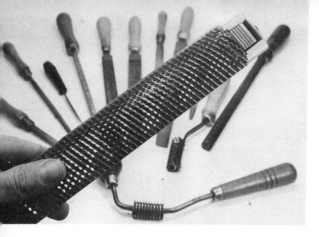

This shaper is an especially handy tool for stockmaking. It comes in flat, curved, and round shapes.

This is the old-fashioned wood rasp typical of those used by stockmakers for generations.

With left hand maintaining its grip, the tool is dipped in water as needed to cool. As long as the grip is the same, the wheel will always grind at the same angle and cut the same hollow. Don't hold on until the edge turns blue, of course, but when a uniform, complete hollow reaches the tip, you're ready to start stoning. Next, the hollow-ground area of the tip is presented to the tone and whetted, moving the tip in a circular motion but not staying in the same spot on the stone. Both the edge and the top of the bevel are stoned away rapidly—that's the idea of hollow-grinding: get rid of the metal in the middle so you don't have to wear away a large surface to renew a dulled edge. When a cleaned

A set of small hand rasps which are used for cutting delicate curves in stocks and inletting.

This tiny parallel clamp is a handy tool for the home workshop. Here it is used to hold a front-sight ramp in place before soldering.

straight edge appears on the ground bevel, turn the blade over and make a single pass on the whetstone with the flat down flat on the stone. Now take a scrap of wood and pull the edge sideways through the end grain, to remove the "wire" edge, or bits of metal adhering. Plane blades are sharpened the same way as chisels.

No, you can't make a hollow-ground knife this way: a grooved piece of metal must be clamped or screwed to the tool rest close to the wheel to slide the back of the knife blade back and forth in.

Pin punches, also called drift punches and just drifts, are used to drift (drive) pins out of firearms and parts. They are hard to locate in

Every home workshop needs an assortment of finishing papers and some sanding blocks.

sizes under $1/16$ inch diameter from normal supply sources, and it is better to buy smaller sizes from a gunsmith supplier rather than try to grind down a larger size. All must be kept square and flat on the ends and kept straight—they do bend now and then. For starting very tight pins, nothing is better than an ordinary nail-set. They are hard, strong, and the cupped end won't skid on a rounded pin end and dent the arm. You can always polish and use touch-up blue on a marred pin, but there's no fixing a dent in a receiver!

Mandrels to hold abrasive cloth in strips or crosses to be turned by a drill or hand grinder are easily made from short bits of rod slotted or

This handy sanding block is made by stapling a bit of felt to a small block of plywood. The soft padding makes it especially effective for final sanding and rubbing on gunstocks.

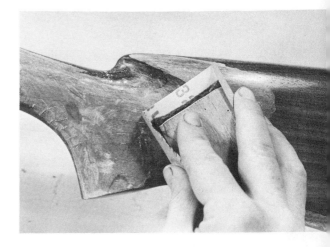

Wrap a small piece of sandpaper around the block and keep it taut with the thumb and fingers.

with a screw in the end to hold the cloth. These are used to polish rough chambers or the insides of bolts or other round holes that need cleaning up. For polishing a chamber, a little cross of 400 grit cloth is made (or 320 if you can't get finer) and always used in a high-speed grinder or hand tool. The cross is oiled lightly, folded back and inserted in the chamber before the motor is started. Passed back and forth from shoulder to rear of chamber—not brought all the way out—for five seconds or so it will clean up a rough chamber. You must use a high-rpm tool for safety because the polishing cloth is thrown out against chamber walls, centrifugal force keeping the mandrel centered so that its metal end or

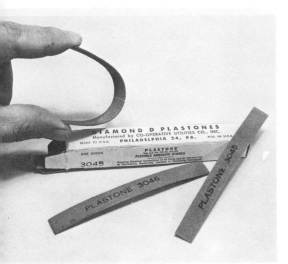

Another handy, but little known, tool for the home workshop are these flexible Plastone strips. They are available in a variety of grits.

screw cannot touch any part of the chamber or bore. At low rpm you lose this protection, although an ordinary electric drill with coarser cutting cloth can be used for preliminary polishing when cleaning up a badly pitted shotgun chamber. The power should always be cut just as the mandrel clears the breech or mouth of the chamber.

A long mandrel can be used to polish the chamber of a bolt-action rifle through the receiver, but you must hold it centered as well as possible in the receiver and turn power on and off every second or two to cut vibration. This won't enlarge the chamber, unless you work hard at doing so. A well-worn cross of abrasive cloth can give almost a mirror finish, but that's about all to expect.

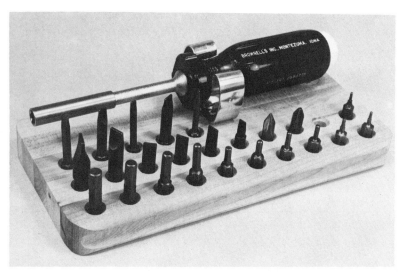

This handy set of gunmaker's screwdrivers includes just about every size and shape that will be needed by the amateur workman.

Here is an ordinary "household" screwdriver compared to a hollow-ground gunmaker's screwdriver. The common screwdriver, at left, may burr and disfigure gunscrew slots.

A tool of my own, which I've never seen anyone else ever make or use, is a hand drift I made by putting an old screwdriver handle on a $^3/_{16}$-inch steel rod. It could also be made by driving a large nail into a block of wood and then cutting the head off. It's very useful for pushing out stuck trigger guards, easy-to-move large metal pins, holding followers out of the way, etc. The end is kept square, but the sharp edge is polished smooth.

To learn to sharpen drill bits, the best I can advise is that you ask a mechanic or machinist to *show* how it is done. It involves a sort of two-phase off-center revolving motion. There are low-cost drill-sharpening jigs made to use with bench grinders, but unfortunately they

Torn-up screw slots can be repaired: Above, three Model 70 front guard screws damaged from much bad screw-driver handling.

The same screws after slots have been peened by a hammer.

After slots have been re-filed and heads have been polished. No, they aren't perfect, but they are presentable. After rebluing, they'll pass as new except on very close inspection.

won't handle the small-size bits you'll need to sharpen. Experiment with grinding them, compare them with new tips and drill experimental holes in scrap material. Improperly sharpened, they either won't cut at all or will cut oversize holes. Holding a bit up and observing the silhouette of the tip will show whether one lip is too long, etc.

Keep files clean with brushes. If possible, keep an extra one or two for use with wood and never use these on metal at all. Watch the switches and plugs on all electrical tools. Never put a hand power tool down until its motor stops completely. Don't overload a circuit, and use common sense at all times. Tools are like firearms: by themselves they never do anything wrong.

5

Rifles

Bolt-Action Center-Fire Rifles

The most common center-fire sporting rifle today is the bolt action, coming in all price ranges, degrees of finish and workmanship, stock design and finish, sights and trigger pulls. Few require major working over, but nearly all require minor attention. Common alterations include adjustment of triggers, removal of burrs and rough areas to permit smoother functioning, stock work such as bedding, rebedding, the butt shortened or a recoil pad installed and sights changed, removed or added.

Maintenance just means maintaining the arm in good condition, keeping it clean, protecting it against rust, repairing any damage or wear from field use and making it ready to serve at full efficiency.

Adjustment can cover little if you want to be narrow about it, but I think minor alterations can be included along with twisting trigger screws and smoothing the safety operation. You can't exactly call such jobs repairs, can you? When something must be fixed, or changed, that's repair.

Adjusting or replacing dovetail sights. Sights are the part of the gun most often adjusted by the gunowner. They are the means by which he shoots so he is very conscious of them. He either wants a better metallic front bead or blade, or wants to get what's on completely off so it won't catch on things. The front may be on a ramp integral with or soldered to the barrel, dovetailed in tightly. Dovetail sights used to be slightly taper-fitted, driven in from the right side, and drive out from the left. Now many are straight-cut, so look at the fitting to see from which side of the ramp or barrel it was driven in. Then drive it back out accordingly. If the sight is in the barrel proper or a ramp integral to the barrel, clamp the barrel in protective vise jaws and use a punch to drive the sight. A short ¼-inch square bar of aluminum, copper or brass is best, with a bit of paper or thin cardboard (as from a match-folder) between this punch and the sight base. This prevents marking or denting the sight, which may be of use in the future on another arm.

Where the sight is in a ramp that is sweated or screwed to the barrel, the ramp itself must be clamped in the vise, usually in vertical position (barrel vertical, that is) just below the dovetailed sight itself, before you try to hammer out the sight. Otherwise, you can knock the ramp off the barrel or at least knock out of line. Quite often, modern ramps are held only with two small screws, but one of them is recessed in the dovetail cut. These, of course, are easily removed once the sight is out, and the holes in the barrel are filled with the 6-48 plug screws you took out of the receiver when you mounted the scope.

Where you have a vacant dovetail, you put in a blank. And do it right away, before you tear your hands or gun cases on the sharp edges. Blanks can be purchased for this purpose, wide or narrow. They also can be made from an old sight, or the slot can be filled with a .22 rimfire lead bullet pounded into it and trimmed off. The latter doesn't look bad

Here a solid nylon rod is used as a punch for knocking out a dovetail sight. They nylon is tough enough to withstand such hard usage and pounding but does not mar blued gun surfaces. It is being driven by a rawhide mallet.

Detail of a proper recoil lug mortise.

at all, as the lead soon darkens in color. This procedure is essentially the same for all dovetail sights, rear as well as front.

Should you want to change the sight, often the replacement will not enter the slot, or it will barely start to enter on the right side. To solve this problem, take your small triangular file and grind one side of it smooth for at least four or five inches. Now you can enlarge the dovetail width without deepening it.

Scopes and mountings will be covered in a later chapter in detail.

Bedding of the barrel, receiver and guard parts is of vital importance in the bolt-action rifle: literally all that have not been custom-made or had special factory provision in bedding can stand work in this area.

This is a stock that has split because of an improperly fitted recoil lug. Since the recoil lug did not bear against the rear surfaces of the mortise, the pressure of recoil was transmitted to the stock screw and this caused the splitting.

INLETTING STOCK
FOR TRIGGER GUARD ASSEMBLY

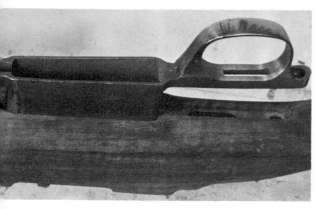

1. The first step in inletting is fitting the trigger guard assembly into the stock.

2. A small hand tool is used to scrape away the black marks left by the forward trigger-guard assembly extension. This spot-and-scrape technique is part and parcel of the inletting procedure.

3. A wood rasp is used to open up the magazine cut. Rasp away a little at a time.

4. Here is a detail of a properly fitted trigger guard assembly. Note the extremely close wood to metal fit.

Receiver bedding. The recoil shoulder on the receiver or the recoil plate or bracket (factories have different names for the steel plate between the receiver and barrel that serves as a recoil shoulder) must fit solidly on its rear face against the inletting cut made for it. If it doesn't, the rifle will force itself back, perhaps split the stock at the rear tang of the receiver or even break out the inletting inside, behind the shoulder. The rifle will not be accurate. The simplest remedy is to place shims between the recoil shoulder and the wood it's supposed to touch. A thin sheet of aluminum is easy to cut with scissors from tear-top containers, etc. It's surprising sometimes how many layers you can use. Thin "fiber" paper—the brownish flexible cardboard used for school theme-book covers—can be used. It doesn't compress much.

George Stidworthy, an eminent-small bore competitive rifleman, once went to Camp Perry and drew an M-1 rifle from the government supply. He used the springs from two ten-cent ballpoint pens to hold the upper handguard in tension and shimmed with fiber to get receiver tension. He won the National Civilian Championship with it.

The best receiver bedding is that done with epoxy. Much more work, but lasts for the life of the arm. Fiberglass was used first and is still in common use, but the epoxy mixtures, such as bisonite, plastic aluminum, plastic steel, etc., are better because they have much less shrinkage than fiberglass and are really easier to work with.

To use any of the synthetic beddings, the metal parts are stripped of small parts—triggers, sears, ejectors, etc.—and then cleaned with solvent and dried. Next, use a little modeling clay, or even putty, to fill up the pin holes and trigger slots. Then coat the receiver bottom and sides with the release compound furnished with the bedding kit. And be sure you get it into the guard screw holes, inside the rails and ramp of the receiver and down in the receiver lug recesses if the front hole goes all the way through. The guard parts receive the same preparation. If you aren't using a prepared kit, see if there isn't some furniture wax around. If it's in a spray can, you have it made. The release compounds (wax in solution) dry fast and leave a coating on the metal that fiberglass or epoxy will not stick to. You must have a dry surface, though. If it's not hard, it will contaminate the surface of the bedding and prevent complete hardening.

Oil will also prevent adherence of the synthetics, but should never be used on any major area because of the contamination angle. It's all right for inside the receiver, etc., if it's used in a very thin coat. Be sure your guard or bedding screws are thoroughly coated with a release agent. Should the rifle become welded together with epoxy, you've got

INLETTING STOCK
FOR RECEIVER ASSEMBLY

1. Some inletting black is brushed onto the receiver just prior to inletting. Wherever the metal parts touch wood they leave a black mark. This is either sliced or scraped away and thus, bit by bit, the action sinks into the wood.

2. Inletting pins are used to keep the receiver in positive alignment during the inletting operation. The complete barrel opening can be inletted as one unit but it is more convenient and exact to inlet receiver first.

Detail of the black smudges left by the inletting black.

3. A small curved chisel is used to slice away the part of the black smudging.

A beveled chisel is used to scrape away the black smudges in the tang area of the cut.

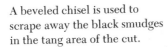

4. The bottom surface of the recoil lug has bottomed into the wood. This indicates the area that must be cut away.

5. A wide flat chisel is used to make the inletting cut for the recoil lug.

Continued on next page

6. The action inletting after the receiver has "bottomed" into the stock. Notice the black smudges on the rear surface of the recoil mortise and the top surface of the action flat.

7. A scribe is used to trace around the partially inletted receiver. These scratch marks will then serve as a guide for slicing away some of the wood.

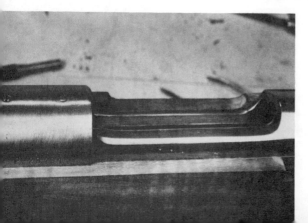

8. A detail of the completely inletted receiver. Note very close wood-to-metal fit.

problems: like having to drill the screw heads off and then slowly driving the receiver out of the stock, very possibly splitting it. If it happens to you, buy a ⅛-inch "easy-out," drill screw heads, drive the easy-out in and use a wrench to back the screws out.

The stock bedding areas are scraped with chisels to them of oil or stock finish so the compound will hold. If scraping even deeply—$1/32$ inch or so—doesn't give clean wood, use a little brush or a bit of cloth held in tweezers to wash it with acetone or lacquer thinner. Either of these will cut oil from the wood surface with a couple of treatments. They will cut and wash off any of the unhardened synthetics from fingers, bench, mixing can, etc., and they'll take off the release compound when you clean up the metal parts for reassembly.

The outside surfaces of the stock around the inletting area must be protected. Either cover with masking tape or use your finger to judiciously coat them with grease or oil. Don't use a release agent! It doesn't come off easily, and you can't use acetone or lacquer thinner without damaging the finish. Any wax will do, of course, probably best of all. A layer of masking or other tape fitted to front of the recoil lug before the release agent is applied and then itself coated, will make future assembly and disassembly considerably easier.

"T"-shaped handle guard screws are most convenient if much stock rebedding is contemplated. They may be purchased or, as the one at right, made by silver-soldering a homemade handle to an old regular screw. The normal screw shown second from right has had a grind-cut made in its threads by corner of wheel, to turn it into a tap for clearing holes in receivers of any bedding material which may be difficult to pick out.

"T" handles speed up the process of inletting considerably and eliminate the chance of burring up the original stock screws. Here is one being used.

GLASS-BEDDING A STOCK

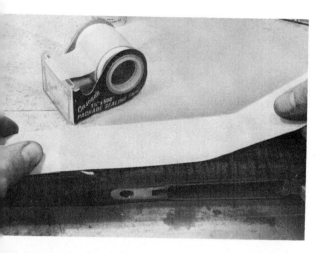

1. Wide strips of masking tape are applied to a finished stock to protect the exterior surfaces during glass-bedding operation.

2. The original inletting is hogged out and roughed up prior to the glass bedding process. This roughing-up operation not only makes room for the glass bedding compound but also makes for a better adhering surface for the fiberglass.

3. The barrel channel has been roughed up by a series of chisel cuts. This opens up the channel for the fiberglass compound and guarantees better adhesion.

4. A coat of paste wax is applied to the metal parts just prior to glass bedding. This keeps the fiberglass compound from sticking to the metal.

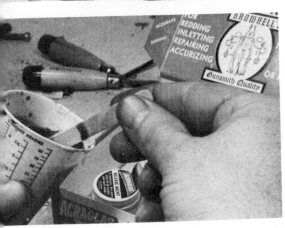

5. A cup of fiberglass compound is mixed. Proper blending and preparation of the fiberglass compound is essential to the project.

6. The fiberglass compound is applied to the barrel channel.

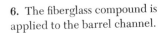

7. The completed fiberglass job. Note that the fit is so perfect that even the serial numbers and tool marks on the metal parts are transferred to the fiberglass.

Barrel bedding. Whether you bed the barrel depends on the barrel. If it weighs under four-and-one-half pounds (the average standard sporter barrel weighs three pounds, the heavy sporter, four), it can be floated—clear of all contact with stock—from the receiver forward. If it's heavier than four-and-one-half pounds, bed the breech just ahead of the receiver for an inch or so. Just a small area on the bottom needs contact; a ½-inch-wide spot is sufficient. The idea is to help the receiver hold up the weight of the barrel. Few rifles have more than a ¾-inch thread contact with receivers, most much less, and a heavy barrel puts a strain on them. Try holding a broom in a horizontal position by gripping only the end of the handle, and you'll get the idea. It doesn't hurt to bed the lighter barrels; it often may help them, but usually it doesn't.

Bedding screws are guard screws with long shanks and cross handles welded or brazed on, for ease and speed in assembling rifles into stocks during inletting and bedding. A synthetic bedding job is hard on the regular screws, though with care a one-time deal doesn't have to be bad. Bedding screws can be purchased from gunsmith-supply companies or made from old damaged guard screws by attaching handles. A few modern arms, the Remingtons for example, use the standard ¼ by 28 thread: you can buy Allen-head machine screws for a few cents each, file the sharp edges of the head to fit guard countersinks and use them. The Allen wrench gives much greater leverage than a standard screwdriver, with no slipping out of slots to mar the stock.

With the rifle and stock prepared and the stock in horizontal position in a vise, mix your bedding compound according to directions. Use a small wooden paddle to coat your inletting uniformly, filling the lug recess one-third full and building a little mound where it will reach the breech of the barrel if you wish. Then slowly lower the rifle into the stock. If you wish to bed the front and rear ends of the trigger guard, it is best to wipe the compound on the guard and then press it into the stock. And if it'll stay in by itself, or you can requisition a third hand to hold it in, put it in the stock before the receiver and barrel. Run the guard screws in immediately and draw them up tight, though you needn't strain the screwdriver. Barrel clearance can be obtained by using cardboard, a bit of leather or anything that holds it above the bottom of the channel while the epoxy or fiberglass is setting up—hardening. This should be just a small piece of material two or three inches ahead of the receiver in the channel.

It is not really vital to bed the complete receiver in this way. It's only necessary for the rear-tang and recoil-lug areas and that under the receiver ring, so the guard screws have something solid to pull against.

In fact, if the rear-tang area of the receiver has a large contact with the stock, you needn't bed it. For example: Mauser, yes; Remington, no.

The immediate problem is always how much stuff to mix up. You usually need about half of what you think you do. Three-quarters of an ounce, liquid measure, will do for most complete receiver beddings and half that for a front-end-only job. If your stock has a vast clearance between wood and metal, of course you need double the amount. But it's messy when the stuff oozes out and runs all over the stock and bench when you put in the metal and draw up the screws. So you want as little overage as possible.

A detail of a .375 H & H Magnum rifle which has been strengthened around the recoil area by fiberglass. This treatment will keep heavy recoiling rifles from damaging and splitting the stock especially around the recoil lug area. Note that in this case only the areas immediately adjacent to the recoil-lug mortise have been fiberglass treated.

Watch the left-over mixture in its mixing cup, or a left-over dab on a piece of paper. When it begins to harden in a half hour or longer, turn the guard screws back a fraction of a turn then bring back where they were. Repeat this another half-hour or forty-five minutes later. This is insurance for getting the screws out when the operation is finished and the bedding is cured.

Should you use fiberglass or a clear or white epoxy, artist's dry pigment—color—can be used to darken the mixture to match your stock color. Only a tiny trace of it is necessary, so be cautious when adding.

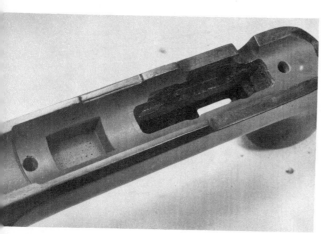

A detail of a very neatly done fiberglass fitting.

Extreme care must be used to avoid "locks," where epoxy or fiberglass can harden in a hole or recess in metal and so lock to the wood. This is why you want the modeling clay. Even polish out deep tool marks on the recoil lug or plate, or any straight-down sides your receiver may have that will be in the bedding, and break—file—any sharp corners so that they will not tend to shave or scrape off fragments of hardened bedding material later when you assemble the arm ready to use. Such scrapings get under the metal and prevent perfect final contact. With a good epoxy job there is room for only a thin film of oil on the metal! This means oiled and wiped off.

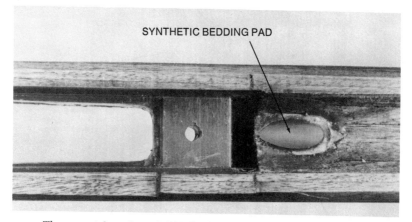

SYNTHETIC BEDDING PAD

The essential synthetic bedding area in a large-caliber bolt-action rifle stock. Note that only a small pad is needed for support of heavy barrel.

Trigger adjustment. Whatever it is to start with, the gun owner inevitably wants the trigger adjustment changed! Military bolt-action rifles have two-stage or "take-up" pulls—triggers having a cam close to their fulcrum. They provide great leverage on the sear and so are able to pull almost out of engagement with the cocking piece or firing pin with little effort. This is the take-up, after which the rear cam, or back-end of the trigger at top, comes into engagement for the harder but shorter final pull-off. This is a safety factor in that the sear can have much contact area with the cocking piece and yet a controllable trigger pull can be provided.

Bolts usually fit loosely in receivers and are able to move up and down a bit, enough to allow accidental firing if engagement is reduced to allow a short or light pull without the double-cam trigger. Where the bolt and sleeve are tight when the rifle is cocked, it is possible to eliminate the first or initial cam, reduce engagement by grinding off the top of the sear or the bottom of the cocking piece to give a short pull-off and therefore easier pull.

To make a nonadjustable trigger adjustable, have the front lip or step on the trigger extended by welding on metal, and then drill and tap for a small screw and locknut. Winding the screw in against the sear body will cause the trigger to lever the sear down and so reduce engagement to the required point. An alternate method is to build up the top of this trigger lip with solder or even a metal epoxy such as the plastic metals sold in tubes at hobby and hardware stores. While easily filed to suit, it should hold for quite a while and is no problem to replace. The only adjustment is by your file—the more you file, the more pull you have! Altering no parts, this is easy to try and is a good way to see if the idea works with your particular rifle.

Commercial triggers—really complete trigger and sear mechanisms in housings—are more popular today. Most fit the arms they are made for with little or no alteration to the receiver and guard and usually only a little stock inletting to give them room. Nearly all are release or drop-sear types, meaning that the sear is held in engagement by the trigger nose or a secondary sear, and when the trigger is pulled, the cocking piece can force the sear down and override it. Where the Mauser-type military trigger pulls the sear out of contact, the patent trigger releases it.

Triggers have springs to return the sear up to reengage the firing assembly, usually not adjustable and usually stronger than needed, set screws to adjust engagement of the trigger nose with sear notch or bottom face and a spring with screw adjustment to return the trigger nose

Detail of the excellent Keyon Trigger. The screw in the lower surface of the unit, just behind the trigger, adjusts the weight of pull down to a very few ounces. The forward screw adjusts the travel.

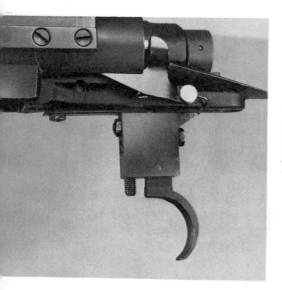

The Timney Target Model trigger for the Model 70 Winchester rifle. The screw just in front of the trigger adjusts the weight of pull.

The Sako adjustable trigger mechanism. The lower screw in front of the unit adjusts the weight of pull and the screw just above it adjusts the sear engagement and overtravel.

The Remington Model 700
trigger mechanism.

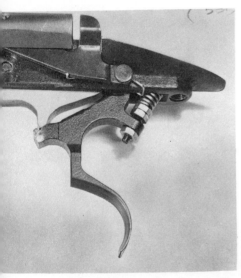

The new Winchester Model 70
trigger mechanism.

back into the engagement position—also usually too strong. You have to pull against this spring as well as against mainspring pressure against the sear contact in order to fire the rifle. The spring being about ⅛-inch in diameter, it's hard to buy a weaker replacement anywhere. So don't buy it. Next time you're in a filling station, walk back to where they fix tires and pick up a couple of discarded valve stems. For a Remington, clip off an end, take off the spring, touch the middle of the spring to the corner of your grinding wheel and you now have two trigger-return springs that allow a safe pull down to a pound and a half if wanted! And adjustment up as wanted. For other trigger assemblies, make light springs slightly longer than the originals.

Regulation of engagement and overtravel is easy if you know what not to do, which is just not trying to be too precise. Move the overtravel screw out until the trigger is felt to move appreciably after

ADJUSTMENT OF WINCHESTER MODEL 70 TRIGGER MECHANISM

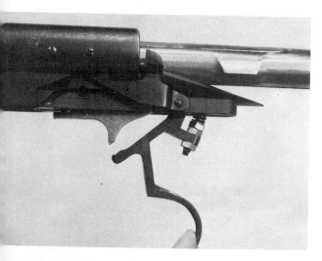

1. This Model 70 mechanism needs adjustment. Notice the wide gap between the sear surfaces when the trigger is pulled to the rear. This makes for a very sloppy trigger pull.

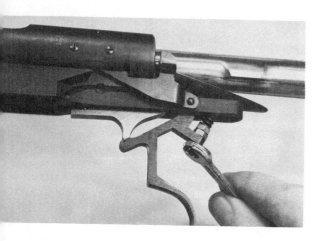

2. To adjust the trigger pull on the Model 70, first loosen the lock nuts at the rear of the trigger unit.

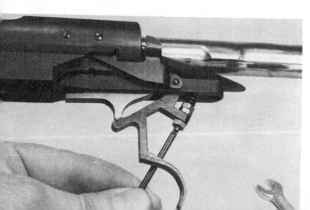

3. With the lock nuts loosened, the setting screw can be adjusted. This determines the amount of travel the trigger will move.

4. Here the surface of the Model 70 trigger which touches the sear is honed down for a more shallow contact.

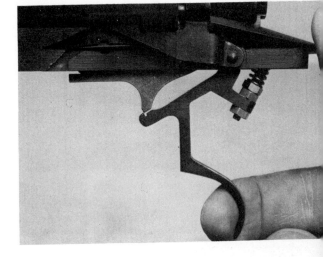

5. After adjustment, the Model 70 trigger has only a very slight amount of travel. This is a crisp, clean-pulling trigger.

the sear is released, and then adjust the engagement until the rifle will just remain cocked when the bolt is slammed and closed with a fair amount of force. This will give a "clean" or "crisp" let-off. The trigger spring will give you the pull-weight.

The great mistake nearly all people make with trigger systems is trying to adjust them so as to get a perfect no-movement trigger pull. They hold the rifle in their laps and slowly squeeze the trigger, usually pulling up rather than back, thus changing the leverage ratio against the trigger pin, or fulcrum. You can feel creep—movement before release—in a set trigger this way! Always hold a gun in firing position to try the trigger, and always allow a bit of overtravel, because if you don't, the mechanism isn't going to last very long. The sharp edges will scrape past each other, and with the pressures on them, one will give. Shooters always worry about this, but seldom ever realize that any after-firing movement of the trigger is only felt when dry-firing or snapping the trigger. In actual shooting, even a .22 has sufficient recoil that such movement will never be noticed.

The modern sporting bolt-rifle trigger nearly always has some adjustment, even if it's not a complex or self-contained assembly. Winchester's various M70's have a trigger-return spring that can vary weight of pull, and its screw guide can be used as a travel stop. Engagement variation is possible only by reducing the top of the trigger nose so it has less contact with the sear. Never work on the sear of a Model 70: only on the trigger. First, any change of dimension on the sear contact changes its seating position against the trigger face in the notch, resulting in the sear moving forward here and down at its upper rear face, contacting the firing pin, which in turn moves a little forward. Result: your safety doesn't work any more. These—and ninety-nine percent of all trigger systems—are based on a ninety-degree angle of the notch face, trigger top, sear face, etc., to a line running through the center of the trigger pin. Change this angle and the trigger can either slip out of engagement when the arm is cocked, or it can be forced to increase sear pressure when pulled, requiring unnatural effort for the pull-off. Should too much engagement be removed by grinding on the trigger nose and an unreliable situation created, reduce the area behind the notch to gain the needed engagement. This can usually be done without throwing out the safety functioning; if not, the bolt must be disassembled and the notch or the cut in the cocking piece for the safety must be moved back to compensate for the new position of the cocking piece.

There is a readily discernible system of operation to any trigger arrangement if you study it a little. Often parts are interdependent, and the alteration of an arm at one area for a desired effect may cause mis-

The Ohaus trigger-pull scale being used to weigh a rifle's weight of pull. A weight of approximately 3 pounds is good for most sporting rifles.

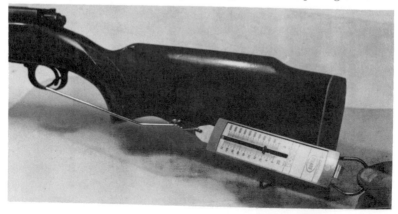

Military and commercial Mauser triggers, the military at left showing the two "humps" at top which give the two-stage, or takeup, pull.

Commercial triggers. . . . Top, a Mauser trigger assembly with side-safety incorporated, showing the adjusting screws, etc. Center-right, the Remington trigger assembly, minus safety and bolt-release parts so that the contact between sear and trigger can be seen through the small hole in upper center. Bottom, the M70 Winchester trigger system, minus trigger-return spring, showing the positions of sear and trigger.

Double and single set-trigger mechanisms, to be fixed into trigger guards. Shown with sear-levers, or "kick-offs," used with bolt-action rifle sears. For other types of arms, similar provision must be made so that the moving trigger can contact and move a sear to permit the arm to fire.

A small, pointed piece of hardwood is used to clean the face of a recessed bolt. Particular attention must be paid to clean under the extractors on this type of bolt mechanism.

functioning when the part moves out of position or connection with another part. Make sure you fully understand everything before using a file, stone or grinder.

With the exception of single-shot target or bench-rest types, center-fire bolt rifles have a common bedding factor to contend with in the contact of the magazine box with the receiver. The magazine box must not contact the receiver directly; the stock must be able to resist the tension of both when the guard screws are tightened. If the magazine box or, in the case of military and some commercial Mauser-type rifles, guard-screw ferrules in stock holes hold the guard from being tightened down against wood, the stock becomes only a handle for the rifle. Much accuracy is lost. Bed so that only the screws make metal-to-metal contact between the receiver and guard. Sometimes guards can be shimmed with paper to gain clearance, but it is never hard to file a little off the top. The magazine box should be as close to the receiver as you can get it without actually touching.

The bolt and its component parts can often be something of a drag, literally, in the operation of the rifle. There are a few easily done operations that can aid the operator. On the Mauser types—those with the long extractor on side of the bolt such as Springfield the old Winchester M70, etc., as well as true Mausers—the extractor may have a tight collar, or ring, holding it, and it may have so much spring tension on the bolt that it resists turning freely. Since it has to make a quarter-turn back and forth as the bolt is opened and closed, this can add to the effort required. Don't remove it from the bolt; instead, put a screwdriver blade under the extractor in front of the ring collar and twist to spring it out from the bolt against the holding tension. Do it cautiously. Now take the rawhide mallet and pound on the extractor over the col-

This is the Canjar single set-trigger mechanism. The trigger can be used as an ordinary trigger or by pushing forward on the rear of the trigger a tiny tab pops out of the forward surface of the trigger shoe. Touching this tab with a pressure of only a few ounces fires the rifle.

lar—take the screwdriver out first!—and see if things aren't a little easier to move around. If it's still very tight, using a screwdriver blade at the rear end of the extractor, lift it straight out from the bolt and try to bend this long leg of it a little. It can be pulled out ⅜ inch from bolt contact without breaking anything. Pulled out any further, you are taking chances.

Modern-design bolts with recessed faces, spring-plunger ejectors and small-area hook or detent contact areas must be kept clean for reliable functioning. Since practically all bolt faces turn 60 to 90 degrees on the chambered cartridge and the fired case won't turn, the extractors very often scrape brass from the case. These scrapings can accumulate and cause trouble with both extractors and ejectors. And a stuck plun-

What may happen if you put the wrong bolt in the right rifle (small part has chipped off from bolt face). Parts removed from arms for safe-keeping should be tagged with a serial number if not already marked.

73

IMPROVING SAVAGE MODEL 99

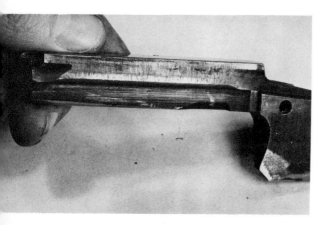

The bright area on the side of this Savage Model 99 bolt shows where it has been rubbing in the receiver.

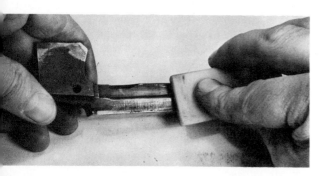

An Arkansas Stone is used to polish up the area where the rubbing occurs.

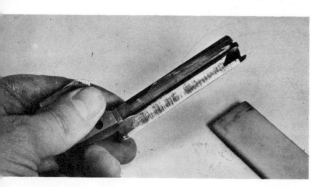

The Savage Model 99 bolt after polishing. This procedure makes lever action rifles work much easier.

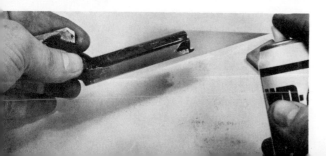

After polishing, the bolt is wiped clean and then lightly sprayed with oil.

ger–ejector can be real trouble to clear. In my personal experience, I have found it best to keep such bolt faces oiled only when the rifle is *not* in use. Before taking the arm out to use it, dip the tip of the bolt in solvent—any kind that cuts the oil and evaporates fast. Oil on the bolt face, in cuts and in the ejector hole will hold brass bits and other foreign matter. You'll have much less trouble if there's no oil. Any unwanted debris can be blown away with your breath if you take the bolt out and examine it now and then during shooting. After shooting, when the rifle is being cleaned thoroughly, use a solvent and a brush on the bolt face, and dry and oil for preservation.

We'll cover stock work on bolt-action rifles later in detail, as it applies to all long arms, not just to bolt actions.

Lever-Action Rifles

In this type of rifle, the operation of the lever sets in motion a number of parts through cams and even gears in some models, in addition to the direct lever contacts. Therefore, there is a lot of friction in working the lever to contend with. After any use at all, even just working the lever a dozen times on a new rifle, examination will show where parts are scraping when they should be sliding. Disassembly and working with Russell's little stones and small files with 320 abrasive cloth wrapped

A gunsmith checks a magazine tube for any dents that might hinder the cartridge feeding.

around them can work wonders in a short time. All you want to do is re-move burrs and edges of rough tool marks—not reduce the size of the parts! Should the action remain stiff and sticky after doing this and cleaning out and reoiling, it may help to coat parts and the inside of the receiver with oil and fine abrasive powder—lapping compounds, not valve-grinding stuff! Then by working the action perhaps twenty times, washing it clean—thoroughly clean—with solvent and lubricating, the action should function quite smoothly. Lapping powders may not be easy to obtain, but silica powder is sometimes available at drugstores, and in a real pinch, you can use ordinary tooth powder. It's a very mild abrasive, of course, and you'll have to work harder and longer with it to accomplish much.

In lever-action rifles with tubular magazines, the cartridge-lifting parts are very important, and an examination of their movements as the lever is operated to slowly open and close the bolt should show any tendency to hang up or drag at any point in their cycle. Study the parts carefully before doing any corrective work, for a sudden increase in tension or resistance to lever movement may be due to another part coming into contact for its proper functioning. Don't change any angles or polish off anything until you are positive such work will not cause changes in the fitting or functioning of neighboring parts.

Keep magazine tubes, springs and followers clean and with as little oil in and on them as possible without their being completely unprotected. And the same goes for rotary and box magazines. Use caution with exposed tubes. Examine them after every hunt for a dent that might have escaped notice earlier. It could cause a follower or cartridge to hang up and leave you with an "unloaded" gun that is able to fire.

Keep locking recesses clean. These are often hidden and may remain unchecked for years. Foreign matter can accumulate here and prevent the block or bolt from being completely locked.

Trigger adjustment.   Most of the older designs will permit good three-pound clean triggers with a little work on hammer notches and lubrication with moly greases. Some of the newer types have the trigger involved with so many additional parts—or as part of the lever assembly and so not maintaining a fixed position or relationship with the firing parts—that good trigger pulls cannot be achieved. There's just too much movement of too many parts involved.

The Savage Model 99 has a straight-line firing pin, rather than a hammer, incorporated in the bolt and moving with it as the lever is manipulated. However, examination of the action with the stock removed

IMPROVING TRIGGER ACTION

The pencil point indicates the amount of sear engagement of the Savage 99 lever action rifle.

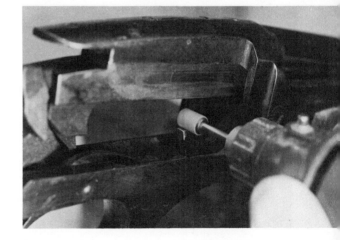

Here a Dremel tool is used to grind the Savage 99 sear.

Here is the Savage Model 99 sear after alteration. By reducing the amount of sear engagement, the trigger pull is considerably improved. If done judiciously this does not in any way interfere with the safe operation of the rifle.

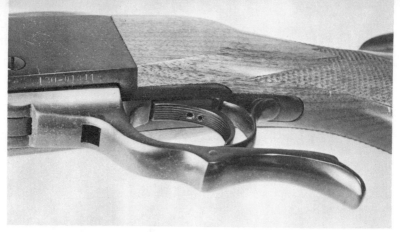

A Ruger #1 single-shot trigger. The two Allen screws in the face of the trigger adjust both the trigger weight of pull and the trigger travel.

clearly shows how parts operate. Usually quite a lot of the top of sear can be ground off to reduce engagement and so give a shorter and cleaner pull without making the arm unsafe. The function and fit of parts in very obvious. Nothing complicated, no hidden meanings!

Safeties on lever-action rifles are usually a safety notch or half-cock notch on the hammer, or a simple trigger block, and thus are not really worth staking your life on. They do not lock the firing pin from moving, as do most bolt-rifle types. So be careful when handling these rifles in the field or on the range. Trigger safeties should be checked often as any wear or play may allow the trigger to move sufficiently to fire the rifle when the safety is in the "safe" position. While the hammer rifles won't fire if the hammer slips from the safety-notch should it be worn or broken out, they will if any hard blow or a fall forces the hammer forward with any force.

The lever does not give any excess power in extraction, and therefore both rifle chambers and ammunition must be kept clean and undamaged to prevent cases from becoming stuck so tightly as to require a rod to drive them out from the muzzle. If reloaded ammunition is used, care must be exercised that cases are sized to enter the chamber freely, are not overloaded and are not used more than three times.

The autoloading rifle calls for the same care on chamber and ammunition and the same treatment for functioning and smoothing of parts and magazines. Trigger work must be done with great care, however, as angles and spring-tensions on sears and connectors are designed to prevent jarring out of contact when the bolt or block slams forward in closing. If all excess trigger movment is removed, engagement of parts may seem adequate on the bench, but be insufficient for actual firing. It's best to do a little at a time and test-fire the gun after each ad-

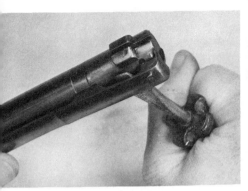

Here is the technique for loosening up the extractor fit and thus smoothing out bolt operation. The screwdriver blade is twisted (left), thus bringing the extractor away from the bolt. Next (right), the extractor is smartly rapped in the area of the extractor collar. A rawhide mallet is used to avoid marring the metal surfaces.

justment. And always test an autoloading arm with at least three cartridges in the magazine. The one in the chamber will always fire—you need to know what happens after that! Cleanliness and lubrication are vital to reliability in auto arms of any type.

The bedding of the fore-end can affect accuracy in some of the new rifles that have two-piece stocks. When pulled tight by screws, the fore-end should not exert pressure against the receiver or any other part. It just fits, with no pressure. And where there is full contact with the barrel—when it's not cut away for gas systems, etc.—the fore-end should have full contact, not just pull down at the front or back. Bedding with a thin layer of epoxy has helped on several types of autoloaders. And this helps Savage 99's, too, as well as single-shot rifles.

The single shot, meaning the old-fashioned kind—not the single-shot bolt actions that are to be treated as any other bolt action—is easy to clean and care for, and reasonably easy to get trigger adjustment. Parts are usually fitted closely and well finished, and little usually has to

Set-triggers, double and single, shown to illustrate their kick-offs, or sear levers, above each trigger. These parts must nearly always be filed or ground to suit a particular rifle, or made entirely new, of flat steel shaped to outline, filed to fit, then hardened.

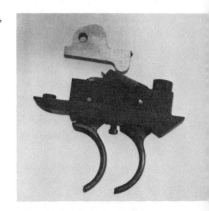

be done. Size and fit of the fore-end can affect accuracy, but it is easy to experiment with beddings to find what helps the most. Sights are obvious in attachment, etc., but any changes from the original may call for matching changes in the buttstock. The buttstocks are almost all designed for a low sight line so that any higher sight or telescopic mounting will leave the stock too low to support the face for steady sighting.

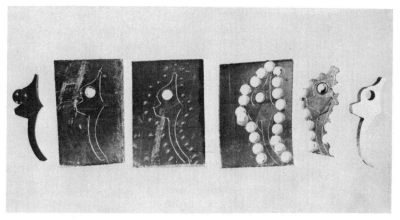

How a replacement part, in this instance a single-shot rifle trigger, is produced. From left: the original trigger, with its screw; the material, of or made to correct thickness, coated with layout dope, proper size hole drilled, then original trigger laid on it with screw through trigger and material to locate, and outline drawn. Then, center-punched around outline, holes drilled, excess broken away, then filed and ground to outline to produce the part at right.

In barrel cleaning, don't let solvents run down into the actions to cut away the oil or grease lubricating the sear or trigger functioning. And, if rifles are stored or racked upright, it is best to have single shots, lever rifles and autoloaders stand muzzle down. This prevents action and/or barrel oils from running down into the stock, deteriorating the wood and weakening attachment to the receiver or frame.

Extractor fitting and function is rather weak on some of the obsolete single-shot actions still in use. Parts have cuts that prevent much strength, don't have much leverage to make them work. All that can be done is to keep extractors oiled, free to move as intended—meaning don't let anything get down behind them, not even a thread from a cleaning patch—and don't slam levers down hard and abuse them.

A cabinet full of rifles and shotguns stood up on their muzzle so that the oil and cleaning solvents will not drain into the mechanism and/or soak into the stocks.

Rimfire Rifles

You can't call them all .22's any more. There are a few variations now such as the .22 rimfire magnum, which is a very potent little creation. It's potent enough that you might be tempted to take apart many old standard .22 rim-fire arms to rechamber for it. Don't try it! Or Remington's little bottlenecked special, which takes rifles just for it and nothing else. However, such cartridges and their rifles need the same consideration with regard to maintenance, etc., so we'll consider all rimfires as rimfires, period. Even the few .25 and .32 calibers still in use are subject to the same troubles as the lowliest .22.

The actions used—bolt, lever, autoloading and single-shot—take the same care, maintenance and adjustment as the center-fire rifles, but with variations. The metal used in nearly all rimfires is soft and burrs, wears and bends easier, so that trouble can develop through wear in use as well as already exist in a new arm.

Wax or greases needed to lubricate the lead bullets builds up around the chamber, in bolt-face recesses and in the cuts for extractors and ejectors and prevents perfect fitting of parts to rifle. The lubricant itself is OK; it's the dust and dirt that mixes with it and makes it harden that cause the malfunction. Keep a box of toothpicks and an old toothbrush on the bench to use in keeping the bolt and barrel breech clean. Stamped metal parts are often easy to bend so they don't work right. They're easy to bend back to correct position also. The spring-loaded feeding gates, cartridge lifters, etc., often are necessarily loose fitting, but still, they have to line up fairly well to work.

If the rifle doesn't feed well, you need dummy cartridges to use in adjusting. These are now usually obtainable from ammunition makers on special order through sporting goods stores, but if not, with a little care you can make them from live ammunition. With a small, sharp drill bit, about $1/16$ inch will do, using a wood block to rest the cartridge on, drill through the case midway in its length and sift the powder out. Drill fairly fast—too slow and you could get too much heat from friction of the drill on the case. Drop these cases minus powder in a small jar of thin oil, thin enough to enter the hole and fill the case, and make sure it does. This will kill the priming compound. Water won't; afterward it can dry out and the primer may be able to fire. Leave them in oil for a day or two, take out, wash in solvent and you have dummies that will function through the arms in safety.

And you do need these dummies to do almost any sort of action-check on a rimfire repeating rifle. Clip-magazine lips can be adjusted for tension and angle, tubes, followers and lifters made to reveal their functions, as well as the obvious chambering–extraction–ejection cycles pursued.

Long firing pins giving excessive protrusion are common on older .22's and probably on some of the newer ones. Dry-firing, or snapping the arm empty, allows them to hit the rear of the barrel and often only a few dry firings can upset the edge of the chamber, forcing metal into it so that while a cartridge will still enter, the fired case will not extract, having expanded to fill the chamber ahead of this burr. Shortening the firing pin is simple as you just grind it off until the tip won't touch the barrel, but you'll need to do some pin-punch work to get the firing pin out of bolt first!

USE DUMMY CARTRIDGES

A ⅛-inch hole is drilled through a cartridge case as the first step of making up a batch of dummy cartridges. The hole in the cartridge makes them easily identifiable.

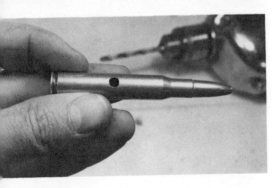

A detail of the dummy cartridge with the bullet in place.

A clipload of the dummy cartridges is fitted into a bolt-action rifle to check the feeding and extraction.

The function of an M-1 is checked with a dummy cartridge inserted in chamber.

SHORTENING A .22 RIMFIRE FIRING PIN

An example of a poorly shaped and fitted .22 rimfire firing pin. Notice that the firing pin is rather pointed and overly long.

This is a result of a misfitted firing pin. Notice how the pin has dented the inner edge of the chamber.

A detail of the firing pin after being removed from the bolt.

The end of the firing pin is filed to a flat shape.

The altered firing pin back in the bolt. Notice that the face has been blunted somewhat and is the correct length.

Fixing up the rear end of a barrel that's been damaged in this way may not be so easy. Old-fashioned single shots and most bolt-action rim-fire rifles will allow you to get at the chamber pretty well to let a small round file tip enter to take away the offending inside burr with a few strokes—and your strokes can't be over ¼ inch long. If the barrel breech is completely accessible, you can even cut the metal clear with the tip of a sharp knife. The face of the barrel can't be changed: you cannot round off or bevel the edge of the chamber at this point because the rim of cartridge must be backed solidly against the firing-pin blow in order for dependable firing.

Removing the lug which locks the receiver and barrel together in this small-bore rifle. Pumps, autoloaders, and some bolt-action rifles have the barrel and receiver fitted together by some means such as this.

In a slide action or lever or some varieties of autoloading .22, the barrel will have to be removed for work on the chamber. Barrels may be held to receivers with pins or screwed in. Removal isn't really too difficult. All parts must be removed, of course, from the barrel/receiver assembly, maybe even the rear sight. Clean the joint of the barrel and receiver and let a few drops of Liquid Wrench or similar penetrating oil work in, from an hour to a week (if any rust around thread or joint is observed). Clamp the barrel in grooved wooden blocks in the vise, if it's the threaded type. If pinned, clamp the receiver. Use the largest monkey wrench or crescent you can borrow—not because you need a lot of strength, but because the larger the wrench the deeper the jaws so you'll have a good area to contact the flat sides of receivers. Pad the jaws of the wrench with hard cardboard and tighten on the receiver and unscrew from the barrel for the threaded type. With pinned barrels having receivers open at the rear, the receiver is clamped and a large hardwood dowel put through it and used to drive the receiver out. You did take the pins out first, didn't you? When you can't get in the rear end, you must clamp the barrel and use hard wood or even aluminum blocks against the front of the receiver to hammer against to drive if off the barrel. It goes back together pretty easily, really, and lining up index marks or extractor slots takes care of position so the front sight points straighten up again.

Most of the .22 bolt-action sporting rifles made in the past fifty years have been held together with just one screw, usually a large-headed coin-slotted type. Combined with the oversized machine-inletting, tightening this screw does strange things to the rifle's point of impact, that is, where it hits, in relation to sighting. This is particularly

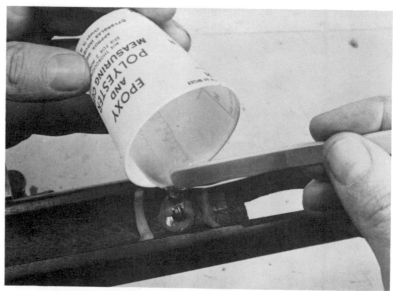

A bit of modeling clay has been used to make a "dam" on each side of bedding area to retard the flow of imbedding compound. This treatment helps inexpensive rifles hold their point of impact better.

true if the rifle has a telescopic sight. Take the rifle apart to carry and put it together in the field, and you may suddenly be shooting five inches high at fifty yards. Full-length rebedding, or bedding in epoxy or fiberglass isn't usually very practical for such rifles. It's best to build modeling-clay dams an inch on either side of this takedown screw, wax the screw, barrel or receiver at this area, etc., and then put a blob of your synthetic bedding stuff in and put the gun together, just tightening the screw enough to pull the receiver into the stock without straining either one. After this, the rifle will always reassemble to the same tension and shoot to its sight setting.

Trigger pulls on most, if not all, .22 sporting rifles are pretty rough and heavy. Only the most expensive foreign-made sporters have decent triggers. As a rule, parts are made of mild or case-hardened steels which wear with use, and to be on the safe side manufacturers provide for much engagement area, which of course makes for long and heavy pulls on the triggers. Examination of the sear and trigger functioning, study of the movement of each part and its relation to others will indicate where you can file off metal to reduce engagement. Usually if you go too far, it is obvious where to take off on the other end or a connecting part to correct the slip. Parts can almost always be filed, but the fine-cut wheel on the bench grinder is always there for the hardened ones. Remember to always lubricate. Parts wear, but they'll wear more if dry than if oiled or greased.

Hard and fast action of levers and slides will wear internal parts, excessively sometimes, and usually there is little you can do except to order new parts and install them. Unless you like to weld and reshape very odd-shaped parts! Which may have to be done for rifles long out of production for which no parts are available.

Should you wish to teach a small son to shoot, you have problems. Not since the days of custom muzzle-loaders have boys' rifles really been made for boys. Any single-shot bolt-action rifle you can get will have too much stock and too much trigger pull, although the barrel length and weight may be OK. It's best to take the stock off and make a stock yourself, kid-size. It doesn't have to be hard walnut: it can be soft pine, easy to shape with knife, chisel and file. If you can't find 1¼-inch or 1½-inch soft clear wood at a pattern shop, go to a lumberyard for ¾-inch shelving and glue two pieces together. Make the pistol grip close to the trigger and small in diameter so the child's hand can really fit it.

Cut the trigger pull down to two pounds if you can. A small boy can learn coordination very quickly; his hand is so small, he gets little leverage on a trigger and his hand isn't strong: A two-pound pull can be as heavy for an eight-year-old as an eight-pound pull for his father. The customary five- or six-pound pull on "junior" rifles is so "safe" the kids can't shoot! The two-pound pull discourages them from pulling the rifle off the mark by having to use excessive strength to get the rifle to fire.

Keep a rimfire rifle cleaned and oiled, and it will last a lifetime or two. Give it no care, and it'll give you trouble. Cleaning the barrel is easy—after firing, a patch or two with solvent will usually take out the little leading even good smooth barrels pick up; then a patch with oil will keep it from rusting until the next day of use.

6

Handguns

Revolvers

There are so many types and variations of revolvers now in existence that it is difficult to make any general comment beyond "keeping them clean," but we'll try to cover those in most common possession. First, the best known, the side-swing cylinder double action, Colt and Smith & Wesson Type. Type, because in addition to the originals, we now have U. S.-, Japanese-, Brazilian- and West German-made arms of this type, not to mention Spanish revolvers. Regardless of origin, any these center-fire arms, made after 1967, are of good and safe construction. Germany's Korth and Sauer revolvers rate right at the top. Until the middle 1930's Spain flooded the world with imitation Colt and S & W's, many of them so poorly made as to be unsafe. After the Spanish Civil War in 1936, however, government standards were set for the arms industry, and for the past generation quality and material control has been excellent. Should any reader have or fall heir to any ancient revolver of doubtful pedigree, don't load and fire it to see if it works: break or grind off the firing pin and keep it for a souvenir if you wish.

Bad handling—rough usage—causes most of the trouble with good revolvers. Thumbing the latch and "throwing" the cylinder in and out is a fine way to strain the crane and loosen things up in general. Tightening it up is a job for a competent gunsmith or the factory. I just can't tell you how hard to hit and where with a lead hammer! Colt and Colt-type revolvers suffer more than S & W-type arms do, the design being rather more complicated and having more parts working and so wearing. The Colt "hand," which engages the cylinder ratchet, has two pins that can wear and throw the arm out of time. Timing means bringing the cylinder around and locking it in position exactly in line with the barrel for firing. Wear on the pins, the cylinder lock or its notches in the cylinder—any one or any combination can put the revolver out of timing. Or cause a worn or burred ratchet.

Probably simply because they are smaller, the ratchets and hands on the older small-frame models are more often at fault than those on the big handguns in throwing them out of time. While a bad ratchet can be recut and a hand tip lengthened by careful hammering ("cold-forging" sounds better!), it is difficult for anyone and impossible for shaky hands on the handgrinder. Get a new ratchet, or a used one in good condition. Peening out a hand tip isn't difficult, and you can't get into as much trouble than if you should manage to get it longer than it was when new and so push the rachet and cylinder so far around that the bolt won't engage to lock the cylinder. You know what you have done, and you can gently file the tip to proper dimensions.

The cylinder bolt, often called the "lock," is the little rounded bar in the frame above the trigger that engages in notches in the cylinder to hold it in time and line. These often drag on the cylinder and may mar the blue on a new gun with just a few turns. Removal and careful stoning down the top, without rounding off square edges, can take care of this if the condition is caught in time. A high bolt may be due to it being oversize, or the rebound lever actuating it a little incorrectly. This is hard to correct, however.

The Colt system employs a V mainspring, one leg for the hammer, the other for the rebound lever, which puts tension on the hand, trigger and cylinder bolt. This V spring can be bent in or out to make cocking easier or harder (in case it should weaken or take a set and thus give poor ignition), but any change affects several parts and functions.

You can see almost all the functions of a Colt or Smith & Wesson by taking off the sideplate. First take off the grips. Then using a screwdriver that fits the screw slots, take out the sideplate screws. Remove the cylinder—the front side-plate screw in the S & W allows the opened

Inner parts of the Colt double-action revolver, 1917 or New Service type.

At top, S & W hammer, trigger, and rebound-slide assembly. The spring showing is the one to shorten to reduce trigger pull. Bottom, the trigger, hammer, sear, and disconnector of the Colt .45 pistol. All must function properly in firing. Trigger shown is long target type with adjustable stop screw to limit rearward travel.

cylinder and yoke to slide out forward. The crane lock and its screw are on the right side of the Colt frame above and forward of the trigger. Removal allows the cylinder assembly to move forward and out. Now take a rawhide mallet or a block of wood and tap the frame at the edges of the sideplate until it raises from its perfect fit. If it doesn't come entirely free, a small, flat screwdriver blade can be used against the hammer and trigger, but don't pry out against the edges of the plate, the inner edges, that is. If the plate is stubborn, you may put dents in its edges. They are not hard metal.

Should you want to watch the timing, put the cylinder back in, cock the arm slowly (both single and double action) and observe the parts moving into position—the cylinder bolt should engage its notch and not allow the cylinder to be turned either way as the arm comes to full cock. A dragging bolt or one with too much tension may wear the edges of the cylinder notches to the point where locking isn't too positive. Peening down the burr that raises on the back wall of the Colt notch doesn't help much, and you can't replace metal worn off anywhere very well. Deepening the notches is a tricky milling-machine setup, and the usual cure is fitting a new bolt that will raise a little higher and harder into the notches.

WORKING ON A COLT SINGLE-ACTION REVOLVER

The pencil indicates the "paw" or "hand" in a Colt single-action pistol. When this becomes worn or damaged the revolver gets out of timing and therefore accuracy suffers.

The Colt hand is "black-smithed" a bit in order to lengthen it somewhat.

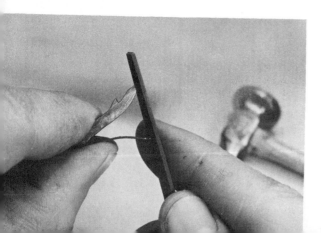

The lengthened hand is filed back to shape.

Dremel tool with a grinder bit
is used to work down a Colt
mainspring and thus reduce
the trigger pull somewhat, as
well as make it easier to cock.
Better to place gun in a vise for
this operation, as in next photo.

After grinding the mainspring,
it is polished as smooth as
possible with finishing paper.

A close-up of the reground and
polished mainspring.

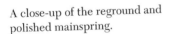

A small Arkansas stone is used
to work down the sear on a
Colt hammer.

A Colt mainspring is being deliberately bent here in order to increase force of hammer fall.

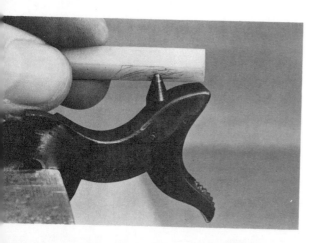

An Arkansas stone is being used to polish and round up the Colt single-action firing pin. Broken or irregularly shaped firing pins cause misfires and punctured primers.

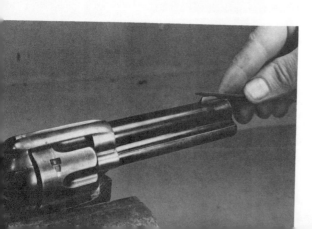

The front sight on the Colt revolver is being filed down here to adjust the point of impact. This is necessary sometimes on handguns with fixed sights.

The Colt cylinder is held at the rear in the frame by a spring-loaded pin connected to the cylinder latch and not surprisingly called the latch pin. It engages in a shallow hole in center of the ratchet. Both pin and hole can wear in time, but a cylinder you are able to wobble a bit at the rear can usually be cured with a new ratchet.

Trigger pulls on Colt or other V-mainspring revolvers depend primarily on the sear face and notch in the hammer. Extremely careful stoning is required to change the pull. If you must try it, clamp the hammer in a smooth-jawed small vise so that the jaws prevent the stone from riding up and over the wrong places!

Many modern revolvers have separate firing pins housed in the frame. These give little trouble. The older guns have firing pins that are pinned into the hammer nose. These are free to pivot up and down slightly, and occasionally have to be replaced. Colt uses a solid rivet, most S & W's a hollow one. With either one, buy a new rivet along with the pin. They fit so tightly that removing the old one will nearly always wreck it.

The Smith & Wesson design is considerably simpler than the Colt; few parts do more than one job, and there is less trouble with timing. A single leaf or flat mainspring works only on the hammer, and some variation in tension is possible by adjusting its retaining screw at bottom of the front strap of the grip. Strength of the spring may be reduced by filing or grinding it thinner, of course, but don't take off much more than the tool marks! Weakening the spring makes the arm easier to cock and to fire double action, but go very far and you'll get misfires on double action, where the hammer does not fall quite as far as in single-action operation.

Trigger pull on the S & W is governed primarily by the rebound slide and its spring, also called the trigger-return spring. The tiny notch area on hammers is almost impossible to stone without doing more damage than good. Most of the weight of the trigger pull is tension against the trigger by its return spring. The rebound slide is a housing for this spring, and both are easily slipped up past the pin-guiding slide: clip or grind off the end of the spring one-third turn at a time until you reach a good pull-off. This and mild application of a moly lubricant to the notch will almost always give a fine let-off to S & W's and similar arms using this system.

Fixed-sight revolvers seldom shoot exactly to the point of aim at the distance the shooter wants to shoot, this being from ten to a hundred yards. If the point of impact is too high or too low, the front sight can be filed down or raised by getting a target sight that fits over the origi-

IMPROVING TRIGGER ACTION
ON A SMITH & WESSON REVOLVER

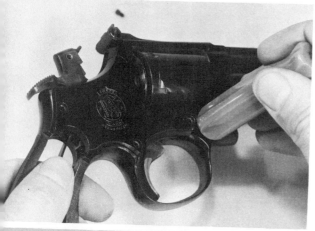

After removing the sideplate screws from this Smith & Wesson revolver, the closely fitted sideplate is snapped loose by tapping the frame with the butt end of the screwdriver.

A detail of the Smith & Wesson revolver mechanism.

The pencil points to the sear-spring housing.

The sear-spring housing has been removed and shows the spring in place.

The spring has been removed from the housing and is being shortened somewhat in order to reduce the trigger pull.

The Smith & Wesson main-spring is being worked down with a file in order to reduce the double-action pull.

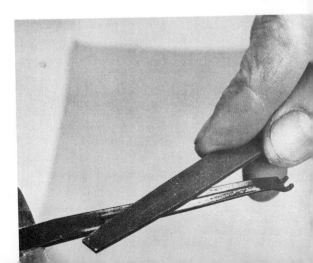

The modern Smith & Wesson large revolver action.

nal and is then pinned to it. But if it is to one side, the gun owner has only one way to go: attach an adjustable rear sight. There is one model today with a side-fitting sight: it attaches with a screw to the side of the frame and requires that one hole be drilled and tapped. A harder way is to cut a little slot in the frame above the hammer and set in a blade with a notch that can be moved to windage zero and then locked in place by peening, epoxy or a setscrew. The attachment of deluxe target sights calls for milling of slots, dovetails, etc., plus higher front sight for a good job. So this job is best left to a professional gunsmith.

"Honing" of handgun parts is often mentioned, but applies only to a sort of a medium grade of revolver or pistol. The very good arms don't need it, and the poor ones have so much tolerance in working parts to start with that there's little gained by smoothing them. Honing is merely rubbing flat parts on a fine-grit whetstone to make them flatter and smoother.

Coil springs are now widely used in revolvers, especially smaller caliber foreign-made types. Their advantage is that they never break; the disadvantage is that they aren't as "fast" as the flat spring. Hammers, etc., that are machined often can stand honing—the cast ones won't need it as a rule. Frames are also often castings, even among some of the U. S.'s better quality revolvers.

Today's gun castings are not even similar to those of a generation ago. They are almost universally investment castings, sometimes called wax castings, and the method used to make them is called the "lost wax process." A mold is made that is in several pieces. The pieces come apart in all directions so that the mold's inner shape can be almost anything imaginable. This mold is used to make wax castings of the part, frame or receiver desired. The wax castings are then connected to a wax column by wax rods until a number are made, forming what is called a "tree." Then this tree is placed in a container and a plaster-like compound is poured in to cover everything except the end of the main wax column. It is allowed to harden, and then it is turned upside down and heated. All the wax runs out, leaving exact hollows in the hardened mold. The mold is then filled with molten steel. When cool, the mold is broken apart and you have a lot of very smooth, exact castings. The advantage is that literally any metal or any alloy, including the toughest steels, can be molded this way, and the resulting castings hardened or heat-treated as if they were machined cold from steel-bar stock. The wax system allows shapes to be cast that couldn't be machined in fact! Revolver frames are being cast that don't even take sideplates, all the parts being installed through hammer and trigger slots. Thompson, Ruger, Dan Wesson, Sterling—these companies use cast parts and frames in all their arms. There is nothing whatever wrong with castings used in these arms or others so far as strength and reliability goes.

In the lower price foreign-made revolvers, parts are often soft, whether cast or machined, and the best thing you can do is to keep them well lubricated to reduce wear. Should a sear or hammer notch wear off, you can usually file a clear notch, and if you dare, case-harden the part in Kasenite. I'd do it: if the part wore too fast in original state, any change will be an improvement. Soft hands, bolts, etc., may need peening out, eventually. Such parts won't be too difficult to duplicate with a file, with the old one to copy, as a last resort. Use any bit of mild steel from bar or flat stock and Kasenite the finished part so that it will be hard on the outside to resist wear and yet not be brittle enough to break, as can happen if you use expensive tool steel and don't get it drawn properly after hardening.

The fit of pins may be poor—a pin may fit tightly in the frame, but the part inside has an oversize hole and can wobble on the pin. And pins may be soft and wear fast. New pins are not easy to make, really, especially oversize ones just a little bigger than the originals. The man with a lathe doesn't have any problem, but all of you won't have lathes. Strip the gun and take the part with the oversize hole to an industrial-supply

KASENITE CASE HARDENING TECHNIQUE

Here the frizzen from a flint-action lock is being hardened so it will strike or spark better. The first step is heating the part until it is cherry red with a small butane torch.

The part is then dipped into the Kasenite compound. Notice that the part is held by a length of wire so as not to burn the fingers. It is necessary to hold the part with a piece of wire such as this. If larger tools were used, such as pliers, the additional metal mass would cause rapid dissipation of heat.

The part is then heated cherry red again and immediately quenched in water.

or hobbby shop that stocks drill rods and find the size that fits perfectly, or even tightly, since you can easily lap the hole with a piece of rod and any abrasive scraped from the cloth until the part revolves freely on your pin stock. The same size drill bit as the rod will be needed to enlarge the hole in the gun frame. Use it to ream the hole slowly, turning your drill chuck by hand. Make your pins the length of the original or originals, polish ends, heat and when red drop in cold light oil or water to harden. Polish a little so you can see clear metal, then reheat to "straw"—the metal turns yellowish—and let it cool slowly. They'll be both hard and tough. This procedure on pins goes for all of the very old Colts, too.

The 1873 Colt Army Revolver, the well-known single action of historical, moving-picture and TV fame, has become very popular. Colt has even gone back to making them, along with a dozen foreign imitators and a few domestic. Even Hammerli, the Swiss maker of super-fine target arms now makes them. Ruger built a big business based on the single-action "frontier" type revolver. Frankly speaking, practically all of the modern center-fire guns of this basic type, including Colt's own, are definitely superior to the originals.

Before the modern models appeared, I can think of only one gunsmith who ever owned one, and he wasn't very bright. The old guns broke cylinder locks, firing pins, wore the notches off hammers, broke out the safety notch, even broke hammers and mainsprings, etc., if used more than a very little. Fire five shots and all the screws were loose. No, it wasn't so rugged! The present-day single actions, excluding some of the very low-priced imported .22's, are better in all respects. Modern steels make some of the old-design parts strong enough to hold up, springs and pins are better and triggers will hold adjustment.

The cylinder bolt is still the weakest part. It has two spring prongs on its rear end, and these do double duty against hammer and trigger, and they get broken or set (lose tension). They can be reshaped and bent a little, but a new one is the best idea. The two-pronged trigger-bolt spring sometimes breaks, as does the flat spring crimped into the hand that revolves the cylinder. It is not too hard to file out a replacement from a bit of spring steel and recrimp in the slot, which luckily usually doesn't break out. Timing depends on the length of the hand and the movement-range of the bolt. Excessive cylinder play can only be cured by fitting a new base pin bushing through the cylinder, which is a fairly simple job, but usually requires use of a lathe to trim to length squarely.

The trigger contacts the hammer directly so that work on the notch in the hammer is obvious and easy, the notch being much deeper than on the double-action revolvers, which, though making direct contact in most instances, have a much different leverage system. A three-pound notch on an S & W hammer is so shallow you can hardly see it, while on the single-action, it has lots of iron in contact. A deep safety or half-cock notch is provided, but in the original revolvers a man could get so much strength through the trigger, he could and did break the notch right out of the hammer, thus losing this doubtful safety factor.

Firing pins are cylindrical, fitting into the hammer nose from the front and held in place by a cross-pin. Removal of the pin allows the broken firing pin to be driven from the hammer by a small punch through a hole in back of hammer. The best of the modern replicas use a separate firing pin in the frame.

Top-break revolvers were once popular, but few are made today. The old Smith & Wessons—a dozen different models—were very good and are practically all collector's items today. The British Webleys were also produced in a good many models, many of which found their way as surplus to the U.S. These are all very rugged arms and not very susceptible to either wear or breakage.

Then, we have a host of obsolete, small break-opens ranging from good H & R's such as the old "Sportsman" down to virtually worthless ones from long-defunct makers. These and their accompanying solid-frame brothers—which require removal of the cylinder to load and unload—are the old "Saturday-night specials," "suicide guns" etc. The selling price, new, was less than ten dollars, and they weren't reliable, even when new. Made of soft, poor metals, parts, pins and springs would wear very quickly. Flat trigger springs would break, mainsprings set, hands wear, catch in frames, etc. They usually have a sear type of part in the rear of the trigger guard that is held in by the same pin that holds the guard. And they have a V or flat spring to break, too. Except in very old models, the handspring is piano wire which doesn't break but gets out of place, bends and fails to function. Timing is practically always bad, but it can be helped by peening or even bending the tip of the hand and putting more spring tension on the bolt. This is done by bending up the leg or leaf or the trigger spring, which usually works the bolt. The latch on the barrel assembly which locks on the frame to hold the revolver in closed position may be loose. You can peen the frame with light hammer to tighten.

Flat and V springs are sometimes hard to make and fit in these arms, but you can't buy the one you'll need. They are literally all of flat stock, what used to be called clock spring, having a mild temper and not very strong. Make a practice of collecting spring steel: old clocks,

wind-up toys, damaged steel tape rules, etc. V-type springs require annealing—heating until red and allowed to cool slowly—before a sharp
bend can be put in the steel and let it be shaped, split, etc. When the
right shape is reached, it is reheated, quenched in oil, then heated just a
little so it won't be brittle. When you have to make one, don't. Make
three—two will probably break after the gun is assembled and snapped
a few times, so you can experiment on those that are too brittle with re-
tempering, and reshaping.

Even in the better grade break-opens, the extractor cams sometimes wear and fail to move the extractor and fired cases back out of the
cylinder when the revolver is broken open. The cure is a new part,
which you can't get. So try cleaning the notch or cam face with a file
and see if you can't make its contact bar or actuating part a little
longer.

Reassembly of internal parts in any arm where they must be lined
up for final pinning through frame, such as the "sears" and cylinder-lock
parts held by the trigger-guard pins is almost impossible without the use
of slave pins. These are short pins that hold the assembled pieces to
each other, allowing placing them in the frame or receiver in line with
holes. Then the proper long pin is driven through, pushing the slave pin
out the other side.

The small, cheap, old revolvers just aren't worth spending money
or effort to keep in shooting condition. Break them up or bury them.
They can't be held or sighted well enough for any form of target shooting and are too unreliable for self-defense.

Vast numbers of .22 single-action revolvers, mostly German-
made, are now in the hands of American sportsmen. These come in two
sizes: full-size, the same as the original big Colt, and a sort of three-
quarter size that is smaller and lighter. The big ones are pretty good in
all respects, but the smaller models have pretty soft parts as a rule and
are subject to the standard single-action ills—hand, bolt and hammer
trouble. The trigger notch in the hammer may wear so that when the
cocked hammer slips off the trigger, it falls and rams the trigger nose
into the half-cock or safety notch, damaging both this notch and the
trigger. Parts are quite uniform, really, and most trouble with the hand,
bolt and trigger can be cured by replacing with genuine modern Colt
parts, full-size for the normal guns, and those for the Colt "Scout" (their
own smaller model) for the smaller arms. Because of varying hammers,
separate firing pins in frame, etc., these parts may not interchange, but
have to be repaired or replaced with new parts obtained from the im-
porter of the arm, reached through dealers handling the line.

Cleaning revolvers. Cleaning after firing can be quite a chore on all revolvers as there is more to the job than just the barrel work—and this alone may not be easy. Today, many shooters like to shoot super-powerful loads in big Colts, Rugers and Smith & Wessons, copper-jacketed bullets sometimes since lead bullets leave lead in the barrel, cone, etc., because of being loaded "hot." In such cases, clean the gun as you would a rifle with metal fouling, using brass brushes, solvents, even the pastes. Brushes made for revolvers are shorter than those for rifles, so that when they are pushed through from the muzzle the entire brush

This cleaning tool (left) utilizes a small brass wire patch to clean lead and other fowling from the bore. Here the tool is used to scrub leading from the forcing cone of a revolver. At right is the complete cleaning setup with the brass scrubbing patches.

can go through into the cylinder opening in the frame and then be pulled back. The barrel proper is rather easily cleaned in any case, but the cone can prove troublesome. In revolvers the bullet jumps forward to clear the cylinder and enter the barrel. Because the cylinder chamber may not line up absolutely perfectly with the barrel, the rear of barrel is coned slightly to funnel bullets into the rifling. This cone gets hit by every bullet, and these being slightly larger than the bore, a little lead may get scraped off and stick in the cone. The brass brush may not get all of it out so get a nonrotating cleaning rod or make one, tap the end for a brush and cut a slot also. Below .45 caliber, life is easier because you put the rod through to the frame opening, screw on a larger brush than your caliber (45 for 38, 38 for 32 etc.), pull it into the cone and turn it. Since pistol brushes aren't made above .45 caliber, you have to improvise for big barrels—an old rifle brush can be bent into a flattened loop, steel wool balled on a brush, etc. Stubborn cases need stronger stuff: look for scraps of copper or bronze screen, as from window, door or sieve screens. You can cut this into strips with ordinary scissors, fold and loop through the slot in the rod to make a wad that will pull into the cone and cut fouling out when turned a dozen times.

Fouling in the frame and around the breech end of the barrel can be reached by a toothbrush and scraper. Make scrapers like little screwdrivers, only not of steel. Copper, brass, even plastic will get the fouling out without scratching the gun.

Cylinders are easy to clean and won't usually need a brass brush, but care must be used not to get rough with extractor–ratchet parts and not to get any lint from patches under these to jam their fit in the cylinder. And oil with light oil afterward. Clean the ratchet with the brush and get rid of all foreign matter.

Because they have so many moving and interdependent parts, revolvers must be kept free of dust, sand and fouling buildup to operate properly and not wear out before their time. Keep them oiled lightly and in boxes, not holsters. To store for any length of time, oil them heavily or grease them and wrap them in waxed paper.

Autoloading Pistols

These pistols are great when they do what they're supposed to do. When they don't function properly, they can be rather provoking. Specific types have specific ills, but here are the general problems.

Failure to extract: broken extractor or very rough chamber.

Failure to chamber cartridge: tight magazine lips, follower angled incorrectly, magazine does not fully seat in frame, rough feed ramp or interfering extractor.

Failure to eject fired case from pistol: everything dirty and fouled up, slide or recoil spring too strong for the cartridge used and so not moving all the way to the rear, worn lip on extractor or a damaged ejector.

Failure to close completely: slide, frame or housing bent or dented slightly, more often a dirty but unlubricated pistol.

Failure to fire a full magazine properly: weak magazine spring, usually.

A Colt 45 Government Model barrel that is badly fouled with both powder residue and lead. For top service it is necessary to frequently clean this model.

Pay particular attention to the locking surfaces. When they become imbedded with grime the barrel does not lock up the way it should and accuracy suffers.

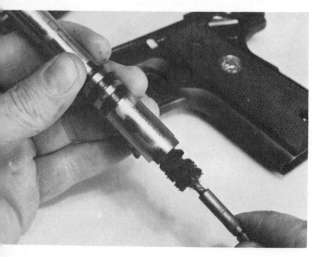

Here a bronze wire brush is used to scrub the metal and powder fouling out of the Colt 45 chamber.

These are the usual malfunctions to be faced. In the .22 autos that use greased or waxed bullets, this lubricant can build up on the face of the slide, under the extractor and around the breech of the barrel to the point of putting the arm out of commission in pretty short order. Dirty cases—cartridges carried in the pocket that pick up foreign matter and carry it into the pistol chamber—can cause all sorts of trouble: sticking in the chamber, slowing down the slide so they fail to eject, etc. A simple cleaning job will keep the average .22 auto going in good order.

Some of the small pocket-type foreign .22's are very critical. These are based on the .25- and .32-caliber arms using rimless ammunition that mechanisms can handle more easily than the rimmed .22 with its soft lead bullet which requires more careful guidance than the larger jacketed types. Magazine lips may need smoothing, tightening up, spreading out, feed ramps need polishing smooth, etc.

Two replacement pistol barrels that are available to the home gunsmith: At left is the lugger barrel with threads for screw-in replacement. The other is for a Model .45 Automatic.

Magazines are the bugaboo for all pistols: often a pistol will function perfectly with one, and not with another magazine, which appears identical in all respects.

The fit of the slide on the frame seldom affects functioning, though one too loose will detract from accuracy.

Trigger pulls on pocket-size autos are usually pretty hard and not too much improvement can be expected, although judicious work on hammer notches, etc., can help some. There are usually just too many corners to turn in the levers and the linkage between trigger, sear and hammer or firing pin. Good pulls can be made on the U.S.-type of .22 sporting auto pistol, and on most large caliber arms with the exception of the Luger. There just isn't much that can be done with them, the original Pistole M'08, that is—without having a batch of parts to switch

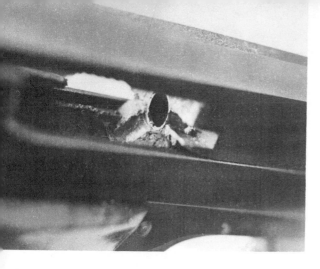

A detail of a .22 rimfire target pistol which has gone too long without cleaning. Notice how grease, lead, and powder particles have accumulated around the face of the breech. In a short time the pistol would cease to function properly.

around and get a workable pull. Some of the modern pistols made in the Luger pattern use an entirely different trigger system which can be improved by hand work in the usual manner, by smoothing notches, honing parts, etc.

Extractor lips, also called "hooks" as they hook over the rim of the cartridge case, may be stoned a very little or their spring tension reduced a little should they too strongly resist a cartridge moving up to full position on the slide or bolt face.

All pistols, with the exception of a few very old military types, have frames and slides of unhardened steel—it may be a tough alloy, but the parts can be bent, dented, filed and stoned easily. Damaged physically, they can usually be put back into working condition. Slides are weak at back ends, as safety cuts, etc., can leave short sections of the milled grooves liable to bending and so clamp the slide on the frame, etc., should the arm be dropped on a floor or bang against something hard.

Occasionally, a .22 will have a long firing pin that can hit the barrel when snapped and burr or peen in the edge of the chamber as described for rifles. Since the chamber is readily accessible, it is easy to clean out the depressed metal and free extraction, and of course shorten the pin tip.

Not too much trouble with defective safeties occurs: the safety itself just about has to break in two to be ineffective, but ignorant persons pulling the trigger very hard with the safety on can bend triggers, pull the linkage out of whack, etc. Unless a pin or stud breaks or is badly deformed, parts can be restored to usefulness by forming them back to their original shape.

Some of the foreign-made small autos break firing pins every so often. These are extremely difficult to make, even for a well-equipped gunsmith, so it is best to look up the address of a foreign parts specialist

This is a Smith & Wesson Model 52, .38 Special target pistol. This autoloader is designed for wad-cutter ammunition only, loaded flush with the mouth of the case.

A .38 wad-cutter cartridge loaded in the Model 52 magazine. Note that if the bullet protruded from the case mouth it would be impossible to load it in the magazine.

Three flat-nosed wad-cutter bullets of the type used in .38 Special target guns such as the Model 52.

and order a new one. And hope you won't have to do a lot of stoning to make it fit!

The pistols used in U. S. competition in 9mm, .38 Special and .45 ACP calibers are top quality, with honed, finely-fitted parts and balanced springs, etc., and are usually suited to medium-power target loads. That is, they are adjusted to function within a fairly narrow range

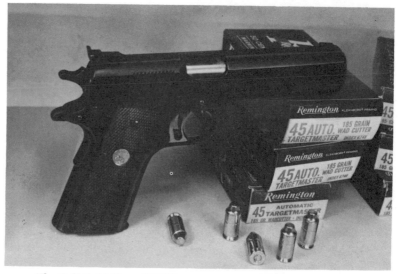

The Colt Gold-Cup .45 ECP government model target pistol with the 185-grain, wad-cutter type ammunition it shoots.

of ammunition variation, and will not operate with very light or very heavy loads, or if they will, are punished by them. A light or weakened slide or recoil spring won't resist the recoil of a heavy load sufficiently to prevent parts from being battered up in time. On the other hand, a .45 set up for normal "hard-ball"—full power military loading—with a new spring may not function at all with mid-range match ammo. The target men know all this, but someone may inherit a set of handguns that seem perfect yet just won't work with what the clerk in the surplus store sold him. Incidentally, just about any spring that can be desired for any pistol can be had from the W. C. Wolff company. *Pistols:* I didn't say revolvers.

Confronted with an autoloading pistol that is apparently OK so far as unbroken parts and springs are concerned but refuses to function, first take it apart and clean and oil it if it appears dirty or any moving parts seem slow in moving as they should—many an arm has been fixed by just cleaning gummed oil from surfaces that should be clean—and then check out the magazine, extractor, all springs and spring-loaded parts, along with close inspection of chamber, trigger movements, etc.

Chambers must be kept clean and oiled. Rimless pistol cases headspace, or stop, against the front end of the chamber. Therefore a worn, rusted or gouged-up chamber just won't do. Working parts, slide rails and the interior of the frame should always have a film of oil unless the arm is being used in arctic or desert environments where oil would freeze or thicken, or pick up and hold abrasive dust. In such environments all types of arms should be dry-lubricated with powdered molybdenum disulphide or graphite to insure reliable functioning.

Single-Shot Pistols

The single-shot handgun is so simple and so exposed to view in its workings that there is little to say about care and maintenance that the reader or owner won't think of the first time he handles the arm. Normal barrel and chamber cleaning is so easy to do that even the laziest shooter won't neglect them! In use and in casual handling, however, make it a habit to check the extractor every time the pistol is opened and closed, or the action opened. Any foreign matter getting down into the extractor slots or recesses behind them, the extractor or any bar or lever connected to it can bend and/or loosen the fit of parts when the barrel is closed or the block raised abruptly.

Very old .22 break-open type pistols may have frail parts. These are worth more as collector's pieces than as operating arms. Don't use, "remodel," experiment with or let any work be done on these arms except by a professional specializing in antique arms.

While parts in modern and replica single-shot pistols are not very complicated to look at, hand-fitting may be needed on any replacement, calling for filing and stoning with much reassembling and testing during the work. Trigger-pull work is uncomplicated but requires attention be paid to what you're doing. As always, study everything before you do anything.

Sight changes and alterations are no problem with most of these pistols. You can do just about whatever you want to in the way of changing front and rear sights.

7

Shotguns

Cleaning and maintenance of the shotgun, whatever the type, grade, value or condition, are basically the same as for other arms—cleaned and oiled barrel, chamber and internal working parts with constant care added in the field. The big bores can plug up with dirt, mud or twigs—every year a good number of shotguns blow off a few inches of the muzzle ends or at least split out at the muzzles just from getting plugged up. And breaking open a single or double gun roughly can wreck ejector rods, or, if a firing pin hasn't retracted for some reason—broken or weak spring, dirt, or stuck in a primer—break a firing-pin tip against the extractor, doing it no good either.

Use ammunition that's suited to the gun. There are variations in shell rims in both material and dimensions, and in headspace of guns. So a shotgun may perform perfectly with some brands of shells and with others fail to fire every time, fail to extract or eject, or both, leading the shooter to think the gun is at fault. If you've changed ammo and the gun suddenly gives trouble, it may have nothing at all wrong with the gun. The ammunition may not be suited to its headspace or to the extractor–ejector system of the gun.

113

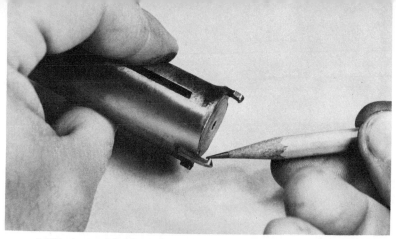

A Winchester Model 12 shotgun bolt removed from the action to show the extractors in better detail. When the extractor hooks become excessively damaged or fouled by powder residue, extraction may fail. They can be repaired by cleaning or, if necessary, by sharpening up the hooks with a file.

For reliable functioning, autoloading shotguns must be adjusted for either standard or high-velocity loads, by a recoil-spring setup provided, or gas-cylinder regulation. Follow the directions of the manufacturer if they aren't marked or stamped in the metal of the arm somewhere—usually on the magazine tube and quite evident when the fore-end is removed. Heavy loads may cycle an auto set for light ones satisfactorily, but the arm is taking unnecessary punishment when the parts recoil more forcefully than they need to.

With the exception of finely-fitted trap guns, the common break-open single-barrel shotgun, even old ones that have seen much use and misuse, are pretty rugged arms. Lever springs break, firing pins both break and get lost—many are held in by a setscrew which, if allowed to loosen too far, just lets the pin fall out when the shotgun is cocked with the muzzle raised. If the hunter is watching a rabbit or quail, he doesn't notice it go. These firing pins are easy to make on a lathe and are not even too hard to just file to shape, providing you can obtain the correct diameter steel rod. Dimensions are measurable in the frame of the gun if the pin is missing or directly from the old pin if it only has a broken tip. Top-lever springs in the old guns are flat or V type and may present a problem. If the correct one for the particular arm is not obtainable, usually a larger spring can be filed and ground to fit and function.

Loose fore-ends are also a common problem on both single and double guns. Since the fore-end usually holds the gun and barrel or barrels together, a loose one affects operation to some extent. There are many variations in the spring and catch systems used to snap the fore-end up tight to the barrel, and examination should clearly indicate what is wrong. A flat spring that has taken a set and no longer exerts full tension can often be bent to restore it for limited further use. (If it set up once, it'll do it again, but not right away.) The engagement hook in the barrel or rib may have worn or even bent. If it's bent, careful work with a hammer can usually move the hook or notch back to a solid locking position without breaking any soldered joint loose. Use a few firm taps, not a lot of light ones or one solid belt! If the hook or engagement slot is worn, extend the end of the engaging part—this can be removed from the fore-end for peening-out or having metal added by welding. Coil-spring plungers or guides may be filed at the shoulder or slot to allow them to move a little farther.

Looseness of the action—barrel or barrels not tight in the frame when the gun is closed—is almost always due to wear in the half-circle notch of the barrel assembly which engages the hardened hinge pin through the front end of the frame. The classic remedy always recommended is installation of a new oversized pin, except that outside of the Pachmayr Gun Works I can't think of anyone I'd trust to do such a job, including me. A high-quality gun should be returned to the maker or a custom shotgun firm for tightening up. Hinge-pin replacement is not a complicated job, but it calls for equipment—powerful press, precision turning and reaming tools, grinding and heat-treating, etc.—beyond that possessed by most well-furnished professional shops.

An old single or double that is loose in the joint is usually black-smithed back to tightness. The barrel assembly is laid on a solid bench upside down and the new top portion of the half-circle hook or notch belted solidly with the steel hammer, bending it closed a few thousandths of an inch. Protect the surface with thin cardboard from matchbook or postcard.

Trap guns and good doubles, side-by-side or over-and-under type, should have breech and extractor/ejector parts fitted very tightly so

Here a double-barrel shotgun is being tightened up by a bit of "blacksmithing." By striking down on this surface, the barrel hook is closed somewhat. This, in turn, makes it fit more tightly against the hinge pin.

they are just able to move smoothly in their slots, etc. This is done so that they can't twist or cam out of position when the gun is opened and closed. The tiniest bit of foreign matter—grains of unburned gunpowder, scraping of plastic, anything—can prevent a good gun from even being closed. Never force a gun shut when it resists a little more than usual. Open it up and see if something is in the way. Extractors break and plungers wear on the best arms, but fitting of replacements or repair of a simple-looking but worn part should be left to a gunsmith because practically every part in a good shotgun demands heat-treatment for lasting strength. And replacement parts usually need careful handfitting.

A malfunctioning or nonfunctioning trigger assembly on a double can be fairly easy to fix up if it has the double-trigger system. With the stock removed, functions of each trigger and connecting parts are easy

A detail of the Model 21 Winchester firing mechanism, with the single selective trigger. The large chunk of metal at the lower rear is the pendulum which activates and functions the trigger selector.

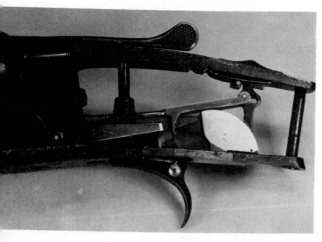

The firing mechanism of the Japanese-made Ithaca SKB over/under shotgun.

The firing mechanism of the Remington Model 3200 over/under shotgun. Notice the rugged simplicity of this mechanism and the use of coil springs. It is not too likely that anything will go wrong with this mechanism.

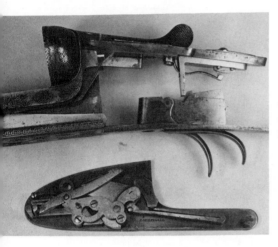

Close-up photos of a sidelock shotgun showing both the frame and the mechanism of the lock. This is the Boss, one of the world's finest shotguns.

to study. Most such guns have the tang safety levering parts to block trigger movement. These can be at fault and may need to be forced to their original position, safety slide tightened, etc. But in any case, after work on other parts, these safety parts must be tested and made to do their job.

A single trigger, either selective or nonselective, can be easy or impossible to comprehend. If you can't observe anything obviously wrong and easily correctable, such as a pin worked out of place or a spring end out of engagement, don't take the assembly apart: such jobs require knowledge and familiarity with the mechanisms. If you can't find a qualified man around or don't know where to ship the disabled gun, go through the shooting magazines to find out when and where the nearest big trapshoot will be held, and take the shotgun to it. Almost always there will be one or more skilled shotgun specialists there who can handle the job in minutes.

Pump or slide-action shotguns have been rugged for the past half-century. Earlier models, with the notable exception of the 1897 Winchester, were pretty sad. Complicated, weirdly shaped parts of soft steel, poorly-designed takedown systems and strange springs made them prone to breakdowns. Don't try to keep grandpa's ancient pump operating—life is too short! If you must make an effort, Christy's Gun Works can provide a few parts for some of the long-obsolete models.

The detail of the Model 12 breech assembly. Looseness in the fit between barrel and receiver is corrected by removing the locking tab and adjusting barrel fit. Note how teeth on the locking tab mesh with those on the barrel.

The average existing serviceable pump shotgun has means for tightening the takedown system, so the barrel need not be loose. Most owners don't even look for the feature, but take their guns to a shop for tightening up. Parts seldom break on these older guns—gunsmiths usd to consider themselves ready for the season for Model 12 Winchesters if they had two new firing pins and a few magazine-tube screws on hand. An extractor or two took care of the Remington 31 troubles-to-be-expected. Even the lower priced Stevens slide guns kept working. Modern pumps use many parts of stamped metal that can be bent rather easily, but are as easily bent back to position.

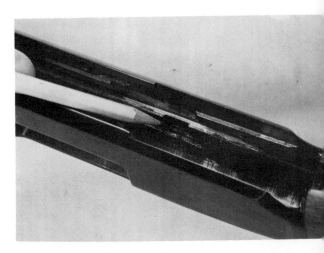

The interior of the Model 12 receiver. The pencil is pointing out some of the action cuts where powder and dirt fouling are most liable to accumulate. This is cleaned by a squirt of solvent and a brisk brushing.

In all pumps the main cause of trouble is foreign matter in the action blocking one or more parts from doing its job. Dirt accumulates mysteriously. It can build up to the point of keeping an action from locking, by filling the locking recess, and by carrying grit, cause the bolt to wear its lock area back and so increase headspace. This condition is common in old M12 Winchesters kicking around today. I can think of remedying only by heliarc-welding hard steel on the back of block and then grinding and polishing to fit, which isn't exactly a home-workshop answer.

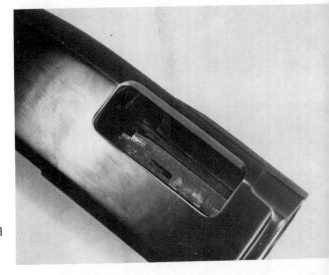

A view through the ejection port of a Model 12 receiver showing some of the action cuts where powder fouling and other residue are most likely to accumulate.

Keep the actions clean. Take the trigger assembly and bolt or block parts out of the receiver after every hunting trip and clean them and the receiver thoroughly. And clean the magazine tube. Any dust, grass seeds, etc., in it will be carried into the receiver by shells cycling through when the gun is next used.

Trigger weight, unless very bad indeed, is not a shotgun problem, as in shooting it is "point and pull," not "hold and squeeze" as with a rifle or pistol. Hammer, trigger and sear notches are large-contact connections, easily reduced to lighten pull if desired. It should never be less than five pounds, for safety, on any type of shotgun.

The autoloaders rank with the pumps for parts reliability. In fact, just about everything said for the pump goes for the auto, especially keeping debris out of them. The old Browning-patent Remington Model 11 was a hard-to-discourage workhorse and would function under almost impossible handicaps.

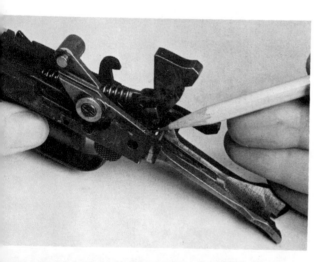

A detail of the Model 12 Winchester trigger mechanism. The pencil points to some of the critical areas where fouling is liable to accumulate and interfere with gun operation.

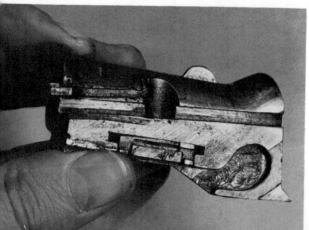

Here is a Model 12 bolt which has been used for a long time without cleaning. Note the accumulated grime. This is best removed by spraying with a gun solvent and then brushing and wiping.

I once saw one that had a copper penny in the action, wedged in, and a moving part had pierced the penny and kept on working. And I personally fixed one that wasn't extracting quite correctly every time. It had the paper tube from a fired shell wedged in the chamber, and loaded shells were being chambered and fired inside this lined chamber. The gun had enough power to force them in and pull most of them out!

Adjusted for adequate but not excessive recoil or gas release, the autoloaders will give little trouble so long as they are kept clean and oiled. Some of the foreign-made ones with hard-chromed parts need little oiling, too.

Chromed shotgun barrels pick up little leading, won't rust and are in general a joy to possess. Ordinary steel barrels lead up readily with high-velocity loads using plain lead shot in just a few shots, though this is easily removed by a brass brush or mop covered with steel wool, finest grade 4/0. Copperized or nickel-plated shot reduces leading and gives better patterns with heavy loads. The autoloaders are not particularly critical as to ammunition otherwise, most functioning with almost any rim, primer, etc., as compared to doubles which must carefully limit firing-pin travel. A friend had a pretty good grade over-and-under shotgun that had one barrel counterbored for rim—therefore headspaced—deeper than the other: one barrel would fire any shell, the other only thick-rimmed ones!

Handloading shotgun shells is widespread, and the handloaders soon learn how to produce ammunition for their own arms, whatever the type, but may not be doing everything to suit other guns. The man who donates a box of his prize product for his friend to use may not be helping the cause. Test-fire before the bird gets up in front of the dog!

The charge-carrying plastic wads now used almost entirely in both factory and handloaded shotshells presents new problems to old guns. While reducing or even eliminating leading in some types, they may also eliminate good patterns by blowing through the shot charge as it leaves the barrel. Strange operations are being performed inside chokes—cutting rings, short rifling-type grooves, other mechanical operations—in an effort to slow up the wad and let the shot get away. Doing such work without it causing too much deformed shot and changing the pattern is the problem. Apparently the type of choke in the barrel to start with is important, the recess close or far from muzzle, etc., as many new guns have no trouble with wads while others do. Innumerable makes of Italian, Spanish, Japanese and Belgian shotguns are being imported, so, along with U.S., German, and British ones there can be a lot of different chokes to suit. The only way to go is to pattern the individual gun with individual loads and see what you get. Take a large cardboard carton and paper at least 36 inches wide to a range or safe place in the country and shoot at thirty and forty yards to check your patterns. (With heavy loads and large shot sizes, "modified" barrels or choke-settings may give "full choke" patterns, incidentally. Don't be surprised should this happen.) Over eighty percent of the shot charge in a 30 inch circle at thirty yards is considered a full-choke pattern, though many guns will consistently give over ninety percent. Break down a loaded shell, count the pellets and then draw a 30-inch circle over the densest area of the pattern shot and count the holes to get the percentage. Try different brands, different loadings, to find the best for your gun.

A further headache the shotgunner may expect is the adoption of soft iron shot and legislation against the use of lead shot for hunting, as waterfowl are dying from lead poisoning—swallowing spent shot as they feed underwater. Iron shot is understandably hard on barrels and chokes, and while new barrel developments may lick this, millions of older and present production guns will suffer. Undoubtedly there will be answers to all the questions that will arise and solutions to all the problems, but right now we don't even know the problems.

The physical fit and sighting of shotguns ties into the buttstock, and will be covered in the chapter on woodworking.

Muzzle-loading Arms

The gun fancier who becomes interested in the muzzle-loader jumps with both legs into the do-it-yourself business at the same time. A serious collector teaches himself to recondition, maintain and perhaps restore authentic old firearms—he's not about to trust them to a modern gunsmith who knows less than he does about them. There are expert antique gunsmiths, but they are few and usually far away. However, for every collector of front-loaders, there are a few dozen shooter types interested in shooting the old arms for recreation, or rather, shooting modern replicas for the most part. In the past few years the sale of such arms and supplies has become a multimillion-dollar business, with such large firms as Lyman, Thompson/Center and Colt now entering the field, for Colt a reentry! Foreign-made replicas of flintlock and percussion-lock rifles and pistols and Colt and Remington percussion revolvers vie with U.S. gunsmiths and firms in supplying the demand. Shotguns aren't quite so numerous as to sources, but demand is growing for them.

The man already in the muzzle-gun game has become something of a gunsmith by necessity, unless he lives near one of the professionals specializing in such guns. He has had to learn to keep the lock and trigger in adjustment, probably make higher or lower front sights, or change the rear, besides the elementary aspects of black-powder living—keeping the barrel clean, nipples clear, flints clamped and edged, etc.

The beginner soon finds he can expect little help from the regular gunsmiths—they don't even have blueing tanks long enough to take a musket barrel! He talks to fellow shooters, finds they are making parts, assembling complete arms from parts acquired here and there, and happily buys a few tools and joins the throng.

And few tools are needed, really. A vise, bench, a few files, a chisel or two and a hand-drill aided by a tap and tap-wrench have been all that hundreds of men have used to turn out complete working rifles, shotguns and single-shot pistols. Octagonal barrels, usually much better than the originals they emulate, are made by Douglas, Numrich, Manley, Mellott and others. Mellott even makes muzzle-loading shotgun barrels, cylinder, modified or full choke. Modern locks by Robbins, Cherry Corners Gun Shop, Hamm and lesser known makers surpass the old ones in materials and reliability. They duplicate original designs and

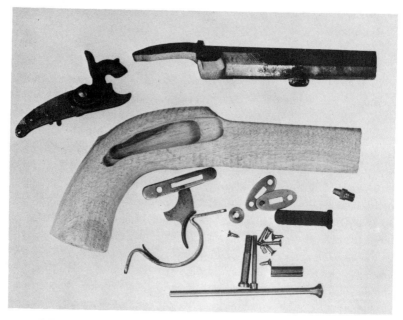

A Dixie percussion "pocket pistol" kit. All parts needed to put together the arm, which, although usable, is really a show or conversation piece. All work can be done with minor hand tools.

A detail of the Dixie Gun Works percussion lock showing the mechanism's engagement with the V-type spring.

are customarily used to make up very authentic rifles of shooting. Thompson's lock is a modern design using coil springs. Smaller locks for pistols and the matched pairs for double shotguns are most often old foreign-made types or modern-production reproductions. The old "hair-trigger" systems are not neglected—perhaps a dozen men are producing them for rifle and pistol-making.

Dixie Gun Works, Inc., is a prime supplier of parts and accessories, publishing annually a 300-page catalog of muzzle-loading arms of all types, from unused 200-year-old ones down to the latest production models, bullet molds, unfinished and finished locks and lock parts, screws, stocks, powder horns, kits of finished and semifinished parts that the buyer can assemble into complete rifles or colonial pistols with few

An assembly of the "raw" parts needed to make a muzzle-loading Kentucky-style pistol. All one needs is a barrel, a piece of wood, a trigger-guard casting, a lock, and a sheet of silver to make inlays.

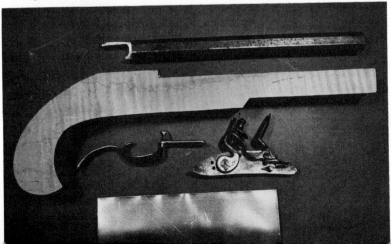

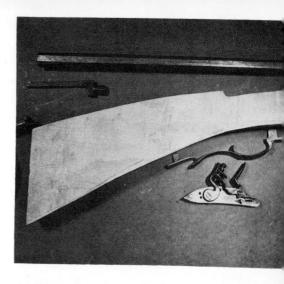

The "raw" parts required to build a Kentucky rifle.

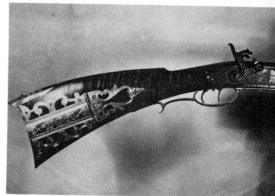

Here is a detail of a butt and patchbox area of a homemade Kentucky rifle. This is very good work, and yet it was done by an amateur.

tools, and a batch of miscellaneous but very useful information. Numrich Arms and several other firms also supply unfinished and semifinished parts and kits.

It is estimated that seventy percent of the black-powder arms in actual use have been assembled and finished by their owners, either from self-accumulated or purchased kits. With the exception of boring and threading for the breechplug, just about every bit of work required to build a percussion or flintlock arm can be done with the few hand tools already mentioned. The kit suppliers and barrelmakers know this, so they'll supply barrels already threaded for breechplugs. The do-it-yourselfer is limited only by his ambition—and bankroll. A pistol kit can be had for fifteen dollars. A set of parts for a true Hawken replica, everything of highest quality, runs well over two-hundred dollars.

Since the man involved with black-powder shooting already knows pretty well all that can be told here, this chapter is directed toward those unfamiliar with muzzle-loaders, just becoming interested

A detail of the Thompson Center Hawkin lock. Notice the use of a coil spring and the simplicity of the lock design.

The Hawkin lock with the bridle removed to show the detail of the mechanism. The home workshopper could duplicate this lock with pieces of scrap metal and a few files.

and just starting out. An incentive is that this type of firearm is legally considered nationally as purely recreational, and so it is not subject to federal firearms laws as regards buying, selling, mailing interstate, etc. With modern arms, all transactions must take place between licensed dealers with only direct local sales from dealer to individual.

Any responsible adult can order a muzzle-loading arm, hang it on a wall for decoration and conversation, or take it out and shoot it by acquiring percussion caps, black powder and lead balls, which can be purchased if he doesn't want to buy a mold and lead and mold his own. If it's a flintlock, he doesn't even need the caps.

Practically all of the hand arms, single shot or revolver types, are made in Italy, Belgium or Spain, and have passed government proof-firing tests. They are therefore quite safe even with overloads of black powder, although some of the very low-priced copies of ancient "pirate" pistols and such are recommended for decorative use only. This is often mentioned in the advertisements.

127

No muzzle-loading rifle, pistol or shotgun of any type can be safely fired with any form of modern smokeless powder. Never, under any circumstances, take any rifle or shotgun powder from a cartridge and try to use it in a muzzle-loading firearm. Even if made of modern steel and very strong, such as the replica Remington revolvers, muzzle-loaders are not designed to handle the pressure curve of smokeless powder.

On the other hand, any *good* front-loader will easily handle a double load of black powder—in frontier days double charges were used whenever the shooter needed more power or range. So, you can't get in much trouble with black powder. However, it can get the gun in trouble if you don't keep the fouling down, as black powder and the water and greases used by shooters do make a mess!

The tyro should start out with a percussion-cap arm and round balls, used with wet or greased cloth patches. Probably seventy-five percent of all shooting is done with such arms. Conical bullets are a step up in experience, and require self-made bullets of exactly the correct diameter for the particular barrel they're to be used in and skilled loading

A detail of a flintlock of the type that is currently being imported by the Connecticut Valley Arms Corporation. This inexpensive lock is a good basis for a do-it-yourself flintlock pistol or rifle.

The other side of the Connecticut Valley flintlock.

techniques. Flintlock shooting is even more demanding, the shooter having to learn about clamping flints, edges of flints, and having to use two grades of black powder (regular and extra-fine for priming).

Muzzle-loading Handguns

Percussion revolvers do not use patched balls as do the rifles and single-shot pistols, but instead take an oversize ball which is forced into the cylinder chambers by the loading levers built into all but a couple of models of the guns. The ball is oversize enough to cut lead around it to make a very tight fit and so not move out of position over the powder charge.

There are two grades of imported percussion revolvers: the brass-framed models are low- or medium-priced; their counterparts with frames of case-hardened steel usually cost fifty to one-hundred percent more. Designs, parts and functions are the same in all. The brass-framed guns are handsome, ideal for decorative purposes, and quite satisfactory for shooting, but they will not hold up in use as well as the steel-frame

A bullet being levered into the Lyman cap and ball revolver.

A close-up detail of the ball being levered into the Lyman cap and ball revolver.

A simple and practical percussion target pistol. Rear sight, adjustable for windage only, uses patched round balls. Loosening two screws forward of trigger guard permits barrel to be pulled out for easy cleaning. Front sight is removable.

models. Brass just isn't as good as steel in resisting wear in pinholes, holes, slots, etc. While I have no real figures to go by, I personally think that the brass-frame revolver has a life of from 700 to 1000 shots. By then it should be so loose all over as to be ready for the bracket on the wall. That's a lot of shots, really, so don't be frightened off this type unless you are already a shooter who likes to shoot a lot and has no plans for quitting.

Keeping a cap-lock revolver going for a long and satisfactory life isn't hard; it just requires a little work: every three loadings (eighteen shots) take the cylinder off or out. With the Colt type, pull the barrel and cylinder so that the base pin and its hole through the cylinder can be wiped clean with solvent and reoiled. For the Remington type, lowering the loading lever allows the cylinder pin to be pulled out so the cylinder can be rolled out on the right side of the frame, and the pin and cylinder cleaned. Cap fouling gets to the rear of the pin, powder fouling to the front; with lubricant and grit they work to interfere with cylinder turning and cause rapid wear on pin and hole.

Most percussion revolvers being sold today take the no. 11 cap, that is, the nipples coming on the gun are for this size. Occasionally, one will have nipples on which the No. 10 will fit better. It is obvious that on a revolver the caps must be a fairly tight, full-depth fit on the nipples. In any case, the smart thing to do is to buy a set of Ampco (berylium copper) nipples. They don't rust, holes don't enlarge and they are made to precise dimensions.

When nipples are the correct length, Colt-type revolvers may be snapped without damage: to check, tear a narrow strip of paper from the nearest slick-paper catalog or magazine, cock the gun, put the strip down over the nipple and pull the trigger. With the hammer down, you should be able to pull the paper out, unmarked. If the nipple is too long, the paper will be caught, and if the nipple top is not filed down, dry-firing will damage the nipple and won't help the base pin as the force of the hammer is transmitted to it every time the hammer falls. For Remingtons this isn't the case. You must remove nipples for dry-firing.

Parts repair, replacement and adjustment—all are basically the same as for the single-action cartridge revolvers. You don't have to worry about timing very often; the Europeans are fitting parts so that the cylinder locks up tighter than on the best modern double-action target revolvers! When new, a Colt replica of the better grade locks its cylinder immovably in line with the barrel. Unfortunately, most percussion-revolver barrels don't show the same level of workmanship in the rifling. However, even when it shows many and varied tool marks, the worst looking one usually shoots very well.

This may not be satisfying, though, as perhaps only one out of five guns hits where the sights point! The rest hit high, low or to the side. High or low impact isn't too bad, as the front sight can be filed lower or a higher one made to replace it. The brass sights, which are pressed into a slot in the barrel, can be pried out, and a replacement made with a bottom to fit the slot. This is inserted and then wedged in by using a medium-size screwdriver placed alongside the sight and tapped with a hammer once or twice. To correct laterally, an off-side blade may be

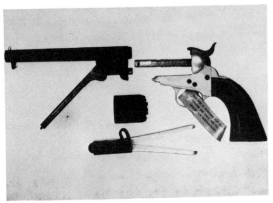

A .31 brass-frame Colt 'Baby Dragon" replica, taken down as for cleaning. The little brass bullet mold is entirely usable—providing extensions are put on handles. They get hot very quickly.

made, and filed before fitting to offset one side or the other. With the Colt types, the rear sight is a little notch in the hammer nose that can be moved a little very careful work with the handgrinder. They are hard, so you aren't going to file the hammer. There isn't really much that you can do with a bad offender and keep it close to original appearance, as there is no top strap, just a cylinder out in the open, with a hammer that comes down through a slot in the frame to reach it.

For serious target shooting, a rib-sight assembly must be made. This is a steel bar reaching from the muzzle to the nipple on the cylinder, with a front sight attached and an adjustable rear set into the rear end. This bar or rib is attached to the barrel with screws. Guns so equipped are sold as units, and probably someone will be advertising the rib assemblies before this is printed. Making the rib unit is no great chore, but requires the use of a milling machine to at least cut the radius—hollow—on the bottom to fit the rounded barrel well. A flat-bottomed rib can easily be placed on the top flat of an octagonal barrel.

The 1858 Remington solid-frame percussion revolver was a much stronger and simpler design, and the modern replicas are nearly exact copies. The front sights are a round-base affair and allow some leeway in replacement for windage adjustment, as does the rear sight, which is a notch in the frame. Filing will open one side or the other, within limits, of course—notches can't be made too wide. However, there is enough metal in the frame to allow the fitting of almost any of the modern adjustable rear sights, though this will usually mean that a higher front will be needed. These Remington replicas are very strong and are

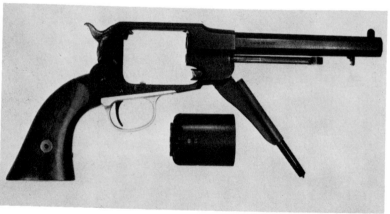

The Remington replica percussion revolver, the .36 caliber model distributed by Lyman. Nose of bullet-ram has had radius opened by filing so round balls may be seated without denting.

The Ruger Old Army Percussion revolver.

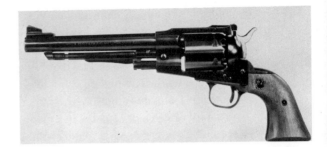

A detail of the Ruger Old Army Percussion revolver. This is the most shootable of all the cap and ball revolvers because it is of modern design and has adjustable sights.

favorites among the serious black-powder pistol competitors. They can be loaded up to compare favorably with the .38-Special and .44-Special target cartridges, although most match shooting is done with medium-power charges. (Cylinder chambers will not hold enough black powder to make an overload.)

In shooting, as with all cap-using arms, the cylinder is loaded but not capped until immediately before shooting if you're on a shooting range or in the company of several people, for the sake of safety. Each cylinder is loaded with the correct amount of black powder from a charger or dipper and balls or bullets are seated down to the powder but not so hard as to crush or compress it. Then the chambers are filled with grease or lubricant over the balls, full out to the ends. A popsicle paddle or a cake-decorator cylinder full of Crisco (one of the more popular materials!) or other lube is used to fill the chamber mouths. This must be done because the lead ball or bullet must have lubrication, and, perhaps even more important, the chambers must be flash-proofed, that is, sealed so that when one is fired with the resultant flame at the mouth of the chamber and diverted around the breech of the barrel, no fire can get back into the adjoining chamber past a loose or notched ball and set off its charge as well. This has happened many times in the past, resulting in smarting fingers and rather bent guns.

Cleaning any black-powder gun can be messy, but it really isn't too much work. The fouling is hygroscopic, meaning that it will attract moisture from the atmosphere and so cause rust if it's not removed promptly. Even a day's delay in a damp climate can result in visible rusting. The fouling itself is readily soluble in water, or almost any other liquid, when a few hours old, but it may harden if not attended to. The amount of grease, tallow, beeswax, etc., used with revolvers, however, makes a fouling that requires the use of some cutting agent, even if it is

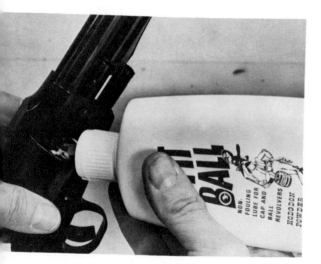

A squirt of Hodgins "spitball" is being applied to a cap and ball revolver cylinder over the bullet. This seals the ball and prevents "jumping fire." It also lubricates the bore so that hard fouling cannot accumulate. This is a significant aid in ensuring shooting accuracy.

only soap or detergent in water. Solvents can be used, with brushes and bits of cloth to clean up the breechs, cylinders after nipples have been unscrewed, etc., but probably most men just take off the barrel and cylinder (from Colt types), put them into a pan of water with detergent in it and just boil awhile. Rinsed wth hot water, the hot parts will almost dry themselves in seconds when removed and laid on paper towels, but it is wise to put them in a pan and dry them in the oven for a few minutes be sure all moisture is gone from nooks and crannies.

Barrels are first given a quick cleaning with brush and patches, of course. The Remingtons can be cleaned well with just an old toothbrush to get solvent around the barrel breech, etc. Remove the nipples and clean separately, either with a solvent bath or the hot-water treatment, for them and the cylinders. While it is not necessary to completely disassemble revolvers and clean every part every time the gun has been used, a pair of tweezers should often be employed to hold bits of patch dipped in solvent to wipe down hammers, hammmer slot in frame, etc.

Trigger pulls are worked on exactly as for the single-action cartridge revolver—cutting down the hammer notch to reduce trigger engagement. The hammers are case-hardened, and to really get any metal off, you must use a bench grinder. Carefully! Before doing this, the face of the notch should be lightly stoned with one of Mr. Russell's sharp-edged Arkansas oilstones. But only a little—on the lower priced arms the case hardening is often very thin. Wear through it to soft metal, and the notch won't hold up for very many shots. The pressure of the trigger is against the face of the notch; the *edge* of the notch may be cut back and might be soft at front, but the hard bearing surface can be maintained pretty well. Any new cap-and-ball revolver should be disassembled completely before using, and parts should be checked for burrs, tool marks that can be honed down, etc.

Nipples should be checked for hole size every now and then. Holes must be uniform in diameter, and not oversize, or the revolver will not be very accurate no matter how much care is used in making balls and in loading.

For all cap-lock arms being made and used today, that is, revolvers and rifles below large musket types, the No.-11 size nipple and cap are proper, and the nipple hole should be $25/1000$ inch in diameter. If it's much larger, excessive—and varying—amounts of powder–gas escape back up the nipple when the arm is fired. Nipple cleaners—wires, steel "pricks," etc.—are commonly used to clear the holes after firing, but probably the best way is to go to a hobby shop and buy a no. 72 drill bit, pinch it in a bit of fine sandpaper and pull it through a time or two to dull the cutting edge on the sides. Then push the shank end into a bit of wood for a handle and use it for a nipple cleaner, always just pushing in and out, not turning it. This drill is $25/1000$ inch in diameter. Should you want a no-go gage, buy a no. 70 bit, put a handle on the cutting end and use the shank to try in the nipple holes. It is $28/1000$ inch in diameter.

Single-shot target and general sporting pistols come in all sizes, shapes and types from large-sized smoothbore coach and pirate flint-lock replicas to modern percussion custom jobs with straight-line firing pins and micrometer sights. The "dueling"-type pistol is fairly popular for plinking purposes and informal target shooting. It's a medium-weight, medium-caliber, long-barreled type, available as either flint or percussion.

The "Kentucky" pistol, so-called because it was often a companion piece to the famed Kentucky long rifle (most of which were made in Lancaster County, Pennsylvania!) is also quite popular—these are heavier, more businesslike arms than the duelers. Small pocket types, the most famous being copies of the derringer self-defense pistol, are popular for decorators, conversation pieces and subjects of home-construction projects. Kits, or complete sets of parts, are obtainable for all of these types of old pistols.

For serious target shooting the single-shot pistoleer either buys a custom-made arm from Tingle or one of the other few gunmakers furnishing these, or gets a good lock, a piece of barrel, set triggers, and makes his own. Or he buys one of the Italian-made .44's listed under various names and numbers—ML5, M1969, etc. There's only one, and it bears an astonishing resemblance to the 1960 Tingle. The barrels are rough, but shoot well and can be easily replaced by a custom worker. Good sights also can be installed. Numrich's "Hopkins & Allen" under-hammer pistol is rapidly gaining favor for serious target work.

The single-shot pistols are all customarily loaded with patched round balls. A few of the old original target types, actually coming at the end of the old muzzle-loading era, had false muzzles and the other equipment for use of conical bullets, but none are made today. Revolvers customarily use a ball $5/1000$ inch larger in diameter than chamber diameter, but patch-ball guns, pistol or rifle, use balls that are .005 inch to .010 inch smaller than bore (land) diameter of the barrel, and employ hard-woven cotton or linen cloth patch to make them fit the barrel tightly. The pioneers used soft-tanned doeskin for patching, but this isn't readily available nowadays.

The patch is moistened by anything from spit to bear grease, inclusive, and can be precut to size or a ball can be placed on it and pushed down the barrel just below the end and cut flush with the barrel, using a very sharp knife. The the ramrod is used to push the patched ball down to the powder charge. If you've forgotten the powder, which happens, the nipple is unscrewed, and all the powder possible is trickled down the hole. The nipple is then replaced, capped, and gun is fired—there will be enough powder to blow the ball out of the barrel.

The thickness of the patching cloth used is therefore important: if it's too thick it will make seating the ball difficult, and the rifling will cut it badly. If it's too thin, it won't make a good gas seal around the ball, and accuracy will suffer. The ball leaves the patch at the muzzle, or should, and the patches blow out a few yards and fall to the ground. By looking at fired patches, an experienced shooter can tell if cloth

By "reading" these patches one can determine what, if anything, is causing inaccuracy with a muzzle-loading rifle. The black marks on the patch at left show that the ball was not properly centered in the patch during the loading operation. The patch in the center is cut along one edge as a result of the fit being too tight inside the barrel. The edges of the land sliced through the patch. In this case a thinner patch is called for. The patch at right shows everything as it should be.

thickness and strength is OK, or whether the rifling is rough, too sharp edged, etc. Fired patches should be marked with streaks (from grooves in barrel) but not cut or badly shredded. Good muzzle-loader barrels have smooth, clean rifling, and need not have lands and grooves as sharply cornered as in a modern cartridge rifle.

New barrel blanks are often too sharp to start with, and rather than firing 200 or 300 shots to wear them smooth, gunsmiths and amateurs building up rifles or pistols may lap barrels before doing anything else. The classic method is to insert a steel rod in the barrel, with a patch or wad of string around it a few inches from the end. Then pour melted lead down the bore to make a plug around the rod 1¼ to 2 inches long. The barrel is then oiled with light oil and lapping powder mixed with it—a very fine abrasive, that is. The lead lap is then pulled back and forth through the barrel, never entirely out of the barrel at either end. The abrasive clinging to the lead polishes the bore and takes off microscopic burrs, too sharp corners, etc. The home mechanic can do a very passable job with a strong cleaning rod using tight cloth patches saturated with oil and dusted with silicon powder, oil–rock dust, paste for metal-fouling or whatever fine abrasive he can come by.

The first step is to insert a common wire brush into the bore. Next, melted lead is poured around the brush. This forms the lapping slug. A patch or wad of string on the end of a steel rod can be used also, as explained in the text.

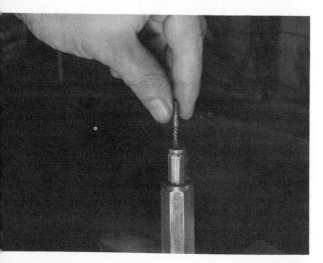

The slug is then pulled from the barrel after casting.

A detail of the lap, showing the "slow" twist of the muzzle-loader rifling.

Next, the lap is dipped in oil and then coated with abrasive dust and lapping compound.

The back-and-forth motion of the lapping rod would damage the muzzle. Therefore, a setup like this is required to protect it. This is a simple piece of leather with a hole that serves to guide the rod.

Here a GI-model steel rod has been screwed onto the lap and the barrel is lapped by rubbing it backwards and forwards through the bore. After every few minutes or so lapping is necessary to recoat the lap with oil and abrasive dust.

An hour's work may not change the appearance of the bore much, but the ball and patch will seat a good deal more smoothly. When a blank or barrel is lapped, the muzzle end should be cut of ½ inch or more because the rifling may be worn oversize or worn to one side a little during the lapping. The slow twist of muzzle-loader rifling—one turn in 48 inches or more—makes lapping quite easy, compared to doing the job on a fast-twist modern cartridge arm .

The Italian replica-revolver makers have copied the old Colt and Remington percussion models almost perfectly—except for the nipples. When they came to the threading on the nipples and in the cylinders, they didn't duplicate the original tooling of thirty-two threads per inch, but went to the 6mm metric (the right diameter) of thirty-four threads per inch. The diameter of threaded portion of the nipple is .232 inch for the .36 and .44 calibers. So be careful about ordering replacement nipples, specifying for "replica" arm or "original," should you be so lucky.

The small five-shot .31-caliber replicas have yet another nipple, this being a 5.5mm coarse thread, in our usage, .216-inch diameter, approximately twenty-four threads to the inch. American-made Ampco nipples in this size are not made at this time.

One point of duplication could have been improved upon. They didn't have to make the screw heads as soft as the ones on the old original revolvers! To take apart the cap-and-ball revolver, screwdrivers with tips fitting the slots precisely must be used: they can't be narrower than the slot, or not go all the way to its bottom, or they'll mar the screw head the first time the gun is disassembled. Considerable care must be taken in all disassembly, of course, The fitting of parts, counterbores for screw heads and threading are usually minimum tolerance, meaning a tight fit. Any burr, bend, foreign matter or dent in an edge will prevent perfect reassembly. Case-hardened steel can be dented, so use soft-metal punches whenever possible, should you need to drive pins.

There should be no hang-up in the loading-lever assembly—the ram should move freely, and there should be no bind or tight spot at any point of the lever's arc. When there is, a few seconds' file and stone work on the points of friction, visible as bright wear-spots on the sides of parts, will clear up the trouble.

Muzzle-loading Rifles

The Kentucky rifle was a colonial American development. Fairly early in the 1700's a lot of people liked exploring better than farming and started moving west. The big-bore muskets were heavy and short-ranged—inconvenient for traveling. So gunsmiths started making smaller calibers and longer barrels, improving both range and accuracy. The flintlock Pennsylvania rifle developed within a few years with barrels often as small as .40 caliber, or eighty balls to the pound of lead. When a fellow took off on a 1500-mile walk to look at the Mississippi River, he had to carry all his ammunition, and too many pounds slowed him down when he met Indians who resented trespassers.

The soft-iron barrels wore and rusted fast, and every year or two the guns went back to a gunsmith who deepened the rifling and enlarged the bore, thus freshening it to new conditions. When the caliber got much larger than .50, the rifle was usually discarded or rebarreled.

Less than 100 years later, the percussion cap lock evolved for general use, and identical rifles were made using percussion locks. Many usable flintlocks were converted to cap use by changing the lock and vent hole.

While the pioneer's principal arm was such a large-caliber rifle, his real hunting gun was usually a "pea rifle," so called because it used a very small ball, .28 to .33 caliber. It was ideal for squirrels, rabbits and capable of killing deer. They made little noise and used little powder and lead, always valuable commodities. This small-bore type muzzleloader survives today as the .31 caliber. As the West opened up, strongly built horseback rifles capable of taking buffalo and grizzly bear evolved. These were .50 caliber and larger, with barrels not over 32 inches long. They were sometimes called "plains rifles." The Hawken firm in St. Louis was the most famous maker. There is currently a trend toward this type, and Hawken-type replica arms and kits are now very popular. These are perhaps the easiest to handle and the most practical rifle for the beginning muzzle-loading shooter. (Just loading a Kentucky rifle with a 4-foot barrel can be an adventure for a tyro!)

With any rifle or single-shot pistol, or kit, or separate barrel purchased for building up an arm, it is necessary to know the exact bore diameter so as to know what size lead ball to buy or mold to buy to make the balls. The barrelmakers maintain the old rugged individualism; each makes each caliber to *his* dimensions. For instance, in the .36 caliber, Numrich bore diameter is .347 inch, Douglas is .363 inch and Manley is .353 inch.

Ramrod cleaning tips, called jags, are button or ringed-button shapes, and dimensions are important since they must positively bring the cleaning patch back out the muzzle every time. In the old days powder was often inferior and didn't burn cleanly or completely every time the arm was fired. Thus it became customary to run a patch wet with water or spit down to the chamber before reloading to put out any smoldering sparks before pouring more gunpowder down the barrel. Also, it kept the barrel clean, and the rifle or pistol shooting accurately. This is standard operating procedure today: after every shot, run a wet cleaning patch all the way down to the breechplug, for safety as well as efficiency. If on a range, the same patch can be used almost indefinitely, wet and squeezed out every time it is used. And even then don't be looking down the barrel or have fingers over the bore when pouring in the powder charge. And give up smoking while you're shooting or handling black powder in any manner. It burns very easy and very fast.

When a patch does come off a rod and lodge in the barrel, a patch-pulling tip or "worm"—a double-pronged corkscrew—is put on the rod, put down and turned to catch in the patch and so allow it to be pulled out. The true old-fashioned worm can also be used to take hold of a lead ball and pull it out when a charge must be unloaded and firing is inconvenient. However, the modern ball-puller is a sharp-tipped wood screw with shank threaded to screw into the cleaning or ramrod. This is forced and turned to make it screw itself into the lead firmly enough to hold it for withdrawal.

The ramrod may be used just for seating the ball or bullet, or for all cleaning chores as well. If the ramrod is all-purpose, the tip base must be firmly fixed to the rod, for if it should pull off, the only way to clear the barrel is to take the gun down and remove the breechplug. So, all wood possible must be left to fill the cavity in the base. Fit the base carefully; then drill through both brass walls and wood, put a little countersink in brass at each end of the hole and then peen the ends of a brass pin to rivet things together. File and sand the riveted ends flush.

Old military arms nearly always had round barrels, and the replica Civil War muskets, rifled muskets, "Zouave" types, etc., duplicate these. American-made rifles and pistols, however, practically all had octagonal barrels, called "eight-square," in early days. These were made in small shops, usually by a lone gunsmith, who made his barrels by heating a straight flat strap of iron and hammering it around a steel rod, forge-welding it into a rough tube which then was straightened and rifled with a homemade hand-powered wooden guide rifling machine. He had no engine lathe, no way to turn this crude barrel round and true, but with homemade files and a simple square he could cut the soft metal to a fairly true octagon with a few hours' labor. The shape, with its flats on top, bottom and sides, made fitting of sights, wedge or pin tenons to hold it in the stock and ferrules or tubes to hold the ramrod much easier.

Modern muzzle-loader barrels are octagonal rather than round to fit tradition and taste for authentic detail, and convey the same advantage to the home gunsmith. Cutting dovetails for sights and tenons, drilling and tapping the hole for the "drum"—the steel fitting that is installed in side of the barrel and itself tapped to take a nipple—these and other operations are almost foolproof to locate and perform on flat surfaces, difficult on round. This is very important to the new convert to the muzzle gun because approximately one week after buying one, taking it out to shoot, meeting other black-powder shooters and reading a catalog or publication for the sport, he's ready for another gun and is aware that fellow converts are making up their own—so why not him?

A decent cap-lock pistol, rifle or musket—or shotgun—requires little maintenance beyond thorough cleaning after each day of use. If locks and triggers are of good quality, little repair or parts replacement is necessary either. Flintlocks demand maintenance of flints—normal American or English flints may not last over twenty shots and edges may deteriorate faster. The shooter must keep flints clamped firmly, with the good edge in line so that when the hammer brings the flint down into and across the frizzen, a shower of sparks goes down to the pan to ignite the priming powder. If the frizzen or the edge of the flint is worn, no sparks and no fire. Agate flints have several times the life of the standard variety. A. G. Russell is now grinding double-end flints from Novaculite that'll last even longer!

Large-caliber—.58 and above normally—military replica rifles and muskets are often used with a minié ball, which is really a hollow-based bullet, small enough to go down the rifling readily. The base expands to fill the bore and groove diameters in the barrel. These bullets are lubricated, having grooves to be filled with lubricating agent. The round barrels on such arms are often quite thin, comparatively speaking, and powder charges are not heavy.

These are minié balls of the type used in muzzle-loading rifles. The hollow skirt of the bullet expands and forms an effective gas seal.

OLD-TIMERS' WAY OF DETERMINING CHARGE

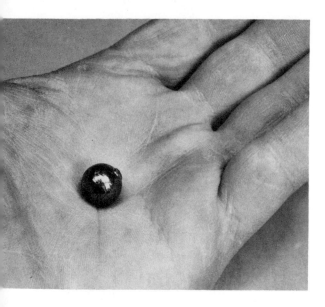

To determine the proper charge for a muzzle-loading rifle, the correct caliber ball is fitted into the slightly cupped palm of the hand.

Next, black powder is poured over the ball until it is completely covered.

The amount of powder that it takes to completely cover the ball is surprisingly close to the correct charge for that caliber rifle.

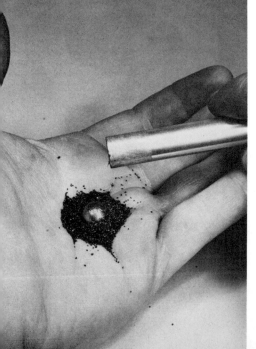

In such large bores a coarser powder, that is, one having larger individual grains, should be used. Today, probably the FFG grade is the most commonly used, though in .69 calibers, etc., FG may work best. The normal "fine" powder, FFFG is practically a standard for .50 caliber on down, including all rifles and revolvers, while the finest, smallest grain powder, FFFFG is used as priming powder for flintlocks.

The beginning shooter should receive directions with a new gun on what weight of powder charge to use, or we should check one of the catalog–handbooks for recommendation. Powder flasks to carry powder in and measure out recommended quantities for pistols and revolvers are commonly used, but separate measures, adjustable or nonadjustable little cups, dippers or tubes, are for the long guns. The ancient rule called for laying the lead ball in the hollow of the palm and then pouring powder on it until just the top of the ball was visible. Theoretically, this is a proper load and cannot be an overload. Heavy loads are seldom as accurate as light ones at the short distances modern muzzle-loaders are fired in target shooting, so there is no reason for heavy loading.

Black-powder charges are really rather arbitrary quantities. In the beginning, they were quantity or volume measurements. Then, for uniformity, weights were assigned, but on the first apothecary's divisions, not on our present avoirdupois system. Your great-great-grandfather may have worked out his loads with grains that went 480 to the ounce instead of the 437½ you get with your new powder scale. Add to this the fact that the different grades or sizes of powder don't bulk the same, so that a full measure cup of FFG may weigh fifty grains, and the same cup filled with FFFG may weigh fifty-four grains. It is a very good characteristic, indeed, that black powder and black-powder arms aren't safety-critical on ten-percent, or more, overcharges!

People are often puzzled by reference to cartridges in writings mentioning early firearms. In fact, the cartridge was invented long before the cartridge firearm, probably early in flintlock days. These cartridges were just packages of premeasured powder charges and lead balls, of plain, waxed or nitrated paper, folded or tied to hold together for ease in carrying for rapid reloading. The paper was torn or bitten through, powder poured down barrel and followed by the ball, the paper sometimes used as wadding, sometimes discarded. Nitrated (combustible) paper powder-and-bullet cartridges were made for revolvers from the earliest days, tapered small at the base so the entire assembly could be quickly rammed into cylinder chambers. These can be quite easily made by soaking thin bond or onionskin paper in a saturated solution of potassium nitrate (all the nitrate the water will absorb), drying the paper and cutting to shape to glue the edges together over a ta-pered wooden form, folding and cementing the end to make a truncated cone to hold the powder and large enough at the big end to take the ball or bullet, which is generally sealed in with stiff bullet lubricant. The nitrated paper is practically a gunpowder itself, and leaves little residue in chambers.

The ultragun of the black-powder world is unromantically called a slug gun. These are .50 caliber and larger as a rule, and are so heavy that they are fired only from shooting tables (a slug rifle weighing fifty pounds is not unusual). They have fine micrometer or telescopic sights, and use very, very carefully made conical bullets, usually paper-patched, but not in the sense of a round-ball patch. The paper is care-fully fitted to the bullet and used as a jacket for it. Great pains are taken in making bullets, even to the point of making them in two parts, soft lead for the base, hardened lead for the nose, the two swagged together in special presses or hand tools made for the purpose.

Many of these rifles now in use were made a hundred years ago. Being target arms they were always well cared for and so remain in near-perfect condition inside and out. Modern-made slug rifles are all individual efforts by advanced muzzle-loader shooters with the metal-work usually done by one of the gunsmiths doing custom work such as making large breechplugs and primer-lock ignitions, etc. Slug-gun com-petition allows use of standard normal large rifle or pistol primers, as well as percussion caps, and special nipple systems that use primers are often made for the guns as the more powerful primers ignite large pow-der charges more efficiently than the old caps.

Most of the usable original and replica rifled muskets and general Civil War class long arms use nipples (modern manufacture) that hold the no. 11 percussion cap, although the thread diameter of the nipple may be $5/16$ inch, twenty-four threads to the inch, rather than the ¼ by 28 size thread on the rifle and single-shot pistol nipple, using the same cap. The latter is usually listed as .250 by 28. When you see ".255" or ".260" it means a larger diameter of thread, to fit tightly in drums or bolsters where the threaded hole for the nipple has rusted or worn over-size a little. A "bolster" is a combination breechplug and nipple socket.

The most direct percussion ignition system is that of the under-hammer arm, in which the hammer is on the bottom of the barrel rather than on the side. The cap fires directly into the powder charge in a straight line, whereas in the more conventional side lock there is a right-angle turn to be negotiated. The Numrich Arms Corporation makes a full line of underhammer target and hunting rifles and pistols,

Jim Carmichel fires the Thompson Center Hawkin percussion rifle. This is a very shootable gun in that it is tough, well made, and accurate.

The complete setup for shooting the Thompson Center Hawkin rifle: black-powder solvent, an assortment of powder dippers for different powder charges, balls and minié balls, bullet molds, patches, an extra nipple and nipple wrench.

which are widely used and highly regarded by shooters. Called "Hopkins & Allen" models, after a pioneer company, they are so simple and efficient in design and with so few parts that they are almost trouble-free. The only criticism I have heard is that the sears should be hardened in Kasenite to prevent fast wear and consequent change of trigger

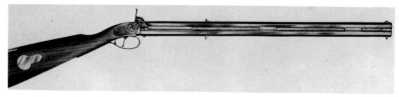

Numrich makes this double-barrelled muzzle-loading rifle. After firing one barrel, the two can be turned to bring the bottom barrel around to lock in position for the hammer to strike its nipple.

pull: the manufacturer probably has taken care of this matter already, on latest production.

Excepting the revolvers, almost none of the percussion arms have any provision for stopping the hammer-fall except by contact with the nipple, capped or not. Therefore, none should be snapped with the nipple or its holding part unprotected. The customary protector is a small leather washer pressed down over the nipple, thick enough so that the hammer can hit the leather but not the end of nipple. Your friendly shoe-repair shop can make you a couple in a few seconds, but you can make your own with a drill and scrap of leather. Cut the leather to fit

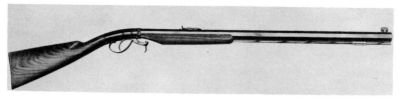

Numrich's "Hopkins & Allen" underhammer rifle, low in cost, very reliable, and made in several lengths, weights of barrel and calibers. This type is eminently suited to the fellow who wants to start black-powder shooting right now.

the bolster or drum with a wood chisel. No rifle or shotgun lock should be snapped when free of the gun or when the barrel or barrels are removed. If you must snap the lock to test the spring, etc., hold it so the hammer will hit a wood block or otherwise be cushioned against a sudden stop beyond its normal travel distance.

An assortment of balls and bullets as well as percussion caps, a bullet starter, and a primer feed for black-powder shooting. The large minié balls are exact duplicates of the big-bore muzzle-loading rifle used during the Civil War.

Muzzle-loading Shotguns

Muzzle-loading shotguns are treated as are rifles and muskets, except for loading and for cleaning of possible leading from barrel. The powder charge is poured down the barrel, and then a wad of paper—old newspaper, generally—is rammed down. Then the shot charge is loaded, and another wad of paper or perhaps a cut felt wad is pressed down to retain the load. There is no patch to protect the bore from leading, and soft shot may cause leading. Peering down the barrels after normal water cleaning should show the streaks of lead if they exist. Removal is by brass brush, etc., as with any shotgun, complicated by the fact you work from one end only and can't look through to see when the job is done! Most shooters soon graduate from newspaper and toilet tissue for wadding to thick cardboard overpowder wads, cut by a stamp and hammer—stamps are made or bought in a size to cut a wad that fits tightly in the bore—and felt, celotex or other semihard overshot wads. These give better patterns normally, and sometimes it isn't wise to blow out a batch of burning confetti when shooting at a rabbit or quail.

Building a Muzzle-loader

There is little restraint on the individual's muzzle-loading building endeavors unless he is a traditionalist who insists on a homemade coonskin cap, self-tanned deerskin clothing and powder horn and bullet pouch to go along with his original or custom-made exact-replica Kentucky rifle—flintlock, of course. The normal black-powder shooter is as ingenious as any ancestor in fixing up his equipment, and isn't proud at all about not using modern components—he'll use double-set triggers from a modern Mauser rifle in a percussion single-shot dueller, or gladly steal the tang sight from uncle's Savage 99 for his .36 caliber offhand rifle. His guns need not be copies of any original type—it is enough that they are loaded and fired in the old way. Guns—plural—because he can't be satisfied with just one, even though it may be a fine over-the-counter job. There is always another caliber to try out. He'd like a smallbore, a .31, and no ready-made rifles or kits being advertised, he has to buy his own lock, stock and barrel and put them together.

The first off-beat fact the novice muzzle-loader enthusiast runs into is color: all the genuine old firearms he sees in museums, at gun shows or in modest local collections are browned, while all the modern replicas are blued. There's a reason for this. While we have to fight rust all the time in maintenance to keep it away, it is a very hard job to rust

This is a Birchwood Casey kit for finishing muzzle-loading rifle stocks and browning the metal parts to duplicate early American techniques.

the outside of the barrel all over to a nice deep brown! Blueing is much, much easier. There are dozens of formulas for browning solutions in old gun books, usually taken from older books (without test by the author), and none of them will work quite correctly. I just spent about thirty dollars for ingredients to check out a batch on a modern muzzle-loading barrel. From corrosive sublimate at four dollars an ounce on down. (Today it is mercuric chloride.) The old guns were of iron: modern ones are of steel, and resist the solutions. They can be rusted of course, but not evenly to give the smooth perfectly even brown the old-timers obtained. The chemicals are often hard to obtain, can be dangerous—mercuric chloride and copper sulfate are poisonous and nitric acid isn't exactly a handwash—and even the nondangerous ones such as spirits of nitre and ferric chloride aren't necessary home supplies. Leftovers are a worry: even a mixed solution must be kept in a glass-stoppered glass bottle—it will rust out a metal cap. The best way here is not the do-it-yourself route; take the easy way and buy a bottle of "Plum Brown," made by the Birchwood Casey Company, available through any sporting-goods store carrying any muzzle-loading supplies, or from any of the mail-order dealers in such items.

The name is a pun of sorts as the most desired finish on the old guns was a brown with a purplish or plum-color tint. The solution is to be handled with care, exactly as directed. Barrels and other parts to be finished should be cleaned, polished and degreased using the Birchwood Casey cleaner-degreaser (wiping with a tissue wet with acetone is also a good final cleaner) and heated before application of the browning solution. It needs to remain on the metal only ten minutes before rubbing down with fine steel wool, and if it isn't dark enough, put on another coat. After rubbing down, the finish may be oiled or waxed. The entire job can take less than an hour, and you need no "damp area" or wet box to help rusting overnight or for days as with most of the old home-mixed solutions.

It should be remembered that before applying the first coat, the surfaces should be free of all grease and provision made for holding without touching with fingers; many a man has found he has fingerprints showing in his browning job after finishing! Wood dowels in muzzles do double duty as handles and keeping the solution out of the bore, and stiff wire hooks through holes in tangs will hold up the other end. Heating a long rifle barrel can be troublesome. Passing back and forth over gas-stove burners will do it, (high over the burners!) and wiping again with a final degreaser afterward is perhaps the easiest method.

It is really quite difficult to do a decent job with even the best of commercial preparations. I didn't want to give up the only good for-

BROWNING METAL PARTS

Since the metal parts must be heated somewhat it is necessary to construct a holding frame such as shown here. This frame, constructed from a bent coat hanger, holds the barrel quite well but at the same time does not rob the heat.

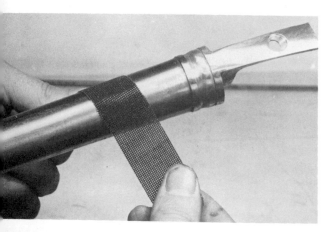

The first step is to polish the metal parts as bright and smooth as possible. Be sure to eliminate all file marks.

Here a fine grade of steel wool is used for the final polishing.

The last step before the actual browning begins is to clean all metal parts until they are completely free of dirt and especially oil. Any oil or grease on the metal surfaces will result in ugly spotting. Since the cleaner and degreaser is a mild acid, rubber gloves are used to protect the fingers.

A butane torch is used to heat a flintlock hammer. Metal is heated just enough to "sizzle" water when dropped on the metal's surface.

While the metal is hot the Birchwood Casey "plum-brown" is swabbed on the surface. The browning effect is immediate.

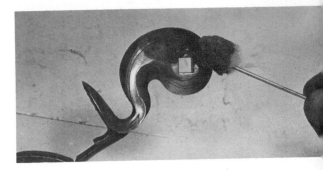

Here the "plum-brown" solution is swabbed on the barrel.

mula I found because of the poisonous ingredient, but with only good sense it can be used without danger. The bad stuff is mercuric chloride, available from chemical supply houses, and it says on the bottle: "may be fatal if swallowed, don't breathe the dust, avoid contact with eyes or prolonged contact with skin, wash thoroughly before eating or smoking after handling, wash clothes after using and take a shower with plenty of soap." The form is small white crystals, there isn't much dust—the material is very heavy—and an ordinary damp cotton cloth over mouth and nose when you open the bottle and pour onto an ordinary powder scale for measuring seems ample protection. Only a very little is needed—you probably will have to buy the minimum amount sold, three or four ounces, but this is enough for many guns.

Get sweet spirits of nitre and straight alcohol at any drugstore. Not wood alcohol or rubbing alcohol. Then a clean wide-mouth jar, a large-size peanut-butter type is excellent. Pour in four ounces of spirits of nitre and four ounces of alcohol. Then add 110 grains (one-quarter ounce) of mercuric chloride, put on the lid, shake it now and then and use it. If you have just one barrel to do, half the above quantities will do.

Stick wooden dowels or pegs in the ends of the barrel and put boxes or bricks on the bench spaced so you can rest the dowels on them with the barrel in between so you can turn it. Make several little swabs—inch-square or round cotton cleaning patches are fine, folded in quarters with a bit of wire clamped on for a handle. Or you can use tweezers if you remember to wash them after using each time. Dip in the solution and run the length of a barrel flat, turning one flat at a time until all have been wetted. Because of the alcohol, the solution dries very rapidly and you see no change in appearance of the metal. (Which should have been polished and washed off with acetone first, of course!)

Close the jar tightly; the swab should be disposed of so no person or animal can contact it. Put a pan of water on the bench and leave it for twenty-four hours. Then repeat the coating. Nothing happens for a day or so, then you notice a delicate brown all over. Before the next coat, wipe down the flats lightly with 4/0 steel wool, and do this for the next five or six days, when you should have a beautiful translucent light brown finish. It can be oiled, waxed or otherwise preserved. There will be no after-rust as with other common browning solutions.

This solution will work on practically all steels, including hardened tool steels. I made a hammer and trigger that took a fine finish after being made very hard. Some modern alloy steels will become very dark brown indeed. Color can, of course, be governed easily—you just stop using the solution when parts get to the right shade of brown.

The mercuric chloride is as stated, very dangerous to handle, but you don't handle it much. In the solution it isn't very dangerous, of course, though it's not advisable to lean over the jar and inhale the fumes. I've had it on my fingers inadvertently, and don't know that it would even sting, as I washed it off immediately. The solution is supposed to keep well, but I don't know as I throw away what's left over, having too many jars of clear liquids around—water, acetone, lacquer thinner, solvent, perchlorate ethylene, to name some of them! Yes, I label the dangerous things, but it's possible not to read labels sometimes, isn't it?

The weak point of the muzzle-loading rifle, and to some extent, the shotgun, and the hardest-to-make component is the stock. The drop or bend at the small of the butt (trigger section) is so pronounced that unless the grain of the wood follows this curve pretty well, the stock is easy to break here. The stock is slimmed down, cut deeply for the heavy octagonal barrel and breechplug, side lock and trigger assembly, leaving the start of the butt curve or angle rather weak. So the long rifles are handled gently: old woodcuts you see showing frontier scouts leaning on their rifles I don't think are very true! They even held the guns tightly between their knees to support them when loading to help take pressure off the buttstock. The plains or western rifles such as the Hawken strengthened the small of the stock by using very long tangs on the breechplug or patent breech tang and long, heavy rear tangs on the trigger plates and guards. Military arms were much heavier through the grip and had much less drop to the butt for strength.

Making a stock for any muzzle-loading long arm from scratch—that is, starting from a blank sawed to an outline out of a maple or walnut plank is beyond any amateur's first effort, but since shaped semi-finished stocks are made and sold by a half-dozen muzzle-loading supply houses (inletted to the desired size of octagonal barrel, drilled for the ramrod, lock inletting if desired and in a variety of styles and types—full length, half-stock, Hawken design—any of which is comparatively easy to complete into first-class finish) he has no need to take on too difficult a project. The Dixie Arms Works provides well-illustrated step-by-step instructions on stock operations. Fancifully shaped patch boxes need not be inletted into the side of the muzzle-loader's first buttstock.

The muzzle-loading gun owner will need his little work area and will find endless projects for it beyond his arms maintenance and repair, such as the adjustment and making of accessories used in shooting. Wooden clamp-stands to hold the rifle or pistol while loading, powder measures changed or made for different charges, flasks and chargers kept in repair or making a powder horn are examples. Parts he can't make, he can buy to build around.

Restoration and Reconditioning of Antique Arms

Old percussion arms and occasionally flintlocks turn up from time to time and too often fall into the hands of eager but unknowing enthusiasts who lower their value and actually damage them through unskilled cleanup efforts. While many shotguns and muskets are reconditioned and rebuilt to use in shooting, nearly all of the rifles and pistols are more valuable as collector's items, but only if restored carefully, not rebuilt with new barrels or locks, etc. A valuable antique doesn't have to be one of the highly decorated museum pieces often pictured; an ordinary, plain, rusted and worn heavy rifle may be a genuine Hawken and worth 1,000 dollars or more.

Should an old arm be acquired, the very first act should be to determine if it is loaded. This is done by checking the depth to which a rod can be inserted down the barrel against the outside of barrel to see if it will or will not reach the breechplug or venthole. If something—load or not—is in the barrel, try a worm if you have one or a screw-type

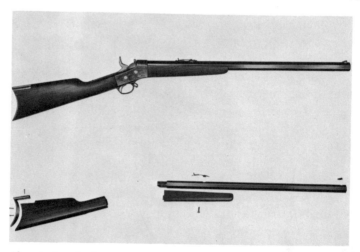

Almost a hundred years ago Remington sold vast numbers of their rolling-block single-shot military rifles over the world, many of which have returned to the U.S. as antiques, but in poor condition and with obsolete calibers. Numrich Arms steps in to aid the single-shot addict with this do-it-yourself barrel and stock kit to make a good-looking .45/70 rifle for target shooting or hunting.

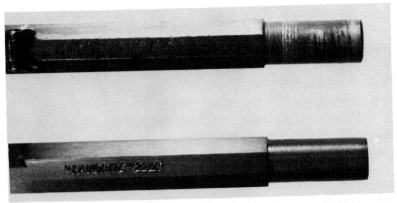

Another Numrich rehabilitation project is making new replacement .22 rimfire barrels for the old Stevens "Favorite" rifles. These are half octagon, half round. Original Stevens barrel is shown at top, the modern replacement at bottom.

puller. As a last resort, straighten a coat hanger, and then bend a ¼-inch hook, hardly more than a right angle on one end and fish down the bore with it. The idea is to get any paper wadding, dried mud from wasp's nests, etc., out before going down with a ramrod and solvent on patches to clean the barrel above the load or obstruction. If the vent or nipple is clear or removable with a little oil soaking, an eyedropper can be used to force water into the breech to render the old powder charge safe.

Now gun oil can be poured down the barrel and allowed to soak into and around the old load or packed wadding. Within a day or two, the ball-puller should be able to do its job. If not, the arm will be safe to work on as long as you get a few drops of water into the breech, and you can proceed with exterior cleanup and disassembly. Wash the entire gun with hot water and mild detergent, drying and wiping with cleaning tissue in a hurry—to keep water from soaking into the stock around locks, etc. With luck, you'll be able to get the arm apart and dry off the interior in an hour or two. If not, a little fresh moisture can't add too much to the old damage. Water will cut dirt and salt; oil won't.

With the arm so cleaned, screw slots should be cleanable with brushes and small strips and picks of brass or aluminum. Don't use small steel screwdriver blades for scraping. Apply one of the screw-loosening agents such as Liquid Wrench to all screw heads, ends, pins and wedges, down in the lock, around the hammer, etc., and allow it to stand for an hour before trying to loosen or remove any pin or screw. When this is done, a precisely fitting screwdriver tip is bottomed and tapped lightly a few times with small hammer. If the screw cannot be loosened, let it soak with the penetrating oil for a week if necessary, and try it every day. If the tang screw and wedges or pins holding the barrel can be removed and the stock taken off without force, the rest comes pretty easily.

When screws are positively rusted in place and heads tear or break off in resisting turning, they must be drilled out, using bits smaller in diameter than the threaded hole or part they engage. Then, above the threaded section, larger drills are used up to the body size of the screw. These are usually the screws holding parts of the lock to the lockplate, and genuine original replacement screws can usually be found to replace the destroyed ones.

The pins or wedges holding the stock and barrel together can usually be driven out with an undersize pin punch of soft-metal drive bar and removal of tang screw or screws frees all attachment—mechanical attachment, that is, whether or not the arm has a hook or patent breech or the one-piece plug with tang. Should the barrel still be stuck firmly to the wood, run a line of bore-cleaning solvent along the joint of wood and metal and tap the top of the barrel with a rawhide or wood mallet for fifteen minutes. If they still refuse to part, use a single-edge razor blade to go down between the barrel and inletting, not pulling it along, but pushing straight down $1/16$ inch or more, then moving the blade to edge of the space and repeating until the entire channel has been opened. The tapping process repeated should now be successful. Barrels usually stick to wood just on the upper edges of the inletting, where metal roughened by rust has wood shrunk to it by age.

Use rust-removing solvents to clean metal, never abrasives. Naval jelly is a must for extreme cases. Used as directed and flushed off with water, it takes all rust and old finish with it, leaving clean metal. Of course, such a badly damaged antique will only be useful as a decorative item, but it can be made into a genuine decoration instead of being left an unsightly relic.

Stocks from old arms should be cleaned with water and brushes, wiped dry and hung by a string from a hook or nail when not on the bench being worked on. They will warp and go out of shape if just placed in a corner, butt up or down. Repeated wipings with cloths wet with wood cleaners will restore a good appearance.

Dents in the wood can be raised by wet cloth and hot iron: heat a bar or rod—an old junk screwdriver is ideal—to dull red (the color will be gone before you can get to the job), lay a double thickness of cotton cloth, such as a GI cleaning patch, thoroughly wetted, on the dent and

REFINISHING A MUZZLE-LOADER STOCK

Here is a fine old muzzle-loader in need of stock refinishing. Note that the original finish has turned black and that grime has accumulated around the fine carving.

Gunstock finish remover or ordinary paint remover is especially effective for removing the old finish from muzzle-loading stocks. It works fast and does a good job.

A brush is used in conjunction with the finish remover to scrub the grime and old finish out of the carving.

Boiled linseed oil is then hand-rubbed into recently cleaned stock. Note how sharp and well defined the carving looks.

apply the iron, moving it around a little and taking away as cloth dries and begins to scorch. This process drives steam into the grain of the wood and expands it to original dimensions.

A stock dark with old oil can be helped by washing in acetone a few times. Old military muskets and pistols may have hardened varnishes on them that require varnish-remover pastes or liquids to be applied, allowed to set a few minutes, wiped off and then wiped with cloths wet with acetone. Do not use scrapers, stiff brushes or steel wool by the handful, yet. Any armory or inspectors' stampings in the stock must be preserved carefully. When the stock is as clean as possible, fine sandpaper may be used to smooth up raised grain or as needed to prepare for a new finish of linseed oil or thinned varnish.

Light pitting on locks, bands, etc., is best cleaned by acid bath—a wide-mouthed peanut-butter jar with a half-and-half solution of muriatic acid and water should be large enough. Use steel or iron wires to hold parts in the solution—a minute is usually long enough—then dip in clean water, dry and rub with 4/0 steel wool dampened with gun oil. If surfaces are almost perfectly clean, just use dry baking soda on a patch. Keep the acid-jar's lid on when not using; fumes will tend to rust unprotected steel items in the room on long exposure.

Cleaned-up parts may be browned or blued, whichever their original finish happened to be. If blue, use one of the cold types. They don't give as nice or even a finish as the gunsmith's hot blue tanks produce, but the appearance may be even more authentic. Also, caustic hot-blueing solutions may turn old metal odd colors and pit surfaces—they are for steel, not iron.

An antique arm suspected of being really valuable should be turned over to one of the professional specialists in restoration, who has tools, spare parts and the knowledge to work on each type of arm.

9

Air and CO₂ Rifles and Pistols

Target shooting for sport with air guns is becoming very popular now that highly accurate arms with good sights and triggers are available. It is easy to make a pellet or BB backstop from a carton stuffed with old telephone directories or packed magazines and shoot indoors. Ranges fired are only 15 to 35 feet. No noise, no smoke, no odor of burned powder. Pistols of all types—purely functional air types or styled to simulate firearms—come in all price ranges, from a few dollars to well over a hundred for the imported precision German models. Rifles range from the traditional boys' BB guns to super-accurate target rifles.

The accuracy arms are .177, or 4.5mm caliber with rifled barrels for the skirted lead pellet. These do occasionally pick up leading in the bore, which is ordinarily easily removed by patch, solvent and cleaning rod. Cleaning rods for air rifles and pistols can be purchased, or made if none came with the gun when purchased.

Almost all the air guns now made are the spring-air type. This has a piston driven by a strong spring that is compressed when arm is cocked and released by trigger to drive air with great force through a small opening and so push out the projectile. With a great deal of use,

161

the springs may weaken and need replacing, but the common cause of failure is deterioration of the leather or rubber washer on the piston. This allows air to escape when the washer moves forward on firing. Over-oiling causes most of the trouble. Follow directions exactly on the oiling and lubrication of air and CO_2 arms. The best—probably most— rifles and pistols use plastics that stand up better than leather, but even so, they can't last indefinitely, and a spare washer or seal should be kept on hand.

CO_2 guns are more for the backyard plinking than for target use, though some of the rifles and pistols are now accurate enough for the latter. Air-type BB and .22-caliber ball or pellet guns are also more for casual picnic plinking than serious practice or competition.

Trigger pulls range from very bad to very good. The true target types have good adjustable trigger pulls, and all but the very cheapest models can be disassembled for filing down notch engagement and juggling return springs to lighten pulls. For those guns that cannot be readily disassembled and reassembled, all that can be done is an injection of moly lubricant in the hope that it will smooth up trigger action.

The good break-open air rifles customarily have a breech seal, a nylon or neoprene O ring that seats in the breech of the barrel, around the bore, protruding a trifle so that when the arm is closed, the ring makes an air-tight seal. These rings compress and in time lose some effectiveness; so they may need to be replaced every couple of years. The old one is caught and pulled out of its recess with a sharp pin; the new one is pressed in with fingers. Many shooters feel the life of the ring can be maintained much longer if the gun is opened just enough to release pressure on the ring when the arm is not in use.

For European-made arms, parts and accessories, the best single source is Air Rifle Headquarters, Grantsville, W. V. 26147. U. S. firms can of course take care of their own products.

CO_2 cartridge arms, using gas-filled cartridges or cylinders for propulsion power, operate on the simple principle of using the trigger to momentarily trip a valve allowing sufficient gas to escape down the barrel to drive the pellet or other projectile out. Valve parts, seals, springs and trigger connections must all function properly, or gas will leak out between firings. Many of these parts are never to be oiled, so lubrication must be limited to trigger pins and other purely mechanical friction points. Except for replacement of an obviously damaged or broken part, guns performing unsatisfactorily should be returned to the manufacturer to be put in order. This isn't difficult, as such arms can be mailed freely, and save for the Hammerli target pistol, I believe all CO_2 rifles and pistols are made in the United States.

At the present time over thirty different air and CO_2 pistols and over fifty rifles, of many different sizes, shapes and designs are in the U. S. market, so it is rather impossible to make sweeping statements about them. Some have brass or bronze-lined barrels—you don't do any careless poking down these with rough steel rods. Smoothbore BB steel barrels can rust—you do oil these bores. Guns must not be knocked around, for a little dent in a thin steel housing may interfere with the movement of internal parts.

Follow the instructions that come with the arm and don't lose any parts lists or diagrams of working parts that may be included. Care is care, but maintenance on air and CO_2 guns really depends on replacement of worn parts.

10

Sights:
Metal, Telescopic, Optical

Sights are the steering gear for sporting firearms: they mustn't be bent, broken, loosened or lost if the gun is to be used effectively. All right, you could figure this out for yourself so why mention it? Answer: Because there are a few reasonably simple precautionary measures not always remembered that can save a hunt or a match.

Check dovetail sights or bases by clamping the barrel in a vise and smacking the dovetail smartly with rawhide mallet or small block of hard wood, first making a penciled index mark across the sight and barrel so you can see if you move the sight. If the sight or base does move under this comparatively mild force, it is too loose. Remove it completely, peen down the top edges of the dovetail cut in the barrel and then drive the sight or base back into its index marking.

Sights or bases held by either one or two screws or naturally dependent on the thread fit for holding tightness. And screws are too often just a teeny bit small for the tapped—threaded—holes in barrels, receivers and scope mounts. With oil in the hole, or holes not threaded dead in line with the holes in the sight or base, they'll loosen. A gun not only recoils, it vibrates all over when fired; any sight represents inertial mass

This is a first step in installing an adjustable rear sight in a handgun which previously had nonadjustable sights. After being carefully measured and marked, the outer edges of the dovetail slot are precisely sawed with a hacksaw.

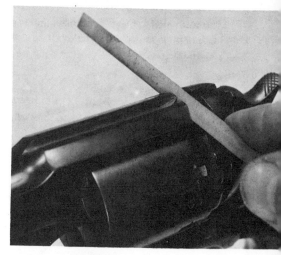

A triangular file is used to cut the inside beveled surfaces of the dovetail slot.

Here is the hand-cut dovetail slot. This job requires care and accuracy but is not especially difficult to perform.

An adjustable rear sight is being tapped into place with a small piece of nylon rod.

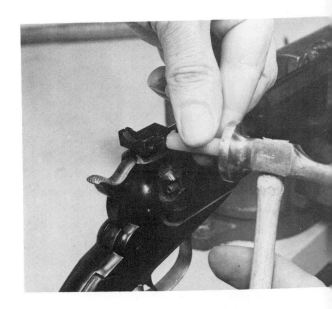

The adjustable rear sight is here shown in place on the Cap & Ball handgun.

Here is the handgun showing the installed rear sight and the new front sight. This adjustable rear-sight mechanism makes the pistol much more accurate and shootable.

resisting movement—the screws take the jolts, and they'll give way if they can. Repeated or excessive tightening of any screw with worn or undersize threads is only a momentary cure, for a couple of shots or even just jiggling in a case during transportation to the range or field may loosen them again. In fact, excessive tightening of small screws, even if they're well fitting, can result in their becoming prone to loosen in some cases. A case-hardened or hardened screw can pull threads in softer steels out of pitch, deforming them. They want to be tight but not super-tight! Ever notice how many of the people whose arms have every screw slot burred and torn are always complaining about their sights loosening up?

Nearly all of the screws used in mounting sights and scope bases are the 6-48 thread, but all of the 6-48 screws aren't exactly the same diameter. A gunsmith can root around in his boxes and drawers and usually find a slightly oversize one to hold in an oversize or worn hole, but there is no way for even him to order such screws. So we use holding compounds such as Loc-Tite, or sticky sealants—linseed oil stock finishes are excellent—first thoroughly degreasing the hole and screw to get rid of all oil in either set of threads. Only a little is needed. A small drop on the end of a nail or drift punch worked into the threads of the hole and the remainder on screw threads is sufficient. Tighten firmly with a screwdriver and that's it. These holding agents insulate from and hold the screw against the vibration tending to turn them back and so loosen. Screws don't loosen from pressure but from vibration.

Where screw holes in receivers are incorrectly drilled and/or threaded, thereby making an angled or off-center meeting, they can bend or break from recoil. This is easily discerned: if the contour of the base does not match contour of the receiver before the screws are completely seated, one hole is off. Up and down doesn't mean much in one-piece scope bases. They can be shimmed (a thin metal washer or plate under the "high" end to support against springing of the base by screw tightening). Off-center, though, can be damaging: a base pulled sideways at the rear by a screw creates tensions that can destroy accuracy even though the rings can be adjusted so as to free the scope from all tensions.

For such scope-base trouble, three remedial courses are open: first, the incorrect hole is welded up, the receiver cleaned and a new, properly located hole drilled and tapped; second, have the offending hole filed or ground toward center until a larger diameter hole can be drilled through the base in the correct location for a larger screw, perhaps an 8-40, or even a 10-32; and last, discard the one-piece base and

Target front sight, equipped with two types of spirit level, is valuable for precision long-range shooting. This device can be made with a drill press and hand tools.

replace it with front and rear separate bases, mounting the rear level and true, straddling the "crooked" hole.

Rifle receiver sights are less trouble to straighten out. Where one of the two mounting holes is out of line, so that the sight is pushed awry when the screw is reefed down, often the sight base can be filed to allow a good fit with no changes in holes except possibly using a tap to change direction a little.

Adjustable metallic sights must be kept clean if much use is being made of the adjustments. Should a hunting rifle be equipped with a simple receiver sight set for one range and never changed, about all that matters is that holding screws be firm and lint and dirt kept out of the aperture. For target use at different ranges, however, keep dust off the adjusting screws and slides, and oil and wipe off frequently. Folding or other types of auxiliary metallic rear sights on telescopic-sight-equipped rifles are practically always neglected by the rifle owner. These should be locked for elevation—sighted in at effective range and zeroed for windage—and kept brushed clean so they can always snap up to correct position. A secondary sight can otherwise be of little use in an emergency. Failure to keep it ready is as stupid as failing to keep air in a spare tire!

Front sights for hunting or plinking usually feature a bead profile, usually of bright metal, the idea being that the bead will reflect enough light to outline itself against a background. The idea was fine a hundred years ago when our eyes weren't reduced to half-effectiveness by clashing lights, jittery TV pictures and air pollutants. Now we need pretty big beads or wide posts to see well enough to distinguish the sight from the mark. The frontiersmen's Kentucky rifles had tiny bead front sights few modern men can use. Today the only Americans left, as a class, who have real vision are the Eskimos and Indians of Alaska. They consider a 4-inch black bull a fine aiming point at 200 yards and for the nitty-gritty, can see and aim at a poker chip at 200 yards. And seeing a small mark and trying to hold aim on it are two different things, really. So put on big front sights! Muzzle-loader shooters usually use front sights over ⅛ inch wide for short-range shooting. Their long barrels, of course, put the sight out much farther from the eye than is the case with the modern sporter, thus making the sight appear smaller. Target shooters always want dead-black front sights—and rear apertures—and so do many hunters, so they blacken them with soot, from match to acetylene (carbide) lamp. This is harmless as a rule, though anyone in his right mind won't bring a flame close to a plastic bead. However, as soon as the shoot or the day's hunt is over, the black should be wiped off, and the sight and adjoining barrel area oiled. The smoking burns the oil off, the

The Conetrol scope mount. These streamlined rings are made up of three closely machined components which interlock to form the complete scope ring. Here they are mounted on a Sako rifle.

Another view of the Conetrol mounts, shown this time on a Mauser action. These are among the best-looking mounts that are available.

soot absorbs moisture, so rust can begin fast. With moisture, or repeated smoking without removal of a prior deposit, a thickened deposit of soot makes an enlarged sight, in itself not too bad, but it enlarges the sight unevenly, therefore changing profile and aiming effect.

Knob-adjusting receiver sights should have windage and elevation scales set after sighting-in, and plates should be screwed down firmly. With the scale indexes zeroed, the shooter can tell at a glance if the sight has changed adjustment by accident. Frequently a rifle carried in a case will rub around inside it and turn windage and elevation knobs a full turn or more.

Scope mounts come in single- and split-base mountings for both hunting and target types. The micrometer-screw adjusting target mounts that allow a long, heavy scope to slide when the rifle recoils are the most foolproof since neither scope, mount or bases take much of a beating from recoil. Actually, when the rifle is fired, the scope tends to stay where it is because of inertia, while the rifle moves back from recoil. Spring plungers and precise bearing surfaces keep the scope tube properly aligned when dust, lint and too much oil or grease—or a rusted or gouged surface—do not interfere. So keep them clean. The base-holding screws are really under no strains, and they usually stay tight. One thing to remember: the mount locking screws are coin-slotted, as are most windage adjustment screws on hunting-scope mounts and target

This photo shows a popular Redfield Jr. mount.

The Leupold mounting system, which is similar to the Redfield Jr. mounts. Here it is mounted on a Winchester Model 70 bolt-action rifle.

171

The Ruger scope-mounting system has rings which attach directly to integral bases that come with Ruger rifles. Since the scope base is part of the receiver, this is a rigid and foolproof mounting system.

front and rear screws so use a coin, not a big screwdriver! The coin is enough. The hunting-scope mounts such as Redfield and Buehler work with off-center tension, a portion of the screw head engaging the scope ring to hold and move it. Excessive tightening simply bends or breaks the screw.

Hunting scopes get bigger and heavier all the time, and the mounts weaker. A generation, or even twenty years ago, mounts such as Tilden and Redfield had perhaps four times the strength and general ruggedness of modern ones, so less care was needed in handling. Today, rings, bases and screws are soft steel or aluminum alloys that won't take long neglect or rough handling. Keep oil off all screws, use Loc-Tite or other gumming agent to help hold, use screwdrivers that are a good fit in ring screws to tighten, linseed oil inside rings if scope tends to slip in tight rings, and handle the rifle so that long overhanging front ends don't get banged about. Alloy scope tubes do bend—sometimes quite easily.

Manufacturers make a big thing out of "fog-free nitrogen-filled waterproof scopes" these days, the idea being that an air-tight scope filled with nitrogen gas can't fog up from interior moisture condensed by temperature and humidity changes. If it's under any pressure at all, the gas eventually escapes as adjustments are made, the ocular cell rotated to correct for the shooter's vision, etc. Interior condensation can occur on a hunt. To get rid of it, unscrew the ocular (eyepiece) completely, let the inside of scope become the same temperature and humidity as the outside and the condensation will go away, usually in minutes. Exterior condensation on the rear lens comes when you get a hot, moist eye too close to a cold lens; this will go away in seconds.

Probably the most widely used rings of all are the inexpensive, but entirely satisfactory, Weaver rings and bases. Another feature of the Weaver system is that the rings are rapidly and easily detached.

Cleaning scope lenses properly is no great chore. All scopes come with directions, including a warning not to rub the lenses, etc. but who reads directions these days? Even with careful use of lens caps when not shooting, the glass does pick up dust. This is best removed with a lens brush, a small retractable brush that's available at camera stores. An ordinary dime-store paint brush, used by school children for watercolors, is cheaper. Don't try to blow dust from a lens if you have a very moist breath—you'll put spots on it!

Inevitable are eventual grease marks, from fingerprints, oil splashes or other sources. I consider the best way to remove these one that the scope manufacturers frown upon: alcohol. Take a bit of lint-free cotton cloth, as from a discarded but washed T-shirt, moisten in the purest alcohol available, make a little wad and wipe the lens. It will dry instantaneously, which is necessary, for should the alcohol run freely down edges it can attack the cement holding the parts of the lenses together. Don't use rubbing alcohol as it will leave more of a color film than it removes. Don't use acetone, etc., as such solvents may remove the coating from lenses.

There are quite a few things you don't do on scopes. Any visible screwheads or slots in a tube, ocular or objective cell you leave alone. In fact, you don't try to unscrew anything completely that is possible to adjust by turning. Most good European, some Japanese and a few U. S. hunting scopes allow zeroing of the adjustment dials so that you can sight in, then move the graduated ring or plate around so it reads 0-0. One or two tiny screws must be loosened or removed, then replaced. This is no problem with a jeweler's screwdriver. Don't try to take elevation or windage adjusting drums all the way out, and don't ever oil the screws. Keep the turret caps on. If one is lost, improvise a substitute from tape or paper with a rubber band, anything to keep dust from collecting under and around the dials. Any foreign matter there can raise havoc with adjustments. Do not allow a scope to become very hot, such as exposure in a closed car with a hot sun bearing on it, and never stand a rifle up so that the sun shines down the objective. This promotes lens separations, first seen as round spots inside the lenses.

Sliding-tube target scopes have to be kept clean and lightly oiled on the outsides of the steel tubes both for rust prevention and to permit free movement. Adjustable mounts, whether for target or hunting scopes, of all types, can best be cleaned by just blowing through with air under good pressure.

Optical sights seem to be coming back again. These are usually plastic-prism reflection-principle instruments that mount like scopes or receiver sights, and are used to provide a single aiming point and do away with the necessity of aligning front and rear sights. They have to be kept clean, or they don't give a clearly discernible spot or point for sighting.

Pistol sights, metallic or telescopic, rate the same as rifle sights in treatment and care, while shotgun sights are something else. As the rear sight of a shotgun is essentially the position of the shooter's face on the stock, about the only sights made are the "middle-bead" types. These are installed usually on side-by-side doubles one-third to one-half the barrel length ahead of the breech, and are used with a larger bead front sight. The purpose is to make the shooter conscious of the rib, or center of the two barrels so he will get his face and shooting eye centered over the gun before pulling the trigger as the front sight locates properly on, under or ahead of his mark. The small bead, usually white, is not concentrated on, but the eye unconsciously is aware of it and tends to find it as the gun comes up. Marble's Bi-Color or Bradley-type front sights are the most popular replacements for factory shotgun sights, as they can be seen very well in any light. They come with tools for insertion, spanner wrenches for screw-in types, etc., and are easy to install.

With the exception of a 200-year-old blunderbuss with a belled muzzle, excellent for point and puncture work on highwaymen at ranges up to five paces, no firearm is much good without sights, and the better the sights are suited to the user, the better the performance in shooting is to be expected. Fortunately, sights are easy to change, substitute and replace, without requiring much in the way of tools. So don't allow yourself to be handicapped with poor sights.

11

Testing, Sighting-in, Range Shooting

Testing

"Testing" takes in much territory. In general it means checking to know that the arm is safe, reliable and ready for use as required. There are a few details to cover, however. Mechanically perfect, a rifle can be almost unusable if its sights are far out of alignment, the shotgun ammunition is not suited to the gun or the pistol ammo is not familiar, so sighting-in and range shooting tie into testing.

Many small but important tests are made at home, of course: trying screws to see if they are tight, trying trigger pulls, checking the movement of adjustable metallic sights, cylinder locking, tightening and clearing the nipples of percussion arms, etc. Trying loaded ammunition in guns made safe by removal of firing pins or in open double- and single-barrel shotguns may save a wasted trip to shooting range or hunting ground. Many a man has happily rushed to the disappointing discovery that his rifle wasn't throated long enough to take the bullets of the ammunition he just bought and brought.

About the only way to find out how a shotgun fits and shoots is to go out and shoot it, preferably at a trap range, with the power of the load and sizes of shot you expect to use most in the field. Any tendency to shoot high or low will be revealed quickly, as will improper length of the butt or fit of the comb. Most shotgun ranges will have some provision or at least an area available for setting up large sheets of paper or cardboard for patterning tests—many ranges offer for sale the NRA patterning target, a large paper target with a black clay bird printed in the center. When patterning, do not try to hold and carefully aim the gun as if it were a rifle—throw it up and pull the trigger as if the center mark were a game bird getting up. This way you can get a pretty good idea of where the gun shoots—center, high, low, right or left. And never shoot less than four separate pattern sheets with each load. Use the average of the four for a rule of what that particular load will do. Shoot the upland–rabbit–squirrel loads at thirty yards, the waterfowl loads at forty. Never mind the classic 30-inch circle—quartering it, counting holes and pellets in a charge, unless you are statistically minded. Just look at your collection of sheets and see whether a quail or dove could get through the no. eight's or a duck could get through the sixes's or four's. And decide which brand of ammunition gives the best patterns for you, and hopefully, functions best in your gun.

Handguns also have to be fired to be known. What feels comfortable in the den, points naturally, etc., just may not be so. A big revolver may fit your fist fine and still damn near break your hand in two when fired with full loads! Magnums have a side effect; their recoil wrecks wristwatches, so don't fire them with the arm you wear your watch on. Revolvers using tapered cartridges—and occasionally standard calibers where the chambers are very smooth and oiled—may tie up (cylinder refuses to turn) should the case move back tightly against the frame when firing. This can usually be cured by simply removing all oil from the cylinder chambers and cartridges, using alcohol, lighter fluid or other degreasing agent. The expanding dry case will grip the dry chamber walls and not move back in the cylinder.

Except for quick-draw afficionados, almost no one ever shoots a handgun without trying to aim it carefully in normal circumstances. In a self-defense position, however, the gun is usually fired hurriedly pointed in the general direction of the threatening assailant, at quite close range. Four times out of five the bullet misses. In such situations, whoever shoots the first and the most usually tells the story. Often the gun is a short-barreled revolver that is very difficult to shoot accurately under the most favorable and unhurried conditions, but noise and flame

The way to test a shotgun's pattern is to fire at a strip of paper stapled to a pattern board, as above.
Then you can check the pattern on the paper and make adjustments accordingly.

177

may be as effective as hits in driving off or causing a thief to surrender, particularly under poor lighting. Anyone owning such an arm should practice with it on an outdoor range if at all possible, pointing and shooting fast, two shots at a time, at a 10- or 12-foot distance from the target. Such familiarization firing will give confidence and teach something of gun pointing. Otherwise he might think he was covering a criminal while the gun was in reality pointing 2 feet to the left of the guy's knees! And encouraging an escape or attack.

Normal sporting handguns may be test-fired from a bench rest or padded table, held in both hands and supported by sandbags to obtain the best groups with various ammunitions, but almost always the point of impact is well away from that of the arm fired in the regular one-hand manner. In doing any such rest testing, care must be observed to keep hands in back of the revolver cylinders and away from the auto slides. In rest-shooting a handgun, people tend to get both hands all over the arm and often place a finger where it can get burned or gouged when the arm is fired and recoils.

Hand loading

While I am striving mightily to avoid the subjects of handloading and reloaded ammunition, these being rather out of the scope of this book, it is necessary to state a few facts since all gun owners are aware of loading whether they do it themselves or not, and usually at some time or other try reloaded ammunition. Handloading can provide special-purpose ammunition not available otherwise, as for target shooting, low-power loads for turkey hunting with a high-powered rifle, or odd-shot shells for a shotgun. When the nonloader gun owner purchases commercially reloaded ammunition, he may or may not have a problem, as such stuff comes in only two grades—very good and very bad. The good stuff will be clean, of good appearance, and present no problem, but the other can be very sorry indeed—bullets gouged and marked, cases dirty and showing sizing marks from rough dies, primers dented, angle-seated and otherwise marked from careless tool use. And if it doesn't look good on the outside, why take it for granted that the powder charge inside is any better?

A visual check of purchased handloads can tell much about quality, and insertion in the chamber can tell if they fit as they should. Except with rimless rifle cartridges, where a long-loaded or over-diameter bullet prevents full case seating in the chamber, if the bolt or block will close without great effort, the cartridge is probably safe so far as the headspace goes. When the cartridge will drop freely into the chamber, check by setting it on a flat surface alongside a case fired in the rifle previously and with your eye level with the case shoulders, see if there is any great difference in height. A little won't matter—new factory ammo is often as much as $10/1000$ inch shorter than the rifle chamber it is intended for, and you can see this much difference.

In matters of comparison, the human eye is much better than you'd think. The lands in a .22 barrel are $2/1000$ inch above the grooves,

At left is a properly reloaded shotshell. Notice how the crimp is even and neat. Next is a crimp which has collapsed due to a short wad column. When the crimp folds in like this the shot leaks out. Next are two shotshells with sloppy crimps. Faulty crimping such as this may result from wornout shotshells or inattention to the loading procedure. Either way, however, it impairs performance.

or less, yet they are as evident as railroad tracks when you peer through the bore. So you can see if a cartridge case has had the shoulder sized back excessively to create a dangerous headspace condition. It's more dangerous to the rifle than to the rifleman, really. Few men have been injured by minor headspace accidents, but rifles can be put out of immediate use. Case separation is the most common trouble—the front end of the case expands to stick to the chamber, the rear end is not supported and blows off. So you get only the case head when you extract, and the front portion is stuck firmly in the chamber. Without a broken-shell extractor made just for this job, and which practically no one car-

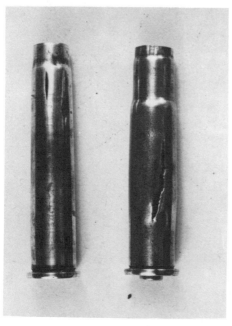

This is what happens when one fires incorrect ammunition in a rifle. Either on purpose or by accident, the results can be extremely dangerous. At left is a .30/30 case which was fired in an 8mm rifle. At right is a .30/30 case that was fired in a .35 Remington rifle. In both instances the case has ruptured and there was no doubt a considerable leakage of gas. This is dangerous to the shooter and especially hazardous to his face and eyes.

ries around with him, the rifle is out of business. Handloaded cartridges loaded too many times and fully sized each time often separate even without headspace present.

A possible error forever with us is getting the wrong ammunition into the gun. Many a shotgun has blown, often with disastrous effect upon the shooter's left hand, when he unthinkingly dropped a 20- or 28-gauge shell into his 12-gauge gun, didn't notice that it slid down the barrel a few inches and stopped and he put a proper 12-gauge shell in the barrel and fired it. This sounds stupid, but remember that the man may have been hunting with his lighter gun the week before and missed getting one of the shells when he cleaned out his hunting coat pockets for the 12-gauge hunt, and with ducks flying, his eyes are on the sky, not the breech of his double. Ammunition makers now try to help prevent this misadventure by making different gauge ammunition in contrasting colors, so if a man looks at all, he can weed out the wrong ammo.

Diameters of revolver cartridges and lengths of pistol cases make for little trouble with handguns getting incorrect ammunition. If it goes in easily and fires, it's OK. Only overloaded or super-power ammo in very old, cheap or poor-condition arms can be dangerous.

Always make sure you get what you really want when you buy ammunition. Clerks don't always reach for the right box. Then you open the package in the woods and find he gave you .303 British instead of .303 Savage, or .300 H & H Magnum instead of the .300 Winchester Magnum you asked for.

People with a number of different-caliber rifles must be careful. It is easy to mix a .270 Winchester cartridge in with the .30/06's, and fire in the .30/06 rifle. This mismatch is safe—for shooter and game both. The bullet goes wide of the mark and if the rifleman doesn't pick up the fired case and look at the headstamp he may never know what happened. The same goes with .243 in .308, or .244 (6mm Remington) in a .257. These are instances of cartridges having more-or-less uniform dimensions and headspace, but with smaller bullet diameters. Where headspace can be very excessive any mistake can be impressive. A .30/06 in a magnum chamber can destroy the gun and shake up the shooter if the extractor holds the case firmly enough for the firing pin to ignite the primer. Firing .308's in .30/06 chambers usually won't cause damage, the shorter case being fat enough to make a fair gas-seal even without a shoulder support, but don't try any experiments along this line.

What has this to do with testing? Maybe just testing your sense of self-preservation. Actually, every factor of using a firearm can be classified as a test, right down to the actual firing at a target or game, when the final test of skill and gun performance comes.

Sighting-in

Sighting-in a rifle can be much easier than most men make it. Checking and OK'ing the ammunition at home, taking a heavy jacket and a towel, the right-size screwdrivers and other tools possibly needed for sight or scope adjustment, having the rifle really ready mechanically—these points are ignored by too many shooters. If the range is equipped with bench rests, sandbags and target frames, well and good. If you have to use a farm pasture, take the biggest cardboard carton you can get into the car to tape targets on (don't forget targets and tape!) a couple of blankets rolled up and tied to use as rests and an old rug or piece of canvas or plastic to lie on, because you'll do the best shooting prone. Place the carton in front of a cut bank or other safe backstop, weighted down with small stones in the bottom. At the desired distance lie down, place the rifle on blanket rolls with the bolt removed and bore-sight, trying to adjust the scope or sight on or just beneath the bull, with the bull centered in the bore. So adjusted, the rifle should put the first shot on the target, making it easy to center up with a few shots. After each scope adjustment, tap the tube with your fingernail or a fired case and dry-fire the rifle a time or two. This will settle the internal scope parts, helping any sticky ones move to the new adjustment. Wear your jacket and fold the towel to make a shoulder pad to protect from recoil. This is not the time to develop a flinch and start jerking the rifle out of line with every shot!

If you aren't using a bolt-action or single-shot rifle and can't bore-sight through the barrel and the makeshift blanket supports make use of

To bore-sight a scoped bolt-action rifle, remove the bolt and lay the rifle, as shown, into support notches of a sturdy box. Then, sighting through the bore, adjust the box's position left or right and elevate it by means of a wood block until the bull, 100 yards distant, is exactly centered in the bore. Next, by means of the adjusting dials on the scope, center the reticle on the bull, as shown here. Tap the scope and dry-fire the rifle to settle internal scope parts. Next, recheck your sight picture.

Then after replacing the bolt and chambering one round, fire a shot from a padded rest, as shown. (You may prefer to fire three rounds instead of only one and consider the center of the three-shot group as the "point of impact.") In this drawing the bullet impacted low and right, though the reticle showed a proper sight picture.

a bore-reflector difficult, you'll have to spend a few extra cartridges to sight-in, that bore-sighting might save. (Everyone who owns a pump or semiauto rifle, or lever-action, should own a reflector.) Just stand about 40 feet from the target and shoot at the bull—this is usually close enough for the paper to catch the bullet even though the scope or rear sight is far out of line. Make necessary adjustment and fire again, repeating if necessary until fairly centered, then walk back to your prone setup and make final adjustments through carefully aimed shots.

The next step is to precisely align the scope with the bore. Remove the bolt again and rest the rifle in the notches of the box. Adjust the box so that the reticle again centers on the bull. Turn the elevation dial until the horizontal reticle lowers into line with the first round's point of impact.

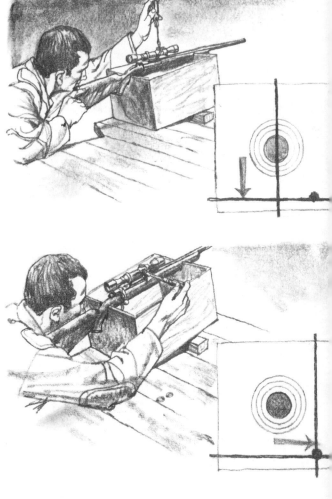

Then adjust the windage dial, by bringing the verticle reticle into line with the impact point. This should leave your scope and bore aligned and thus *sighted* at 100 yards. A test-fire will tell you whether you should make fine adjustments by repeating the process described on these pages. (To sight-in rifles other than single-shots or bolt actions, begin test-firing by aiming through the scope at 25 yards. This ensures against missing the target paper completely. Then proceed as described in the foregoing drawings.)

183

For a true point-of-aim setting, the rifle should be allowed to cool, then a three-shot group fired from as steady a position as possible, one hand holding the fore-end with the wrist against a tight blanket roll or sandbag, and final sight adjustment to the center of the three-shot triangle. If a firearm is allowed to rest free on any support, it will nearly always shoot to a higher point than when held in a regular shooting position and gripped with both hands. Where ground is soft, push stakes in at each elbow-point for them to rest against when aiming. The rifle can be held much steadier. Don't do this in hard ground, or use rigid elbow supports when firing a heavy-recoil gun. You'll hurt. Use sandbags or any object of weight sufficient to keep elbows in place yet willing to give or move when the rifle recoils.

There are allowances to be made when open metallic sights are used: proper sight picture shows the front bead or blade centered in the rear notch with the height even with the top wall of the sight, or sides of the notch, whichever is level. In the excitement of the hunt, the hunter often does not pull the front sight down in the rear notch to its proper position and so shoots over the game. In sighting-in, the rifle must be sighted to hit where the top of the bead or blade locates on the target with sights correctly aligned. If field shooting, if the hunter remembers, he will place the top of the front sight exactly where he wishes the bullet to strike. If he rushes and gets the sight a little high, he may still register a satisfactory hit. Should the rifle be sighted so that the bead covers the point of impact, any deviation will be too much!

When testing a rifle in the field, always use a rest of some kind. Here Carmichel uses a rolled-up sleeping bag.

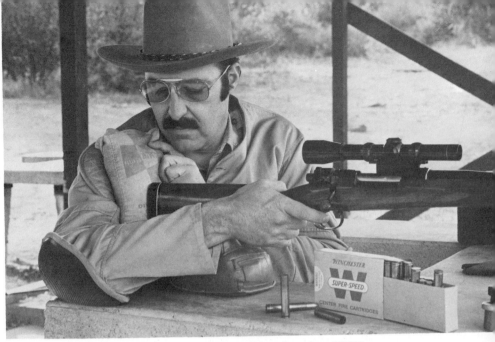

For test firing large-caliber, hard-kicking rifles such as this .458 Winchester Magnum, a sandbag can be placed between the rifle butt and the shooter's shoulder. Excessive recoil causes flinching and flinches often are responsible for misses.

Firing from a shooting bench. Notice how the shooter sits in a loose, relaxed position with his left hand on the bench and lets the rifle lie on the rest rather then trying to hold it himself.

Shooting uphill or downhill at a steep angle means a change of elevation, but make no allowances at short metallic-sight hunting ranges. Invariably the hunter will overcorrect. An unhooded front sight in sunlight will be affected by direction of light, the shot going a little toward the sun side—the shiny side of the sight not being clearly visible, the tendency is to hold farther toward that side. This is why veteran hunters—and all target shooters—smoke shiny front sights when shooting in bright light. The dull black sight outline becomes clearly visible.

Parallax is the bugaboo of the telescopic sight. Almost all, if not all, of the variable-power scopes have it, some to excess. Also, many of the variables change the point of aim when power is changed. Test yours when sighting-in. With the rifle supported by sandbags or other rests in position so the reticule is on the target or other fixed aiming point, move you head back and forth while looking through the scope and not moving the rifle. If the reticule moves against the target, you have parallax. Should the movement be slight, say an inch total at 200 yards, you have no great hunting problem. More, try to have it corrected. The higher powered scopes now often have an adjustable focus on the objective lens which can be moved per manufacturer's directions to eliminate parallax. If not, you may be able to help yourself by eyepiece adjustment. A slightly fuzzy reticule is better than one that moves all over! Fixed-power scopes are set at the factory to be free of parallax beyond minimal distance, say one-hundred yards for 4X, 150 yards for 6X, 175 or 200 yards for 8X. At shorter distances they will show some parallax, but will have none at longer ranges, and the error at short range is not enough to blame misses on, though it won't help group shooting from the bench. Most hunting scopes now made 8X and higher power have focusing front objectives and can be adjusted precisely to eliminate parallax at any range. Old scopes permitted correction by loosening adjustment bases on the tube and moving them forward or backward as needed, but the fixed-turret modern types require lens adjustments by the factory or an optical expert.

For change of setting through change of power in variable scopes, there is no cure. Learn to live with your own scope. Normally, such changes are uniform, that is, if the rifle is sighted-in with the scope set at 4X, and shoots 2 inches low and 1 inch right when changed to 7X, it will go back to center when reset to 4X, then back 2 inches low, etc., whenever it's changed to 7X. If the rifleman can remember such impact changes and correct his holding for them he's in fine shape. Most men will be better off by sighting-in at the power they can hold and shoot best with, say, 4X or 5X, then use the higher powers for observation, checking legality of game, etc., and then change back to their sight-in power for actual shooting.

Range Shooting

Group shooting, or testing from bench rests has become a popular sport among rifle owners in general, as well as the organized competitive bench-rest men who use ultra-accurate special rifles made to meet specific weight classes and rules. The gun owner who likes to shoot seldom if ever can find enough hunting to satisfy himself. Therefore, he gravitates toward ranges where he can test his holding skill and his rifle's accuracy and usually his hand-loading ability. The bench equalizes strength and experience in holding the rifle steady for many shots, doing away with most of the "work" in shooting and leaving the fun. The shooter learns the value of careful trigger control, what wind can do to move a bullet over, can see what happens when he goofs one and misjudges the other.

Where no public or club ranges are accessible, the gun owner who really wants to shoot may have to really extend himself, to building his own. Anyone having a cousin with a farm or other possible shooting area can set up his own recreational range. Safety in all aspects must govern the layout. Everyone will think of a backstop—cut bank, steep hill, old railroad-tie wall, etc., but this is still secondary to a safe fallout area for the bullet that might miss the backstop entirely. This means at least a mile of uninhabited country (fenced and posted so hikers won't wander around in, either) behind the backstop, and at least a half-mile wide. And you don't want anyone living within a quarter mile of the firing point. Talk to all the people who will be within earshot of the gunshot. They probably won't object to the sounds of occasional distant firing, but don't strain relations by trying to beat the wind by shooting a magnum at dawn on Sunday morning! A sound barrier around the firing point can be made by erecting a framework on which old carpets, blankets, etc., can be attached to wall-in the noise. It should reach from the ground to 2 feet above the height of the gun muzzle in use. The closer to the gun, the greater the muffling effect. Such a barrier will cut a sharp, ringing report down to a dull thud when heard from a couple of hundred yards to the rear or sides.

Wood for such framework, target frames and even the shooting bench can be picked up at low cost from lumberyard cull piles. In fact, if the pile is getting big, they may give it to you. Culls are the warped, split or otherwise unsalable lumber that yards accumulate, usually in

Author's "prone rest"—a 12″ x 33″ piece of ¾″ plywood with shaped wooden blocks to support and prevent movement of elbows when shooting rifle prone. The block for right elbow is adjustable to suit size and position of individual. Except for wing nuts and screws it is entirely of wood. Used with sling, this rest is practical for sighting-in and informal testing, as it makes possible steady holding. It is also portable.

long lengths that will permit good short lengths to be cut from some section.

The informal target frame is just a couple of timbers, from 2-by-4 size on up, set in the ground and braced, holding soft-wood crosspieces to make an open frame 6 feet or more wide, enough space to hold several targets. Nail corrugated cardboard from old cartons to the face of the frame. Appliance and office-supply stores throw out nice clean big cartons. Cut round holes the size of target bulls, or a little larger, so that when you staple targets to the frame there will be no cardboard back of the center and so allow bullet holes in the black bull to be seen easier, with a spotting or high-power rifle scope. An 8X will ordinarily show holes at one-hundred yards in almost any light. At 200 yards, a spotting scope is almost a necessity at all times. Unless you like to walk a lot.

A shooting bench, table or bench rest is literally a must for the informal range. A T-shape that will permit use by both right- and left-handed shooters is easy to make. Use 4-by-4-inch or larger legs that are long enough to be set in to the ground 8 inches or more and hold the top of the bench 40 inches high. Frame, top and bracing can be of 1-inch lumber, but 2-inch is better. Surface the top with smooth plywood ⅜ inch or thicker and paint everything well, and often. The plywood will deteriorate rapidly out in the weather unless it's well protected. A ramada, or shade and rain roof over the bench will help a lot.

A built-in seat won't be stolen, but a separate heavy stool is best, and you won't move the bench while fidgeting around on the seat. Make the height to suit your own sitting height, of course. Muzzle-loading shooters have to have separate seats as they must stand up to reload for every shot, and if the firing point is covered, the roof must be raised quite high for ramrod use in the long rifles. Also, their shooting benches must be a foot or more longer fore and aft since they bench-shoot with rests under the long barrels, sometimes with muzzle rests.

The gun supports can be anything from a wadded-up gun case to the elaborate screw-adjusting mechanical rests used by competitive benchresters. The sandbag in one form or another is almost a must, since it provides firm but not hard support to the firearm. Cloth makes a poor bag, though shot bags from a shotgun-shell reloader, or coin bags from banks hold up pretty well. Leather bags are best, but stitching is the weak point. Should you try to make your own, say from sleeves of an old leather jacket, have the ends sewn by a shoemaker or leather shop with a double seam and wide-spaced stitches. Leave ½ inch at one end open so you can fill it with dry sand through a small funnel, and tie or hand stitch this opening afterward.

Fairly satisfactory bags can be made at no cost by picking up old inner tubes, cutting sections from them, filling with sand, and tying both ends with heavy cord. Only two quite small bags are necessary for the immediate support of butt and fore-end—raise to desired height by use of wooden blocks. Building sites or lumberyard scrap boxes yield short ends of 2 by 6, 4 by 6, 6 by 6, etc. Nail a strip of old carpet on one face of the block so that the sandbag placed on it will not slip off when the rifle recoils under fire. Such blocks can be combined to make any desired height above bench desired.

Range shooting is not only year-round recreation for the man who owns and is interested in using firearms. It is also the most sensible preparation the once-a-year hunter can give himself. The deer hunter may be bored shooting at a paper target, but if he spends fifteen of his twenty new cartridges on the range, he has a far better chance of hunt success with the remaining five than if he just heads for the woods with the full box and a rifle unfired for a year or more.

The competitive target shooter will use the bench to test a new rifle or barrel or ammunition, and then do his practicing without a rest to test himself, his range shooting simulating as much as possible the conditions of match competition. The nontarget man who likes to shoot is limited to paper targets of one type or another. Even plinking at tin cans or rats at the city dump is frowned upon today.

A New Target Sport

Spreading north from Mexico is a shooting sport that almost every U. S. gun owner who really enjoys shooting would embrace if he could: metal-silhouette shooting. Sporting rifles only are used—as in a gigantic outdoor shooting gallery—in shooting at steel silhouettes of chickens, turkeys and sheep that fall over when hit with a bullet. You see what is happening as it happens! Shooting is at long ranges, 200 meters for chicken, 385 for turkey, 500 for the ram, in standing position only. Any hit is a vast satisfaction. Knocking over a slightly oversize hen turkey at 420 yards just isn't easy, so no one ever hits everything. But you absolutely know that if you could shoot the last series of five over again you'd get at least three! While a competitive sport with fixed rules in Mexico and Arizona, the principle of the game is flexible. Ranges can be varied, require little change to natural landscape, point in any direction that's safe, silhouettes can be of game appropriate to the area, etc. The shooting is a challenge to every type of rifle owner: big-game hunter, target man, varmint shooter, group-test man. There are silhouette courses for the .22 rifle and .22 pistol also, so it isn't limited to the high-power rifleman. There are several ranges in the southwestern states, and a few have started at other areas, but the sport is literally unknown to most of the people who would enjoy it.

12

Accurizing and Improving Sporting and Target Arms

"Accurizing" is both rather a new word and new in the work it means, this simply being to make a firearm more accurate. It's not applicable to shotguns, of course, and in handguns it's pretty limited to target-type pistols and revolvers. To some extent, however, it's possible on all rifles. Until a few years ago the only rifles receiving much extra attention were bolt-action and military autoloading rifles being used for match competition, but now almost all sporting rifles can be improved in performance, regardless of type. Incidentally, accurizing was discovered by gunsmiths and rifle owners borrowing from target-rifle tune-up procedures.

Many of the alterations involve rather advanced gunsmithing, particularly those concerning the large-caliber center-fire autoloading pistols, so I will give only light coverage to these. A real pistol-accuracy job calls for specially-made parts and special fitting of them, extremely careful and experienced hand and machine work and parts substitution possible only to the professional gun shops specializing in this type of work. The cost of such a job is usually more than the new target gun cost to start with, indicating it isn't an easy semipro undertaking!

In contrast, a rifle-accuracy job is quite inexpensive, ten to twenty-five dollars in a shop, and except for the M-1 (Garand), practically every rifle can be worked up with the home-shop equipment. And, with a good bit of filing, the M-1 parts can be handled, as well.

In reality, we do not improve the accuracy of the arm: we are simply removing or subduing factors that are preventing it from delivering maximum accuracy.

I will repeat much of the bedding data of Chapter 5, but detailed more as to specific rifles and their needs to achieve improved accuracy.

Such factors are, of course, many, varied, often interdependent or allied and may be pretty far out. Because of this multiple-choice aspect, you have no choice: you take care of every little thing and trust that they add up to accuracy. Any operation omitted might cancel out beneficial accomplishments of the others! Stocks, also called "grips" when belonging to handguns, are the most obvious features of any firearm to the user, since they're what he holds on to, the part contacting him physically. So stocks figure very much in accurizing, just on fit alone, to start with. All the precision fitting of a pistol slide and the balanced springs and tensions of a fine accuracy job can be nullified if the grip allows the gun to twist or pivot in the hand under the recoil of a shot fired, or too much or too little wood interfering or not supporting the trigger finger as the trigger is squeezed. For a handgun begins to recoil before the bullet leaves the barrel. If the stock doesn't permit uniform control of recoil from shot to shot, the shooter can't get a good group, even if the pistol shoots phenomenal groups from a mechanical rest!

On a rifle, the external dimensions and shooter-fit of the stock are very secondary to the internal bedding to the receiver, though of course they're not to be neglected. It is possible but difficult to use a rifle having too long a pull—buttstock—or too low a comb, or even too small a pistol grip.

Concerning metal parts, many of the ordinary smoothing-up operations done for easier and better parts functioning also contribute to accurizing. Polish the body of the firing pin, the nose and sear face of the cocking piece, and notch in the bolt, and the rifle not only cocks easier but shoots better—friction has been reduced, and the pin can move without interference. Cleaned-up locking blocks and bolts can seat better, springs that do not bind give uniform tension or force every time. Fine abrasive cloth over files and a buffing wheel used on a grinder motor or portable drill will take care of nearly all metal work desired, with a file and hacksaw doing any real alterations.

The bolt-action .22 rifle needs little beyond good stock bedding, smoothing of the firing pin, etc., perhaps a new mainspring if the gun is more than a few years old and the customary trigger job. There really isn't much more you can do save recrowning the muzzle should it show any signs of abuse. Any dent or burr affecting rifling at the muzzle is very detrimental to .22 accuracy!

Except smoothing of action parts and perhaps restocking to a better fit, not much can be done to better pump-action rifles, but fitting of fore-ends, cleaning up gas assemblies, etc., can help the autoloaders quite definitely as a rule. Glass- or epoxy-bedding fore-ends of rifles such as the Savage 99 and various single shots very often results in pronounced accuracy improvement. The fit of fore-end against receiver and holding screws can often be helped; the fore-end should not fit tightly against the receiver, nor should the screw be difficult to screw in. It should go straight in, smoothly, until tight.

The bolt-action center-fire rifle is the principal subject of accurizing efforts for two reasons: the bolt-action rifleman is the type most interested in accuracy, and the rifles are usually immediately responsive to the work. He can see results. The work is not complicated, it's understandable and he can do it himself, even to completely restocking the arm to his individual measurements.

The first step in improving the accuracy of a firearm is to check the barrel to see if it is worn at the muzzle, pitted, or otherwise deficient. If it is obviously in bad condition, you can't improve it very much. Clean and dry the bore then use a magnifying glass to check the rifling at the muzzle for the first inch or so—this is the most important area in most rifles and handguns.

Should you be buying a new rifle, insist that the grease be wiped from the barrel, a patch with solvent put through, then a dry one so you can inspect the rifling before you pay for the gun. In 1973 quite a number of new arms with defective rifling were sold, and I'm sure there are quite a few men who are disappointed in their new rifles. Out of a dozen purchased, I got three myself, but since I was rebarreling them to start with I wasn't really hurt. Looking down the muzzle of a clean, new barrel made by the Appel hammer or swage process as used by Remington principally, one can observe a pronounced waffle effect several inches back from the muzzle, a corrugated surface over both lands and grooves. From the breech end, the barrel appears perfect, so you must examine it from the muzzle. I do not know what causes the trouble in manufacture.

The other type of defect, if it may be called that, is found in the button-rifled barrels. Examination from the muzzle reveals concentric rings—toolmarks—in the bore. Unfortunately, these rings show up best after a few bullets have been fired through the barrel. However, they can usually be seen with a glass. They are caused by using a reamer of too large a diameter prior to button-rifling; the button doesn't remove them. They do not always really harm accuracy—the arm may be quite accurate—but they do promote metal fouling and require that the barrel be cleaned with a brass brush every ten or twenty shots, to maintain accuracy.

In doing a job of improving a bolt-action rifle, much of course depends on what you start with. Say you have a .243 Remington, Savage or Winchester rifle, new, but shooting 2-inch groups at 100 yards: not good enough. Remove the firing-pin assembly from the bolt, polish the inside of the bolt with abrasive cloth on a mandrel, polish the cocking notch in the bolt, wash with solvent, dry and oil. Disassemble only the Winchester firing-pin assembly—the others are smooth enough, and so is the Winchester, except that you want to polish the top of the cocking-piece opening in the sleeve and nose of the cocking piece. This, with trigger adjustment, is all you need to do to moving parts.

The rest of the work is on the stock, and with a new or comparatively new stock, there isn't much of it. On these rifles there is sufficient support—or rather area of tang and guard parts to be supported—so that the stock wood will do the job without help. Therefore, you need only to take care of the front end of receiver and the recoil lug, which is called barrel bracket when it is a separate part from the receiver, as in the Remington and Savage. Use a bedding compound: the epoxys such as bisonite, plastic steel, etc., are better and actually easier to use than fiberglass. Use acetone, lacquer thinner or such solvent to clean the inletting in and behind the recoil-lug recess in the stock of all oil, dirt, grease, etc. Then scratch the varnish or plastic finish off by scraping with wood chisel and finish with a few deep cross-scratches in this receiver-ring inletting area. Degrease the metal parts at this point also and cut any high points out of the barrel channel so the barrel will not touch the wood when the screws are tight.

You can shim up the barrel when actually bedding to gain a little clearance also. To do this, you use strips of cardboard or cut a wooden wedge to lay in the barrel channel just ahead of the receiver, regulating thickness so that with the guard screws tight you can pull a piece of thick paper freely all the way from the breech to fore-end tip, between the barrel and wood. Use only the front and rear screws, of course.

With this done, use a thin coat of wax or the supplied release agent to cover all of the receiver, lug, etc., where the bedding com-

A detail of a glass-bedded M-1 Garand rifle stock. The pencil points to the neatly fitted recoil surfaces. Correctly fitted surfaces aid accuracy tremendously; thus glass bedding is necessary for top performance from target rifles such as this one.

pound might touch later, in the guard-screw threads in receiver, inside the receiver around the hold, on the feed-ramp, lugs, etc., as well as covering the screw itself and the guard part or plate underneath. Also cover the front section of the magazine box if you wish to use it, which isn't necessary. While these are drying, use a heavy wax or two or three coats of linseed oil on the inside of the front inletting for the magazine box, being careful not to get any on the scraped, dry area, and on the top edges and sides of the stock (outside) at the bedding so that any of the compound extruded out when the rifle is seated in the stock won't adhere to the outside of the stock. Oil or wax will allow lifting off hardened epoxy or glass without damage to the stock finish underneath.

Mix the compound per directions, and use a small paddle or tinner's brush to paint it over all surfaces desired, well into the lug recess, then add more, to half fill the lug recess and a good puddle or raised portion in the stock (which should be held in padded vise jaws and remain there until the compound is set up fairly hard). Try to keep it from running out of the guard-screw hold, which you won't be able to prevent completely. Then seat the barreled receiver in the stock, not forgetting the wedge to hold the barrel clear of the channel, and tighten the screws, not excessively, just enough to pull the receiver down into position in the stock. Keep the paper cup or tin can with the excess compound remaining for a check on hardening. When it gets tough or semihard you can remove the "flash" or extruded compound from the sides of the stock or wherever it is it shouldn't be that is accessible. Usually, it can be cut easily with a wood chisel easily, but go straight in, don't try to run the edge along the top of the stock. You'll cut the finish and scratch the receiver for certain.

Back the front guard screw off a turn and retighten. This should prevent it becoming locked in place by epoxy or glass should some of the release agent have been worn off.

When your leftover mixture is hard, the bedding is hard and the metal parts may be removed, which isn't as easy as it sounds. The rifle stock is clamped in the vise with its toe resting on top of the bench; bring your left arm up strongly under barrel just ahead of the fore-end, catching it in the bend of elbow. This will pull the barrel and receiver partially up out of the stock. By inserting a bolt to use as a handle on the rear end, you will be able to lift the rifle clear of the stock. Clean up with acetone or lacquer thinner, oil lightly, assemble metal parts completely, that is, put on scope base, mounts, etc., and you're ready to put the rifle together for trial. The stock should require only clearance of unwanted epoxy or glass from the front screw hole and front of the magazine inletting. No bit of epoxy should block the fit of box or guard parts and prevent the guard screws from exerting tension on both guard parts and receiver when fully tightened. When a screw threads in well but suddenly stops, see what is wrong. They should tighten gradually. It is really fairly painless to do a job on a new rifle.

On an old or well-used rifle there is much more to stock preparation, depending on the condition of the inletting. Wood may be cracked at the web (the small solid portion ahead of the trigger assembly) or even in back of the recoil lug or plate. This isn't really a problem: the bad factor is the old oil and solvent which has contaminated the surfaces of the wood so that bedding compounds won't stick—perhaps deeply. Use a ½-inch wide natural bristle cheap paintbrush to introduce lacquer thinner over the oil-bearing strata, and, ten seconds or so later, blot it up with a wad of cleaning tissue. Keep doing this until you're tired or drunk from lacquer fumes: most of the oil will be dissolved out of the wood surface. You can't just put solvent on the wood and let it dry—oil residue will be left. Blow solvent through cracks as best you can. If the wood is very deteriorated, just cut a slot with chisel where the crack was, so you can degrease the wood well. Small holes may be drilled in the bedding area, at varying angles, up to ¼-inch deep and not under $3/32$-inch diameter or over ⅛-inch. These will provide anchors for the bedding compounds. With all metal parts ready and the compound mixed, use acetone liberally to wash the wood surface two or three times to give a dry surface for the bedding to grip. In extreme cases where you've had to cut a sixteenth of an inch or so of oil-soaked wood away, do all this but only a preliminary bedding: prepare the stock, then put a thin coat of epoxy or glass on the wood, working it into holes and cracks but not building it up to a level where you might have trouble replacing the barreled action in the stock. Let this primary coat of compound harden and check it to see if it is holding well. If not, cut out the offending areas and put in more material. Then, with a solid foundation, you have only to wipe it with acetone, which will only degrease the hardened surface, put more on and bed the rifle with confidence.

Old M-1 Garand stocks are often so oil-soaked as to be worthless for rebedding unless the above is done. When I was accurizing these in numbers, I made a stock-shaped aluminum tank to just hold a stock, for soaking in solvents. Accurizing an M-1 is today a rather difficult job because of the parts shortage. When new National Match barrels, sights, gas cylinders, rods, etc., were plentiful, it was no problem to build up a very accurate rifle. The accuracy work to be done, however, is the same whether the basic rifle is a World War II relic or an unfired National Match model from the front end back.

The front sight itself is filed to a sharp, square top profile, with thickness (width of blade) to suit the owner. The gas cylinder is made to fit the spline cuts on the barrel tightly by peening the latter, and the rear ring is drilled or filed out so that it does not touch the barrel at any point around it. The small lip in back of the stacking swivel is narrowed so that it cannot touch the handguard. The handguard itself has a ring at the front opened (by reversing and putting down to taper on a barrel and turning by hand to expand it). The barrel band, removed from barrel, which it should fit tightly, is attached to the handguard by screws. The best screws are 1-inch no. 7 flathead sheet-metal screws, so that the band and handguard form a unit.

The rear handguard is cleared of any wood that may touch the barrel or operating rod, and is fitted rather loosely under the barrel band. The barrel itself is to be polished on the bottom at the breech, where the operating rod may touch. With the rifle assembled, the operating rod should lie in the center of the operating rod cut in the band and groove of the upper handguard; file clearance in the band.

197

The front end should lie in the bottom of the gas-cylinder hole, and the middle should not touch in the stock ferrule tip. The rear should lightly contact the bottom of the barrel, and the contacting surface should be polished. The spring tension should be such as to tilt the handle up. No words can tell how to bend an operating rod; you'll just have to experiment. Operating-rod hooks are polished, the nose of the bolt and the face of the hammer are buffed, the hooks on the hammer are stoned to shorten it to get a crisp pull and all metal surfaces contacting each other are polished. The trigger-guard assembly must lock solidly into receiver—the little lugs do wear, so a new loop and and operating-rod spring may be needed. The rear-sight parts may have to be reworked, such as peening the curved T slot in which the peep or aperture slide rides to eliminate loose side play, and the cover spring bent to bring sufficient tension to prevent vertical displacement. This covers most M-1 metalworking.

Glass or epoxy bedding of the stock again may or may not be a difficult chore, depending on whether or not the stock is old and oil-soaked or reasonably clean. If the wood is clean and solid, it's not a hard job at all. The safest method is to do the bottom first. Scrape and cut to dry wood under the rear tang of the guard and sides of the magazine opening, where the edges of the plate bear. Then mix a small amount of bedding material—you hardly need more than a couple of bottle caps full and coat the guard assembly well with the release agent, put the compound on the bedding areas and assemble the rifle, but not closing the trigger guard completely. Use a large rubber band or even a string to tie it with the rear tip about ¾ inch from the closed and locked position. Set the rifle horizontally, bottom up, for the hardening period. All that is important is that the bearing surfaces of the guard are supported by hard bedding. When the material is cured, remove the metal parts, clean up excess and use a sharp narrow chisel to clear the engagement-notch area at the back end of the guard inletting so the guard can lock.

Preparation of the stock for action bedding requires quite careful use of a narrow wood chisel, no wider than ¼ inch and preferably ⅛ or ³/₁₆ inch. A horseshoe shaped channel ¼-inch wide and ¹/₃₂-inch deep is to be cut under the rear of the receiver, straight channels in top stock walls at sides under the top bearing surfaces of the receiver and the wood scraped to a clean surface under and at the sides of the lower front side walls of receiver. The recoil shoulders of the stock, where the straight-down rear surfaces of the receiver's magazine section contact must also be channeled back, ¹/₃₂ to ¹/₁₆-inch deep, leaving a thin wall of wood at the inside but cutting sideways into the stock walls a bit. You make channels instead of just cutting clearance to keep the bedding compound from running out of place when you seat metal parts for bedding. Clean all these channels well with acetone or lacquer thinner and a small brush, as they must be free of oil. Roughen channel bottoms, drill anchor holes if called for and undercut edges where possible. Masking tape may be used in small bits to seal channels inside and out if edges are broken, and modeling clay in the little notch inside the horseshoe area—this must be clear as the rear end of firing pin enters it when the bolt recoils.

A thin strip of metal, say ¾-inch wide and 3-inches long, perhaps $25/1000$-inch thick, (less than $1/32$ inch) is needed, plus a V or sharp U with legs an inch or more long must be made of round rod not over ¼ inch in diameter, of any metal—aluminum, brass, steel, anything except lead. The strip of metal, aluminum is best, can be cut from an old pan, lid, etc., and straightened out in vise jaws. Small bits of the same metal may be doubled for making thick little strips about ¼-inch wide and ¾-inch long. The stripped barrel and receiver—without the barrel band or any other parts—is coated with a release agent all over the receiver and the metal strips are also coated.

A rather thick glass or epoxy mixture is required for a good job; and the best thickening agent for either is a substance called Cabasil, a talc-like white powder that is very light—don't sneeze in its presence or it'll float in the air! It can be obtained wherever glass resins are sold or used industrially. A couple of ounces will last a long, long time. Only a very little is needed to bring an epoxy to stiff-butter consistency, much more for glass resins. Just add until your mixture will stand up in "points" as for cake frostings.

Before thickening the compound, it is wise to use a small water-color brush to paint the thin mixture well into all channels. Then, with a paddle, fill in the top channels of stock—it should be held in vise top up, horizontal. Build up a high ridge of the compound, well above the surface of the wood. Now lay in the thick ¼-inch wide metal strips across the front end of channels, opposite each other (this will leave the left one perhaps with the channel forward of it, while the right-hand one is against the stock wall forward). The wood should be left solid under these, not channelled out. If it is cut out, make small wooden blocks to fit in the channel to support these metal strips.

With the top of the stock holding the bedding material and strips in place, quickly fill the recoil-shoulder channels with material, again providing excess, lay the 3-inch metal strip across the stock just ahead of the horseshoe and put the barreled receiver into the stock. Wipe off the amount of compound forced out at the bottom, put in the trigger-guard assembly (it can be complete or minus the hammer and trigger, but it must have the safety in place) and engage the guard locking lugs, pulling the guard to within ¾ inch of closing. Hold in position by using the U-shaped rod, one leg through the hole in the safety, the other around the guard.

When semihard you can cut any big runout of material, but if there is little, leave it alone. You can clear it with files after it's completely hardened.

This is the best system for the home gunsmith. An armorer would not use the strip wedges to obtain the receiver angle needed for tension; he'd have little metal bars and rods to lay across the ferrule tip at the fore-end, extra machined-out barrel bands, etc., as well as other parts the average man won't have. The end achieved is the same: the little metal strips tilt the rifle up a little at front, in the stock; the wide metal strip prevents the horseshoe from sinking down into the bedding too far, in the rear. When the job is done and the M-1 is ready for putting together, it won't go so easy. The trigger guard won't just push down and lock. A heel may be used—I use the side wall of the bench top, hold the butt with one hand, the fore-end in the other and slam the loop of the guard against the bench.

You now have much barrel tension against the hold of the barrel band on the stock ferrule, and that's what you want. Should things not quite have worked out and you positively can't lock the guard and assemble the rifle, you file the forward top bedding surfaces of the stock, thus reducing the angle at which the receiver and barrel are being held. If this doesn't work, you have too much top-to-bottom distance, so you file the guard bedding down a bit—not the tang, just the side-rail sections.

See that the operating rod does not touch the stock at all in the rear position; cut and file wood away to give complete clearance. It is best that the stock be given two or three coats of waterproof lacquer with a brush so you don't get any on the bedding. Use a moly grease, not oil, to liberally lubricate the M-1 at all metal-to-metal friction or contact points, including rear and front ends of the bolt, the operating-rod runway on the side of the receiver, and the bolt lugs.

When the arm is finished and assembled, test-fire it. If the rod seems to lie right in its channel, everything is smooth. Shoot standing, holding the fore-end tightly in your bare hand. If it's OK, solid recoil will be felt. But should you feel a bad vibration, persisting for several rounds, the rod is bending or is improperly shaped and you must must recheck it, bending perhaps at the junction of the hook and handle, and trying again. You must not put any horizontal curve in the straight slide-and-handle rear section of the rod. This makes the rifle shoot a wide, flat group.

The Garand rifle was originally designed for medium pressure ammunition, primarily 150-grain bullets. Anything heavier punishes the operating rods. The 172-grain National Match ammunition was loaded to medium pressures as much as possible, but even so special rods become necessary. You do not use heavy bullets or heavy handloads unless you take some of the load off the rifle by bleeding off some of the excess gas pressure. An old type solid gas-cylinder screw is required, which is easily vented by drilling a $1/_{16}$-inch diameter hole through it, back to front. This will take off sufficient gas pressure to prevent hard slamming of the rod to the rear, yet allow full and efficient semiautomatic functioning. The later-type screw with valve action (made to allow firing rifle grenades without damaging the rifle) can't be so altered unless the separate parts are soldered together first. Complete removal of the valve allows almost all of the gas to escape forward, and the operating rod will not function. Target shooters sometimes do this, using very heavy loads and operating the rod by hand for each shot.

A match-conditioned—accurized M-1—should not be disassembled often. Repeated takedown will damage a tight bedding job in time. The barrel is always cleaned from the muzzle anyway, so clean it after firing, preserve and use tweezers and tissue to clean the bolt face, magazine well, etc. Equal in cleaning importance to the barrel is the front end of the operating rod. With the rod locked in the rear position, the front is sufficiently exposed to allow wiping with solvents to clear off fouling. Wet it well with solvent, let the rod carry the solvent forward into the cylinder and set rifle away muzzle down.

Accurizing of the M-14 service rifle is along similar lines, but requires more alteration of metal parts on the front end. Since these are restricted military weapons, they aren't allowed in civilian hands and never will be because their design permits easy alteration to full-automatic performance. Thus there is no need to get involved talking about them.

Nor is there much to be said for the M-1 carbine, many of which are legally possessed by nonmilitary people. Like jeeps, carbines seem quite popular with men who were never in military service. Any ex-soldier experienced with either usually exhibits a stunning lack of enthusiasm about them. The carbine caliber is, to all effects, a higher velocity .32/20, for which cartridge no rifles have been made for many

A custom stock Model 70 Winchester in .220 Swift caliber. This accurized rifle, which was restocked in French walnut, and checkered by Jim Carmichel, is a super gun for long-range varmint shooting. The scope is a 10-power Unertl Vulture model.

years. While attractive stocks are available from stockmaking firms, good sights and scope mounts aid much, bedding the receiver and rear tang with glass or epoxy helps a little and smoothing metal parts a trifle more, real accuracy depends on the individual barrel—which, since it was produced for military use originally, may not be too good. The gas cylinder, or piston housing, is shrunk onto the barrel. Every now and then one shrunk a little too much, and the barrel has a tight spot there. Bullets are reduced in diameter at the tight spot so they're a little small for the rest of the barrel and therefore wander off a little in any direction. The only remedy is another barrel. Reliable functioning depends mainly on magazine lips and keeping the piston assembly free of hard fouling.

All autoloading arms must have clean and smooth chambers to permit proper chambering and extraction of ammunition and fired cases. M-1 and carbine chambers must be maintained well and always be well oiled to prevent rust. A weakened operating or slide spring will allow moving parts to move too fast and hard and abuse each other. A too-strong spring may not allow the bolt to recoil far enough to the rear to pick up a fresh cartridge from the magazine and reload the rifle. This is common with new M-1 springs; just clip ½ inch from the big end, and see if it doesn't cure the trouble.

Accurizing bolt-action target rifles, which includes varmint and bench-rest types also, simply calls for added stock bedding. Where the sporter job is satisfied with just the front-end areas and possibly the rear tang supported, these more specialized rifles usually see much more use and general handling, and usually are rebarreled several times. The complete receiver is bedded and usually the trigger-guard assemblies, as well as 1 to 2 inches of the barrel ahead of the receiver. When a barrel is replaced, the old underbarrel bedding is scraped to give good clear-

Here is another super-accurate varmint rifle. The scope is a 6 to 18X Redfield Variable on a Mauser action with a Canjar single-set trigger. The heavy stainless-steel barrel is made by Hart and the caliber is .224 Clark. The stock, which has a beavertail fore-end for best holding and bench shooting, is stocked in beautiful Claro walnut.

ance to the new one. The surface of the bedding is cleaned with acetone, and a small amount of bedding compound is mixed and used to seat the new heavy barrel. Receiver screws are pulled down tight, and care is taken that no fresh material gets into the old bedding and hold the receiver up out of its solid original seating.

Even .22 rimfire match rifles should be bedded with fiberglass or epoxy. The round receivers are easy to work with, and while there is little recoil to be countered, solidly mounted rifles shoot better.

Many .22 match rifles absolutely require bedding of the receiver and barrel breech to shoot well when a target telescopic sight is mounted on the barrel. Most of the foreign-made rifles have full-floating barrels that are unsupported from the receiver forward. They usually shoot well with metallic sights, but often not nearly so well when a 1¾-pound scope is placed on the barrel. A bedding job practically always accurizes them.

This accurized long-range job is built up on a Winchester Model 70 action with a stainless-steel Atkinson barrel in .280 Remington Improved Caliber. The stock is laminated walnut for extra stability and the scope is a 20× Redfield Model 3200.

PART II

Advanced Alterations and Repairs

The following chapters concern operations requiring more complete sets of hand tools, shop supplies, a drill press, an acetylene or propane torch and an ambitious operator. They involve minor to major changes in firearms, adaptations to special-purpose uses, improving the overall quality and value of arms and making possible rifles the gun owner might not otherwise be able to afford.

They are for the firearms owner who finds himself not satisfied with adequate maintenance and strictly utilitarian improvements such as sight changes, and begins to aspire to a complete change of stocks, deluxe refinishing of metal, etc.

A larger shop or working area than the basic is not really necessary. It is nice to have lots of room, of course, but remember the home-workshop application of Parkinson's Law: "Contents expand to fill available space." With more equipment to place and store, careful planning may be needed to utilize all space, and neatness becomes a necessary virtue. If at all possible, purchase one of the small shop or utility vacuum cleaners and make a home for it under the bench. These high-powered vacuums save much time in cleaning the bench, floor and air, and can be reversed to use as a blower. Coming as small as 12 inches in diameter and 18 inches tall, they do not take up too much room.

If a window is available, the ventilation question is answered. If not, and an outside wall can be tapped, try to put in a small exhaust fan—an inexpensive bathroom or kitchen type will do fine, and comes as a complete unit. This will permit work with lacquers, solvents, etc., which are offensive or dangerous to use in a closed room.

As in just starting out in the home-arm-care hobby, material and equipment will be accumulated as needed and wanted.

13

Woodworking: Restocking Rifles and Shotguns

Refinishing, altering and replacing the furniture, or wood components, of firearms, is in one form or another nearly always the first major undertaking of the home gunsmith. They can be done with hand tools if no power equipment is available. Compared to metal, wood is easy to cut, shape and finish to individual tastes.

Taking the practical viewpoint first, we have the obvious changes in original wood fittings for firearms: fitting recoil pads to shotguns and rifles, which more or less combines with the desire for shortening or lengthening buttstocks, repaired cracked stocks and replacing unrepairable broken or deteriorated stocks.

Recoil pads are most often fitted to new stocks on new arms, or rather, on new arms that have been fired and found to need pad or butt-length change. The simplest method of lengthening a butt for a tall person is to put a pad on his stock, which he probably wants and needs anyway. For shortening a butt, it is easier to install a pad than to try to cut the butt down and refit the original buttplate. This new or first-class gun condition is no help at all—much more care must be taken in reducing the oversize pad to exact fit to the outside of the butt than with an old beat-down stock or an unfinished one in the making.

Here we should mention "pitch," a word used to describe the relationship of the bore-line of the barrel to a line running across the rear top and bottom points of the buttplate or pad. Think of an L-shaped carpenter's square with a long leg that can be placed on top of the barrel of the complete rifle or shotgun, with the short leg down across the buttplate. If both heel and toe (top and bottom) portions of the plate touch the short leg which is ninety degrees—a right angle—to the long, there is no pitch; if the top of the pad or plate only will touch, the pitch

PITCH

Stand a gun on its buttplate on the floor with its breech touching the wall. The distance between the muzzle and wall is the pitch.

is called negative; bottom only, positive. Now, to make for real confusion, pitch is not figured as an angle, which it should be, but rather as a distance between the barrel and the long square with the buttplate seated on the short leg! Stand a long gun on its buttplate on the floor with the breech touching a wall. The distance between the wall and muzzle may be anywhere from 1 to 5 inches! Maybe I should never have mentioned pitch, anyway, from now on we'll call it the angle of the buttplate.

On a rifle the angle really isn't very important. Factory rifles almost always have a slight negative pitch, or angle, the idea being that this will tend to hold the muzzle down when the rifle is fired and recoils against the shoulder since the top prong of the buttplate digs in to counteract the upward movement. Personally, I find that no angle—buttplate or pad at 90 degrees to line of bore—serves best for all-around shooting.

On shotguns the angle can be very important—too much on the negative side leads to undershooting. Normally, the original factory angle will be correct, and the pad can be lined up to duplicate it. However, if the gunner believes he has trouble with undershooting or overshooting, now is the time to check out stock fit, as concerns the angle: saw the butt, per the original angle but ⅛-inch long. Drill for screws but do not cut pad sides or do any finish work on the butt, and attach the pad. From any soft wood handy, make a wide thin wedge, 5 inches long, around 1¼-inch wide, and $3/32$ inch thicker at one end than at the other. Split or saw it lengthwise, and head for a trap range or the field with a box of shells. Shoot with the pad as is, then with wedges under it. Loosen screws, slide a wedge up under the pad on each side, trying with thick ends up and reversed. A few shots with each at clay birds will tell what is best. Back in the shop, with drawn lines on the side to show which way the angle is to be changed, cut the butt to the correct length—either heel or toe can be moved in ⅛-inch easily.

As with most undertakings of any sort, doing a really good job of putting on a recoil pad is quite difficult and laborious. Just sawing off a stock can be frustrating. The edges of the saw cut want to splinter out on the far side and there isn't too much that can be done to avoid this. Even hardwood crosscut blades on a table saw tear a little. On the home bench, go the long way around: use a new, sharp hacksaw blade and cut the stock $1/16$-inch long; then, with a sharp cabinet-scraper and files, reduce to the length wanted, cutting away the splintered edges. (Or hold the butt against a belt sander.)

Prepare the pad, cleaning off any lumps from the backing plate, locate it, drill and tap pad holes in the butt and attach to butt. When the firearm is a takedown-type shotgun or rifle, remove the barrel assembly, etc., before starting the work. Where you have a solid-frame-type arm with the buttstock held by a screw through the butt from the back end, the pad job is a little harder, as you must take off the stock to fit the pad, do all work, then remove pad, reinstall the stock on the firearm and then reinstall the pad on the stock.

Just to show that a recoil pad may not fit perfectly flat on the butt; a few minutes in warm water allows it to be straightened in fingers so it will draw down to wood with screws for a perfect fit.

Where no necessity of removing the pad once on exists, you may use thickened linseed oil (boiled oil exposed to air until it becomes syrupy) prepared stock oil, or clear varnish to the wood butt end, immediately before the pad is screwed down. Do not do this when the pad is to be removed.

Wind two layers of masking tape around the stock from the pad base to 3 inches ahead to protect the stock finish from the pad cutting-down work. The resilient portions of recoil pads are resistant to cutting except by abrasives: a belt or disk sander is required, the latter being

A handle soldered to a screw-head makes a perfect 'tap' to thread the pad screw holes in the butt. If this is not done, there can be such resistance to the screw entering the hole when attaching the pad that bottoming will not be felt, and a further turn will destroy the threads in wood and screw will be loose.

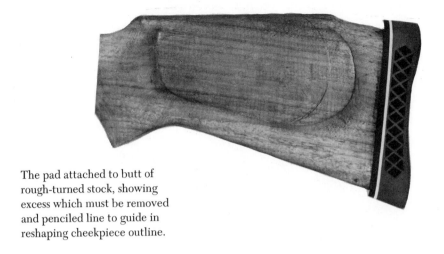

The pad attached to butt of
rough-turned stock, showing
excess which must be removed
and penciled line to guide in
reshaping cheekpiece outline.

best. Not having these, you can make do with a sanding-disk attachment
on a portable drill, or use the bench grinder to rough off pad edges and
finish with much use of abrasive paper and cloth backed by wooden
blocks. Should the bench grinder be very small, it may be necessary to
install a pad, scribe an outline of the stock on its base, remove the grind
down to $1/32$ inch or so of outline and then replace on the stock for finishing. Remember when doing such roughing away of the pad that the
top and bottom lines of the stock must be continued through the pad as
well as the sides. The toe will extend down and back quite a bit.

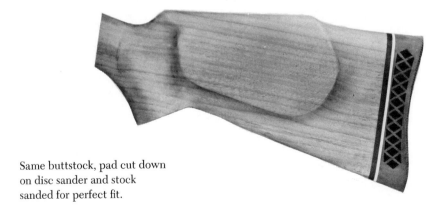

Same buttstock, pad cut down
on disc sander and stock
sanded for perfect fit.

211

A correctly fitted pad: No gaps between butt and pad base, stock lines carried out through pad depth, pad sanded down to smooth edges and sides.

The abrasive disks backed by their flexible backing plates cut pads rapidly, and great caution must be observed to keep them from cutting through the masking tape protecting the stock. When working down close to the final fit, use the medium-grit disks, shaping the pad, etc., and then put on fine-grit disk for the finish. With a new disk you can cut down to the tape and even into it without going through. The motor and disk are always stationary—you handle the stock and move it, using mostly the outer ½ inch of the disk, bringing the pad into it at a slight angle and drawing the stock forward. A little experience helps a lot, but few individual gun owners have old stocks and pads to practice on. A fine-grit disk can become worn almost smooth around the edge; this is ideal for finishing—the smooth part can be brought into contact with the masking tape just ahead of the pad/butt joint and just smear the tape while still cutting down the pad a bit. When the disk work has progressed as far as is dared, remove and replace the tape if worn almost through in spots, use strips of sharp, clean cutting cloth or sandpaper on a long narrow backer, finest grit possible if the pad edge is really close to the wood, and sand across the pad and tape. Then reduce to one thickness of tape, finally to one thickness with the rear edge ⅛ inch ahead of the pad-stock joint. When it's really down to fit without marring the finish, you have a great victory!

So you couldn't do it and the disk scarred the wood: with fine paper wrapped around a small flat file clean up the spot and refinish the wood. Some modern stocks have a thick plastic finish which may be marked itself on the surface—the 4/0 steel wool can polish out minor markings. Winchester stocks are usually stained, and if the wood is cut,

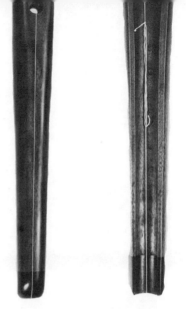

An easy way to pick up center-line of stock of locating swivel hole. Make a string with rubber-band spliced in, move to center of barrel channel at tip and guard inletting.

a lighter color appears. A tiny bit of artist's coloring, burnt umber in oil, rubbed in with your fingertip, will make a color match after which a touch of stock oil will restore gloss.

Wood finishing, of course, means the final operations, final sanding grain-filling, application of surface finish—oil, varnish, lacquer, plastic, etc. Refinishing means a complete repair job on the original finish, or a complete removal and replacement of it, very often a much more difficult undertaking than finishng a new stock.

The four drill bits needed to install two swivels: Left, body diameter for starting hole for butt swivel, run in as deep as the non-threaded base of swivel-shank; next, the actual hole diameter bit to take the threaded shank full depth. . . . For the forend swivel, drill for full diameter of shank, then, in barrel channel, the big drill which is same diameter as the smooth part of the swivel nut. The raised knurled part will then draw down into the hold and lock against the turning when swivel is screwed in from bottom.

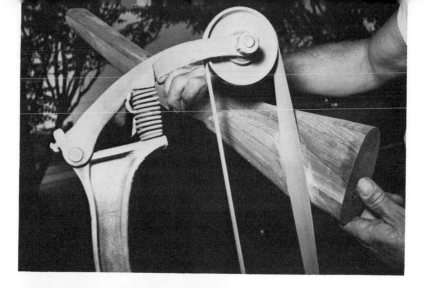

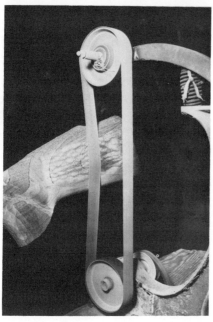

A band sander with table removed and used outdoors so as
not to fill the room with dust
can in minutes smooth up
rough-carved stock blanks,
even to polishing curves
around cheekpieces. It can't
work in the hollows, but can
reduce stock-sanding time 75%.

It may seem that the cart is getting a little ahead, in talking about
stock finishing before inletting, shaping and other basic stock work done
first, but the fact is that many arms owners today purchase almost
ready-to-use rifle and shotgun stocks and need only work on the finish
end. E. C. Bishop can supply stocks, fore-ends and slide-handles for almost every type and model of long arm, in all stages from unshaped
blank to finished, checkered semicustom ready to install and use. Fajen
has also almost as large a selection along similar lines, and Sile Distributors' Italian-made stocks for military actions and pump and autoloading
shotguns come finished and checkered, at very reasonable prices.

The finish-inletted stocks, otherwise unfinished, usually require only a little chiselwork here and there, to accommodate a patent trigger system or a larger barrel than the maker could anticipate. Do all such fitting, assemble the rifle or shotgun with the stock, etc., to try for functioning and make sure of it, then remove the wood and finish.

After any minor shaping desired on the grip, fore-end, comb or cheekpiece, and installing a pad if wanted, sand to a smooth, unscratched—and unwavy—surface and finish with 6/0 or 220-grit garnet paper. Being old-fashioned, I always raise the grain now, wetting the wood with water and drying rapidly over the stove, 8 inch over a gas burner, 1 inch over an electric coil. The glass-smooth surface is now rough again, where the moisture expanded wood fibers at the surface. Now the road forks: with oil-type finishes you start them, but with plastic, varnish or lacquer in mind, you sand the stock smooth again, giving a final go-over with 7/0 (240) or even finer abrasive, taking care not to go across the grain. Should a filler be used, this latter sanding is done afterward. If you do use a filler to fill the open pores and grain lines, be very sure you obtain the correct type to be used with the finish liquid. An oil-base filler is pretty worthless for anything. One made for varnish will be dissolved by lacquer. Epoxy or plastic finishes have their own fillers. All these are very difficult to apply, and involve much polishing down with abrasive compounds in the case of lacquers to make a really nice clear surface all over. Practice on fair-sized scraps of wood before starting on stock.

The fastest and easiest way to sand hollows—with a strip of abrasive cloth pulled out from under thumb and held to contour.

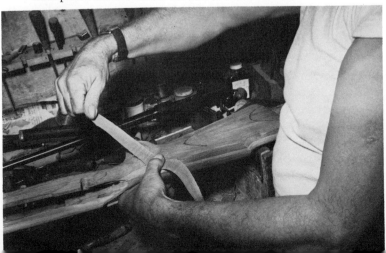

Varnish finishes are easier to work with. Most factory finishes are varnishes of one type or another, though Remington's present one seems to be a plastic type. For gunstock finish, only marine or bar-top types should be considered. These are virtually weatherproof and are not easily damaged by oils and powder solvents. The spray gun is, of course, the best method of applying either varnish or lacquer, but it requires skilled use to prevent building up of the agent on the wood and allowing "runs." However, varnish, thinned with the best quality thinner, can be applied with a brush. Several coats may be needed, with bad spots sanded in between (each should be allowed to dry before the next is applied) and final rubdown with wet or dry 400 or finer grit paper.

Many a factory-varnished stock has been refinished in oil by the owner. The old linseed-oil finish has always seemed to me to be the easiest. I started out using the best boiled oil I could get and adding Japan drier to it to make it dry faster. However, when George Brothers brought out his "LinSpeed" oil, already prepared, I switched to it. LinSpeed has many competitors today, the best known being TrueOil and Genuine Oil, similar quick-hardening oil-base finishes, as a rule a little stickier than LinSpeed. They all begin to thicken with exposure to air, so containers should be tightly capped except when you are using them. You can't even store them for more than a few days with air space in the container—use half a bottle, and you'll lose the other half unless you can find a bottle that can be exactly filled with the remaining oil. It is supposed to be possible to fill a partially used container with benzine (lighter fluid) and keep the unused oil in diluted form, but such oil will not be as efficient as in its original form.

Using LinSpeed, finishing a new stock is very simple, indeed. The stock, straight from the grain-raising operation, may be given a surface-saturating coat of oil, or, first, a coat of sealant—a wood-penetrating liquid moisture resistant. About the best I've found is McCloskey Varnish Company's "Tungseal," which is available in clear or wood colors. Brush it on the stock, allow ten hours or so to dry, and then give the wood a full coat of stock oil, reapplying to end-grain areas where it may soak in quickly. The Tungseal will greatly reduce this, as it has sealed up most of the grain openings just under the surface. This sealant should always be used where the stock wood is figured American black walnut, or of any soft wood or any with fiddle-back or end-grain areas on the sides. It will prevent the wood from soaking up so much oil as to darken it too much.

After this basic coat of oil, and a bit of drying time—an hour or so in hot sun or warm-air outlet for a minimum—get your working supplies

HAND RUBBING A STOCK

Fine finishing paper is used with a felt block to rub down the finish on a fine sporting rifle during the hand-rubbing process. Between coats the finish is lightly rubbed.

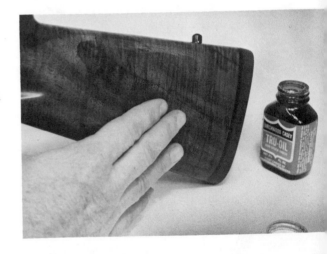

Here Birchwood Casey's Truoil is hand rubbed on a stock.

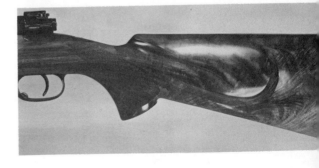

This is a hand-rubbed finish on a stock of American black walnut. A rich luster has been brought out to the fullest.

together: a box of Kleenex (so you can pull out one at a time with sticky fingers), 6/0 sanding paper (fold a sheet and tear into twelve small pieces), a well-washed old cloth large enough to cover your lap and a chair or stool to sit on. Wear an old sweatshirt and remove your wristwatch—many a stock has been scarred by watchbands, buttons and belt buckles!

Apply oil over a small area at a time with your finger, say over a cheekpiece, or half the side of a butt, or the top or bottom of butt, or one side of a fore-end. Give one rub with your hand and then take the small square of sandpaper and sand the oil-wet area in the direction of the grain. Use fair pressure, but don't do a lot of back-and-forth fast sanding. A minute or so of trial will demonstrate. The raised grain and surface are mixed with oil and smeared into the open grain structure. As you finish each spot, wipe off across the grain with tissue. Discard the tissue as it fills full of oil and wood. Do not stay too long on a small spot—you can pull out the filler you've just sanded in! This wet-sanding is easy and fast, and less than half an hour is needed for a rifle stock. If convenient, let it stand a few hours before repeating, but it is possible to just keep on sanding in oil and wiping the smears off until you can see that the surface is full. However, it now must set eight hours or more so that the oil–wood filler is hard. Linseed oil doesn't "dry" as does water or solvent: it hardens. At this point you apply the oil all over the stock fairly liberally, and wipe it down with the tissue. Don't put on a few drops and rub with your hand! Close inspection under good light will show where the grain surface needs more filling—so put on a little oil and sand it in. On coarse, open-grained wood you may have to do three full oil-sandings to get a fill; very close grained dense stocks may fill on the first try.

With the surface filled and clean, put on oil and wipe off with tissue once a day for three days. It takes about five minutes at most. You now have a genuine real oil finish that will resist almost anything except a fire! It will have a pretty good gloss and will look better if it's dulled a little. You can go over it very lightly with 4/0 steel wool, and then rub with clean burlap. Or go old-fashioned and use a cloth with rottenstone or pumice on it. I like then to apply another coat of oil and wipe it off as dry as possible with the tissue and do a few minutes' hand-rubbing. The stock won't be shiny, but it will glow with light and life. A good finish will make the most colorless, plainest grain stock a joy to behold.

Dirt and sweat may be washed from an oiled stock, the harshest solvents may take off the gloss or patina, but add another touch of oil and the finish is restored. A true oil finish is in the wood as much or more than it is on it. The durability of an aged finish is remarkable. I once sold one of my own rifles to a friend, who decided he'd refinish it. He tried lacquer thinner, acetone and commercial semiliquid varnish removers with no result except for surface dulling. So he sanded the stock all over. After about ten hours' work he gave up and put the oil back on.

Refinishing a varnished stock in oil is usually easy, in that about all the preparation necessary for most is just washing off with a solvent, or even warm water with detergent, to remove all the dirt and grease from the wood. Once in a while the varnish will be thick, built up here and there and require sanding down. Maybe even a varnish remover will be needed, and if so, be sure to wash the stock with acetone, lacquer thinner, or alcohol before starting to sand in stock oil.

The fastest of all stock finishes is the ancient "French Polish," almost unknown today. Originally used on fine furniture, it was a popular stock finish fifty years ago, when an oil finish could take weeks to complete. Of good appearance and fair durability, the French Polish is simplicity itself in concept: take a small, shallow pair of containers, such as 2-inch diameter jar lids, put pure, clean thinned white shellac in one, pure boiled linseed oil in the other; fold up little 2-inch pads of well-washed lint-free cotton cloth, dip first in the oil, then in the shellac and rub on the finish-sanded stock, covering a hand-sized area until tacky, renewing the pad with oil and shellac and progressing until the entire stock is covered. The grain fills as you work. Theoretically, you can have a well-finished, dry stock in two hours or less, allowing for clearing buildups and all. The idea is that the shellac bonds and dries, while the oil keeps the finish from becoming brittle. I gave up early, on finding out how to use the oil, but the finish has some merits for highly figured woods that oil may darken. Bob Owen, America's first great stockmaker—he practically invented the sporter rifle stock as we know it—was a master of French Polish. A good friend of mine, I once asked him how he managed to do such clean jobs. All I got was a laugh and a comment to the effect that it was all in being apprenticed to an English cabinetmaker when ten years old. So perhaps it does take practice.

The actual manufacture of a rifle or shotgun stock from unshaped blocks of wood is not recommended for any home gun enthusiast unless he is willing to make three. After two learning-how attempts, the third should be moderately successful! Basic professional-gunsmithing books will be needed to learn the techniques. With or without them or prior knowledge of how-to, I strongly advise making a pilot model: Obtain soft, easily worked wood, such as pine shelving. Two or three ¾-inch

A stock-finish drying chamber made from a steel drum by Ron DeWarf, a capable home gunsmith, from a steel barrel, ordinary photo-light reflectors and a barbecue-spit motor.

Lid with stock attached to motor spindle so it is turned slowly inside the drum.

Inside of the drum showing the large heat-producing bulbs. These big floods create a lot of heat for stock drying.

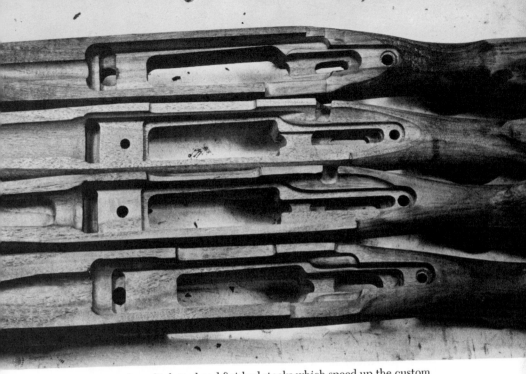

A group of semi-inletted and finished stocks which speed up the custom stockmaking process. The inletting in the stock at top is for the Mauser Model 98. The two center stocks are for Winchester Model 70s, and the one at the bottom, again, is for the Mauser.

thicknesses can be glued together to make a stock blank, or fore-end block. And a can of plastic wood, wood dough, any of the easily worked wood-patching compounds available at paint and hardware stores. Sharp chisels and drill bits, cabinet scraper, spoke shave and rasps make quick work of inletting and shaping, with the wood dough repairing mistakes in dimensions—where you removed more wood than later found desirable. Making such a dummy pilot model will teach the use of tools, many what-not-to-do acts and give a perfect example of what proportions and dimensions are necessary to work to.

More work in the line of stock replacement will be done on semi-finished wood, available at present for almost all long arms in various stages of manufacture, from rough-shaped blanks with rudimentary inletting to 90-percent finished models requiring only a touch of inletting and finish sanding. The Bishop people can provide a choice of half a dozen different patterns for the more popular rifles, for instance. The gun owner is not limited to one style. He can obtain a stock with or without the fore-end tip, the recoil pad fitted and shaped, or with a left-hand cheekpiece if he's a southpaw. Perhaps a dozen stockmaking firms

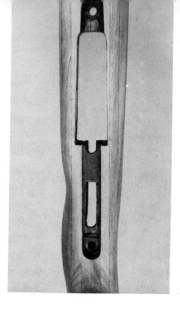

Triggerguard bedding for Winchester M70, giving support to all three receiver screws.

are presently supplying well-made semifinished stocks of all types. Inletted blocks and inletted rough-shaped handgun stocks are also made for the more popular large pistols and revolvers.

In connection with pistol stocks, the semipro magazine gun writers always blithely say, "With a drill press it's easy to rout grip inletting and make your own beautiful custom handgun stocks." It not only isn't easy, it's very dangerous. Normal drill presses don't turn fast enough for good routing, but they do turn fast enough to grab instead of cut and pull fingers in, which will cut, but good. Trying to handle a small block of wood under a turning router bit or end mill is much different than cutting little grooves and designs in panels, as shown in the home-mechanics magazines. So buy the inletted pistol-grip blanks.

Cleanliness is vital to work with new wood: no gun oil or grease can be permitted on a fresh, sanded surface, or even one unsanded but close to finish dimension. When you do absentmindedly handle such a stock with oily fingers and leave prints on the wood, clean immediately with acetone or lacquer thinner, and wash your hands. Just sanding the surface lightly may not do the job—later there may be a spot or spots showing under the final finish! Leather vise jaws pick up oils and will appear clean, but they can stain a clean stock clamped in them. Use a double thickness of paper between the leather and the stock.

Often a sanded stock ready for finish will have surface blemishes—short cracks, checks, openings, etc. Look for these before the final sanding. Small ones will fill with oil-sanding, but larger ones need prior treatment. If very large, bits of wood of as close to stock color as possible should be inserted and held with fiberglass, epoxy bedding compound or epoxy cement. If bits of wood are medium size, mix them with scrapings from inside the barrel channel or other source on or in the stock with epoxy or other hard cement and fill with this paste.

Stockmaking for percussion and flintlock arms means real work. The inletting is comparatively simple, but there's a lot of it, mostly the barrel channel which can be from 15 to 50 inches long, almost always for an octagonal barrel. The stock blanks usually purchased are flats, band-sawed to stock profile. A table saw is very often used to do most of the barrel-inletting by squaring the top and sides of the long fore-end so the sides will slide true against the saw's guide plate. The saw is set to first cut to the depth of the bottom flat for the barrel in the center of the blank. Successive cuts are made, moving the guide for each one the kerf-width until this deep slot is the width of one barrel flat—⅜ inch, $7/16$ inch or whatever—back from the muzzle end to the approximate forward end of the lock-plate location. Then the depth is reset so the saw blade will cut to the depth of the barrel's side flats and used the same way, cutting now a wide shallower groove, to the size of the barrel across the flats. These saw grooves are quite deep from the top of the stock, as the top must be lowered greatly for the conventional flintlock or percussion rifle or shotgun to leave a high step at the breech of barrel. Figure out the approximate true height of the fore-end when finished, allow $1/16$ inch over and saw off the top strips, being careful to preserve the now-raised section at the breech.

The fore-end is now inletted for bottom and side flats. You chisel, file and scrape the square shoulders of the sawn channel to obtain the two lower angled octagonal flats, and continue all by hand back to the breech, which must be squared at the rear face for the barrel or patent breech, next to be inletted. The barrel must be breeched and have the nipple or vent installed, and be completely inletted before the lock can be located and inletted. Trigger parts are then inletted to proper relationship with lock. Wedge-tenons or other loops are fitted to the barrel, and the stock is inletted for them.

The stock is now shaped down to approximate finished contours and dimensions, the buttplate fitted, muzzle cap if any, the groove for the ramrod cut in full-stock types, wedges or pins located and holes for them drilled and filed so they may be fitted and so assemble the firearm. Inletting for patchboxes or ornamental inlays comes after the first sanding.

The half-stock muzzle-loader requires drilling a hole back into the bottom of fore-end for holding the ramrod. The surest method I know of to do this in alignment with the thimbles or ferrules to hold the ramrod along the bottom of the barrel or rib is to use them. Solder, braze or weld a ramrod-diameter metal-cutting drill bit to a long rod of the same diameter, put it down through the thimbles and drill the hole with the gun assembled. An alternate method would be to just inlet a deep groove in the bottom flat of the fore-end to take the rod. This would weaken the stock a bit. If the barrel is to be bedded in glass—and I firmly believe all shooting muzzle-loaders should be so bedded to water-proof the inletting, strengthen the stock and just, maybe, make it shoot better—the rod can be wrapped in wax paper, be in place during the bedding, and the fiberglass will mold itself around it, filling the slot, etc. This would really strengthen the stock.

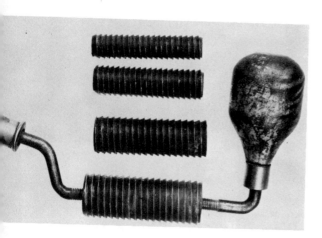

Barrel-channel cutters, by Zene Denman. All sizes may be used with the one set of handles. Such tools are literally indispensable when doing rifle stock work.

Because of their length, full-length muzzle-loading stocks often warp and twist after inletting, but being no more than thick shells, the barrels will hold them straight when the arms are assembled. The long stock fore-end adds no strength at all to the gun.

Several firms make semi-inletted muzzle-loading stocks in many styles and grades (none of the "modern" stock manufacturers do), usually shaped and with the barrel channel cut for any of the standard-size octagonal barrels being made, most of the half-stock types with the ramrod channel drilled, but almost none with lock-inletting, since the buyer has a choice of many locks of different types and sizes. These are comparatively easy to finish up, of course. Anyone getting this far along will learn of the various parts needed, details on finishes, etc. One thing—don't try the often-told business about burning a tar-soaked string wrapped around the stock to make it tiger-striped. It doesn't work. Such effects can be gained by using a small brush to paint acid solutions on the wood or—practicing first, by the "Suigi" method, using the torch with a tiny soldering tip to give a small, soft flame which is moved across the wood rapidly at such distance as to only discolor (blacken) the wood without actually charring it. Very fine effects can be obtained with a little practice on light-colored woods such as maple. It is done after sanding, just before applying finishing oil or varnish. The dark spots or stripings are not affected by finishes—any may be used over them, including lacquers and plastic types.

Ornamentation and Checkering

Stock ornamentation and checkering interest most rifle owners and a few shotgunners. Ornamentation became quite a fad a few years ago, and kits for inlays of wood and plastic, and some for liquid-metal inlay remain on the market. The precut inlays, of course, demand only careful chisel work to install them. Metal inlays require even more careful cutting. However, with the stencils, pattern-transfers, etc., the metal amalgams are not too hard to handle. For a good job the surrounding stock area must be resanded and refinished for a good appearance.

Checkering is today both ornamentation and useful addition. Originally conceived and executed to provide a nonslip holding area, it quickly became dressed up with detailed borders, and today we have imitation (pressed-in) checkering, skip-line and flat-top types, all more for appearance than any practical purpose. Checkering on fine custom stocks has become an art form of sorts, but with the actual checkering so well done it fulfills the nonslip clause in the contract. Few gunsmiths and few specialist stockmakers today care to give time, skill and eyesight to checkering stocks. Even checkering machines take skill and time to use. Yes, there are hand-held electric tools to cut checkering that are used by many professionals, and they do a good job. You can buy a good rifle for the price of one, too. Most checkering today, even on custom stocks made by hand, is done by men and women who do nothing except checkering. It is another specialist field.

I learned about checkering from the late Thomas Shelhamer who was perhaps the best at it who has lived yet. He evolved the difficult borderless decorative patterns, unbroken patterns around pistol grips, and produced work that was flawless when viewed with a magnifying glass. I never learned how to do it fast, though. About twenty years ago, after spending over two days putting about a square foot of checkering

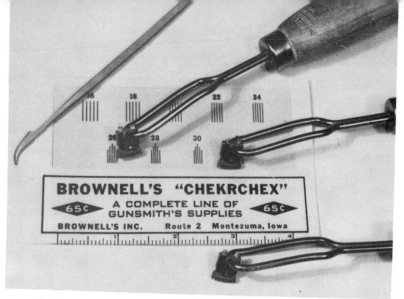

To do a good job of checkering all one needs are these few simple tools: a flexible ruler, a scribe, a V-tool, a spacing tool, and a boarder tool. If the checkering is neatly done the boarder tool is not needed.

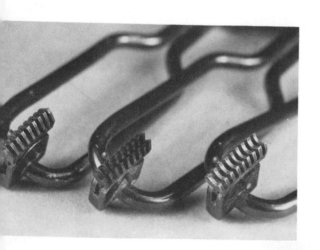

Here is a close-up detail of the cutting edges of checkering tools. At left is the V-tool, at center is the spacing tool, and at right is the boarder tool.

This is a V-chisel which is handy for cutting borders around checkering patterns.

on a deluxe target stock, it occurred to me that I was donating about one-hundred dollars worth of time on each job. I haven't checkered anything since! Which means only that doing it requires time and patience. Cutting the diamonds in the wood requires only normal manual dexterity, a good light, the tools and willpower enough to practice a little, go slow and quit at the first sign of eye or hand fatigue.

The tools are inexpensive and can be had in sets. The Dem-Bart, with its replaceable cutters, is perhaps the most popular type made. Some consideration must be given to the stock wood in relation to the tools purchased. One may read a write-up on some super-deluxe job with thirty-two or even thirty-four line checkering, but you need wood about as dense as ivory to hold diamonds as tiny as these sizes. The hardest, choicest imported walnut may take twenty-eight line, but for good wood all around, twenty-four lines to the inch is it, and most "good" grade American woods take even coarser. The common open-grain black walnut is for eighteen or twenty. The time spent in working may be almost the same—with the finer checkering you cut more grooves, but shallower, requiring fewer passes with the tools. The stock finish is also a factor. It is almost impossible to checker stocks with lacquer, plastic or epoxy finishes if a hard or abrasive filling agent has been used.

Checkering must be done after the stock is completely finished, or otherwise it is almost impossible to do a finish on a checkered stock without damaging the checkering. So, you're limited to oil or thin or rubbed-varnish stocks. (Varnished stocks rubbed down with paste abrasives.) Checkering can be cut through these finishes, and the finished checkering oiled or treated by brush.

As for the actual operation, the first stage, of course, is figuring out how to hold the stock so you can work on it. The checkering cradle is almost—not quite—absolutely necessary. This is a frame with sockets or pivot points to hold a stock at each end so it can be turned and therefore work can be done always on the top, or horizontal plane. Professionals use quite elaborate types that are adjustable to take short shotgun buttstocks, small fore-ends or long rifle stocks. These are entirely impractical for someone to try to duplicate who intends to checker only one or two stocks. However, if you are willing to spend a few dollars and a few hours, you can make one to handle the individual stock to be worked on, almost entirely of wood, to be screwed or bolted to the top of your bench. The illustrations show the general construction. The three butt positions give six stock positions since the stock can be placed bottom up or down in each, and the tip-socket tightened to hold

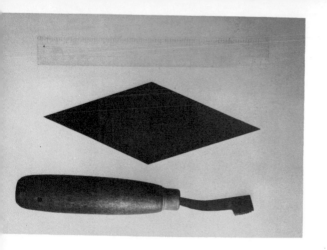

Checkering layout equipment: diamond (this one is of spring steel) and homemade lining tool for outlining and for starting basic checkering lines.

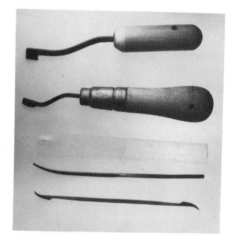

Top tool is groove-deepening tool, having edge filed to make it cut a shallow V, and beneath it, with curved profile, a two-edged or grooved spacer, like a little saw, to space and begin grooves. At bottom are curved triangular-shaped files used to clean out and touch up the finished checkering.

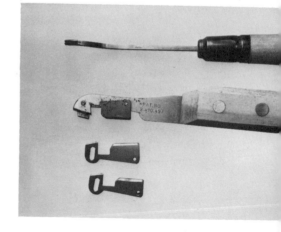

Commercial checkering tools: At top the Dem-Bart, which features little interchangeable cutters, and below it a single-edge tool having two extra spacing guides below, allowing it to be used as spacer for 18-, 20-, or 24-line work.

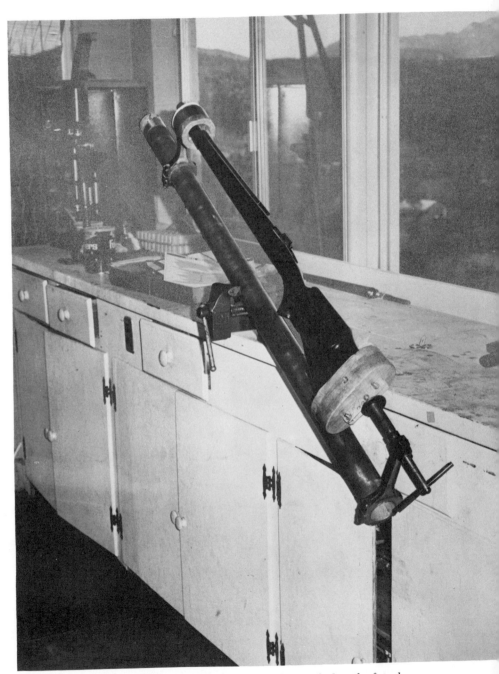

A convenient but simple checkering fixture made out of a length of steel tubing and a couple of automobile connecting rods.

The author's own checkering cradle can be adjusted to hold short or long stocks, fore-ends, etc. It is used bolted to the bench or, as in this photograph, held in a vise.

it firmly enough for the pressure of checkering-tool use. This setup will allow work all around the grip and fore end areas without physical strain.

Actual checkering begins with the layout of the pattern. Patterns may be your own creation, copy of standardized ornamental-border types—there are books and tracing sets sold just for this purpose—or simply an area with shallow S-curve borders. It is very difficult to transfer and absolutely duplicate a pattern from one stock to another unless they are precisely the same size and have all the same curves in the same places. So, don't be surprised to find a pattern traced or purchased doesn't lay quite right on your stock. Put the borders where they should be on your stock, center any uncheckered panels within the pattern and so adapt to your dimensions.

The individual attempting checkering from scratch should have a flexible transparent ruler and wood to practice on, preferably bits of walnut, maple, etc. An old stock is excellent if you have one, but even small flat blocks will teach a great deal. Outline the pattern lightly with a pencil first, then scribe lightly on the wood after making any corrections desired, with a sharp metal scriber. With some dark woods a white pencil does well.

A quickie all-wood checkering cradle, easily made for a one-stock job, construction evident. Fore-end tip to be wedged in notch with piece of innertube. The three butt notches allow six stock positions, and, padded with more of the old innertube, butt can be wedged below the butt "sockets" to give horizontal stock position, either side.

Use the layout tool or single-edge checkering tool to cut a groove at the border, where the checkering lines will end, not too deep. Later you will need to go over it again, perhaps with a special bordering tool.

The proportions of the small wood diamonds formed by checkering have much to do with both appearance and durability of the job: Too often the diamonds are too short, making them weak and easily broken down. When a design diamond is used, this seldom happens. Fold a small piece of heavy paper two ways and make one cut with scissors to produce a diamond 3 to 4 inches long and about a third as wide. The ideal is approximately two and a half-times as long as wide, but a three-to-one ratio will do. When you have your large paper diamond, duplicate it in flexible plastic about $1/32$-inch thick. This diamond is used to lay out the basic lines for checkering within the pattern. The tiny diamonds you cut with the tools will be the same shape as the layout diamond.

With the pattern borders marked, use masking or plastic electrical tape around them to form a defense against tools running over borders. Use the layout diamond to cut two starting grooves with the grooving or lining tool, setting the diamond so that it is in line lengthwise with the grain of the wood as best it can be. Holding the diamond

1. The first step in doing a checkered panel is attaching a paper pattern to the stock. Here the paper pattern is held in place by cellophane tape.

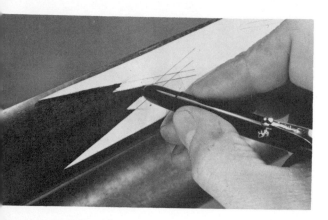

2. A wax china marking pencil is used to trace the outline of the pattern onto the wood. The wax marks are easily wiped off when checkering is finished.

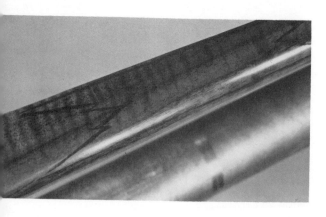

Here is the pattern after it has been traced onto the fore-end.

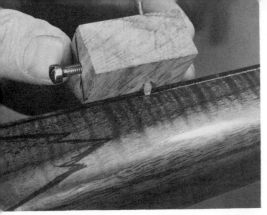

3. This simple tool, made from a block of wood, a sharpened nail, and a screw is used to cut the top edge of the checkering boarder. Since it rides along the top of the stock, the line will be straight and even.

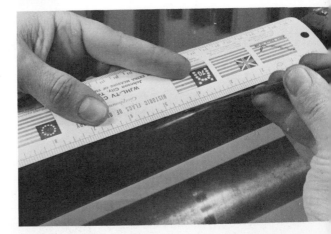

4. A flexible metal ruler is used as a guide for the scribing tool which, here, is cutting the bottom edge of the panel.

5. One of the most important steps in the checkering process is cutting the master lines. The lines should intersect at an angle so that the diamonds are about 3 to 3½ times as long as they are wide. Here the flexible plastic ruler is used because it follows the contour of the stock but still holds a straight line.

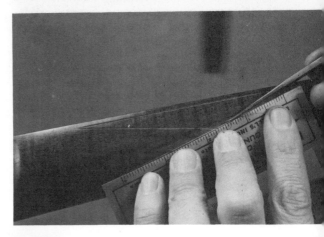

A detail of the panel to be checkered after the master lines have been cut.

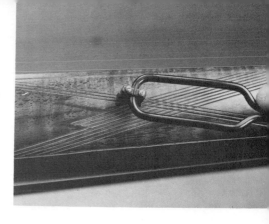

6. The spacing tool is used to begin the spacing. The lines are cut one by one with each previous line acting as a guide for the succeeding line.

7. The work is continued across the pattern with the spacing tool. This close-up shows the tool at work.

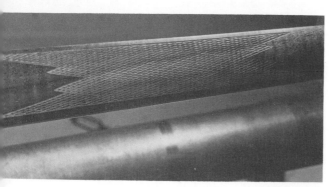

Here is the panel after the spacing is completed, but before the diamonds are cut to full depth. Notice that the diamonds are still flat-topped.

8. The V-tool is used to deepen the lines. About two passes usually bring the diamonds to full depth.

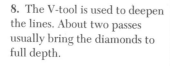

234

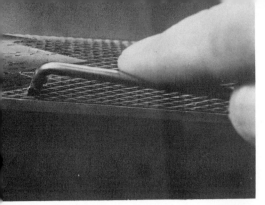

9. A small close-quarter tool is used to work in tight areas such as the extreme corners. Extreme caution must be used here to avoid overruns.

10. A Brownell edging tool is used to cut a straight line along the edge of a border. This tool deepens a border and adds a "finished" look, although this step is not necessary.

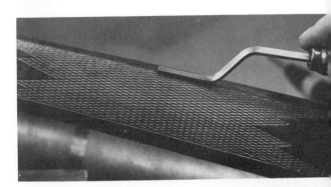

11. A toothbrush is used to scrub the dust and wood fibers out of the checkering.

Here is the finished checkering pattern after all the lines have been cut to full depth, but before final finishing.

12. Now stock finish is brushed into the checkering.

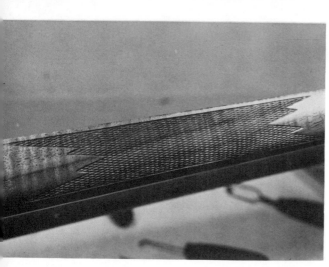

This is the finished pattern, an accomplishment the home work-shopper can indeed be mighty proud of!

against the stock, cut these grooves well inside the pattern, using one point only, front or rear—no need to make them meet at the point. Now use the flexible rule to continue these two lines, a little at a time to keep them straight, both ways to the borders of the pattern. Deepen these guide lines just enough to get a clean uniform depth. Then you are ready to use the spacer tool. Starting with the guide grooves, cut the entire pattern, each fresh line guiding the next. Deepen the lines one way first, using checkering cutters to deepen, half to two-thirds full depth in softer wood, almost full in hard. Then do the crossing lines, and working each way alternately, deepen until the checkering comes up to points and is completed. Use a very soft, fine wire brush to keep the grooves clean while cutting them. Concentration must be constant, and hands steady, to prevent a tool from jumping a groove or crossing over.

When satisfied with the checkering and each line has been cleaned to the border, and the border line deepened at least to diamond depth—it can be deeper and wider than checkering lines of course, or made a double line, etc. Remove the protecting tape and give the job a final brushing. Then brush a slightly-thinned stock oil or well-thinned varnish into the checkering, and you are finished. If you can find cheap toothbrushes with very fine bristles, they will do.

Checkering can become fascinating; there are many amateur home gun artisans who have become very skillful at it. People either enjoy doing it or can't stand the thought of it after one trial!

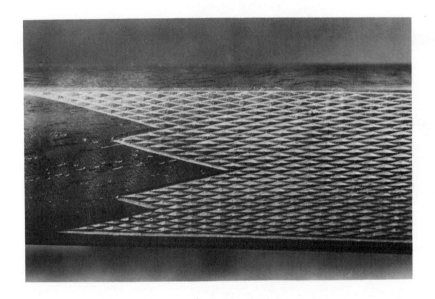

A detail of near perfect checkering. Notice that there are absolutely no runovers at the edge of the panel. This shows good worksmanship and care and adds considerably to the value of the work. If runovers do occur they can be hidden with a bordering tool.

The wood involved can have considerable bearing on the work. In all stock work, soft, poor wood is much harder to work on than good hard stuff with close grain; in checkering this is particularly true. The hard, fine-grain stock takes checkering very well, diamonds don't break during checkering as they will with coarse-grain wood, and the tool cuts cleaner and faster. When diamonds do break off, there's no real repair: you have to deepen all the checkering to get points on all of the diamonds. The actual checkering tools really saw the pointed grooves in the wood, and when they get dull, they'll tear out diamonds during the finishing stages, so, don't try to get too much mileage from the cutters.

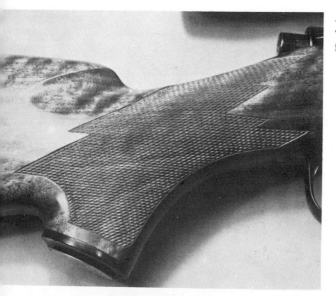

A detail of the grip pattern which matches the preceding fore-end pattern.

This is top-notch checkering by ace stockmaker Clayton Nelson, of Enid, Oklahoma.

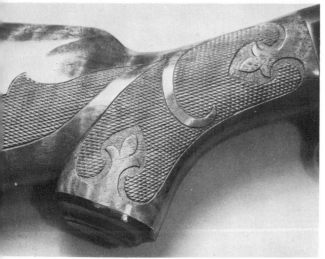

Examples of fancy checkering patterns done on a shotgun grip and fore-end (opposite page at top) by Jim Carmichel.

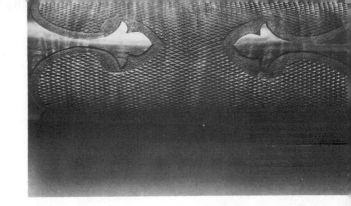

Stock Design

No book on the subject of firearm stocks should omit a discussion of stock design and engineering so that the firearms owner can gain some idea of how they affect him.

Stock design—shaping, proportions, dimensions—affect handling, aiming and accuracy of manually-handled arms whether they are pistols, revolvers, rifles or shotguns. The angle of the butt and the shape of grips on a pistol—the stock—determine whether it points naturally when aimed, or requires a consciously maintained bend of the wrist. The Colt single-action revolver and the Luger pistol have survived for generations because they handle well. They have good stock design.

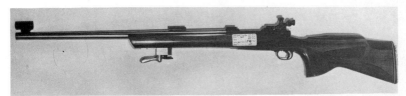

Left view of a well-known Dunlap target rifle. This stock style is extremely well accepted and one of the most successful designs.

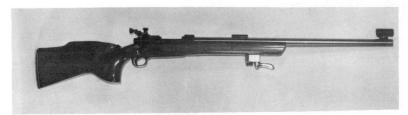

The right side of the Dunlap target rifle. The fore-end handstock assembly was also designed and manufactured by the author. This particular rifle was a Model 70 Winchester action in .308 caliber with a Douglas stainless-steel barrel.

239

With shotguns and rifles, buttstock design affects and is affected by recoil. The sight line on a shotgun is low, literally the top of the barrel: to get the sighting eye down to proper level, the comb, or top of the stock, must be proportionately low. When this low comb was carried on to the buttplate, very often a quite excessive drop was attained, that is,

A detail of a reworked Mauser action. Notice the gracefully altered bolt handle and the neat checkering on it. Also notice that the original Mauser safety has been replaced by one which operates very similarly to the Winchester Model 70 style. Notice further the reshaped trigger guard bow with the floorplate release button inside the front edge of the bow. This is a fine custom rifle.

This is very neatly done checkering in steel on a bolt knob by ace gunsmith Clayton Nelson. Checkering steel is very difficult but adds a nice touch.

a pronounced downward angle for the buttstock. While the design allowed guns to handle and point well enough, muzzle-jump and recoil were bothersome. It was not until the 1930's that shotgun stocks began to straighten out, following the lead of the deluxe models that received more engineering attention. Therefore, your late-made, prized Winchester Model 12 may be a dream to use, while shooting grandpa's Model 12 that he bought in 1919 with his mustering-out pay might be a nightmare! Cheekpieces on shotgun stocks have never become very popular, although many muzzle-loading guns had them, and many European guns are still made with them. The reason is that if the cheekpiece doesn't exactly fit the shooter's face, it belts him in the chops every time he fires. If it's too high or too low, it's bad. This is because the necessary drop for sighting contributes to the gun jumping, or recoiling up and back when fired. Imagine a wheel with your shoulder as the hub and the buttstock as a spoke: the barrel is at an angle to the spoke, so recoil being in line with the bore of barrel, straight back, it forces the spoke, or butt, up. The whole arm moves in an upward arc. The arc serves really to reduce the recoil against the shoulder, but the up-and-back force against your face hurts.

When the buttplate can be raised to the line of the bore, as in most modern military autorifles, recoil is a straight push back. Where powerful cartridges are used, spring or padded buttplates or a counteracting recoil system is needed to protect the firer. But the muzzle doesn't jump, so the arm is controllable.

The Monte Carlo, or raised-comb type of shotgun stock was designed to provide a better support for the cheek, yet allow sufficient drop to give fast butt placement on the shoulder in quick aerial shooting, as at clay and live pigeons.

To the modern rifleman, used to scope-height cheekpieces and full pistol grips, the old flint and percussion long rifles, and muzzleloaders in general for that matter, have horrible, ill-fitting stocks. The basic American long-rifle stock design, what we see on the Kentucky rifle, was developed in a short period in the middle 1700s to the demands of the frontiersmen. Muskets, even rifled muskets, were heavy, inaccurate, short-range arms. Stocks were metal-bound heavy affairs, and sights were just barrel aiming points as we know on shotguns.

The early American rifleman wanted an accurate arm he could kill game with up to 150 yards, light enough to carry, to be shot almost always from a standing position as he had to see over the underbrush and comfortable to shoot. The gunsmiths made the rifles long and slim: long barrels for balance and to burn black powder well, and comparatively light in weight. No one knew much about sights, but everyone had good eyes, so they made both front and rear sights very low. The style of shooting was head erect and back. Therefore, the buttstocks were sharply curved down so the barrel-top sighting plane could be seen. Deeply-curved small buttplates were developed that were

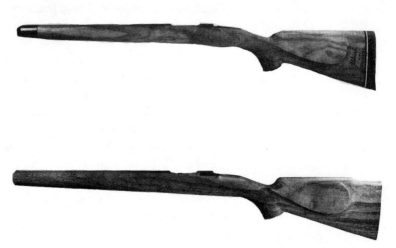

Top-quality stock designs, by Pachmayr Gun Works, for classic sporters and varmint rifles. The machine carving, by Petersen, is very good, inletting very close, so that finishing entails little labor.

never to be placed against the shoulder, but always on the upper arm. Since most rifles had hair- or set-type triggers, there was no need for a pistol grip or other shooting-hand support. The rifles had to be reloaded for each shot, so nobody cared about the muzzle bouncing far above the mark when a shot was fired. I am quite sure that the gunsmiths would have preferred to make stocks straighter and thicker just for strength, but the customers undoubtedly told them to "make 'em light or keep 'em."

In the 1830's the plains rifle developed, shorter barreled, stronger and straighter stocked. I believe the present great popularity of this "Hawken" type (the Hawken Brothers, of St. Louis, were the top makers of the original plains rifles) due to the fact that modern riflemen do not find them especially different to handle than modern rifles.

The bolt-action rifle was known for over thirty years before it became popular with sportsmen. A California gunsmith, Wundhammer, made a few sporter-type stocks for 1903 Springfields before World War I. They are crude affairs viewed today, and he is chiefly remembered as the originator of the "Wundhammer swell," a rounded bulge on the side of pistol grips to fill the palm-hollow of the hand. From 1920 on, with war-surplus bolt-action rifles selling cheaply, with Bob Owen and Tom Shelhamer developing the beautiful classic sporter stock design, rifles began to fit the shooters. Telescopic sights came slowly into use, and stocks developed raised cheekpieces so the shooter didn't have to hold his head up in the air, unsupported, to see through them.

Today we have an infinite variety for consideration: actions, stock designs, calibers and sighting equipment. What seldom occurs to many men is the fact that caliber can affect the choice or use of any or all of the other factors, especially the stock, due to design for recoil control. For example, say you purchase two Winchester M70 barreled actions. One is a .243, the other .300 Winchester Magnum. The .243 you custom-stock for deer and smaller game; it may have a feather-light stock with considerable drop and say, ¼-inch offset (the vertical center line of the butt is ¼ inch to the right of the bore line, on the right-hand side for a right-handed user) a high-power scope with short eye-relief and perhaps a shorter buttstock than normal so the rifle snaps up in sighting position very easily. The rifle handles perfectly, and you want nothing at all improved.

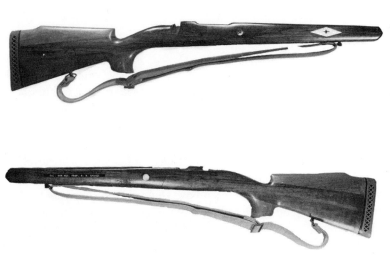

What can be done in remodeling. A military Mauser stock with pistol grip and high comb added, refinished, and recoil pad fitted.

For the Magnum, or it could be a .270 or .30/06, for getting a trophy mountain sheep at long range, you don't duplicate the .243 stock! It'll kill you: with pain. The larger cartridge needs a stock with a straighter butt, fore-end and pistol grip large enough to hold onto, a recoil pad, a cheekpiece exactly the right height to hold your eye in line with whatever scope is used (with a long scope, enough eye-relief not to dent your brow when it comes back!) and sloped so that in recoil it moves away from your face instead of into it.

A scope mounted too high or too low for the rifleman's cheekpiece–cheek relationship leads to poor shooting for the first, and facial punishment for the second. If the scope comes before the stock, you can

A Sile completely finished sporter stock, fully inletted. These are available for most varieties of Mausers, 1903 Springfield, 1917 Enfield, Sako, Savage 110, BSA and Lee-Enfields, for less than $30 delivered. The only work necessary is to open up barrel channel to fit your own barrel when it happens to be a little large for the small channel provided.

alter the design to suit the sight line and your face, of course. It is obvious that a person with a narrow, thin face needs more comb or cheekpiece than a man with wide, heavy face, just as a man 6-feet, 5-inches tall needs a longer butt than a man 5 feet 8 inches.

Yes, even the "pull' or butt length is a part of proper design. Years ago in a bull session, Jack O'Connor made a comment I have never forgotten: "Everyone wants his rifle stock too long and his shotgun stock too short!" This is too true too often. There should be an inch difference! The 14- to 14½-inch pull on the shotgun really means 13 to 13⅜ inches on the same man's rifle. For many years the normal factory rifle pull was 13$^7/_{16}$ to 13½ inches. So most people—and gunsmiths—copied it. This distance is correct, providing you are 6-feet 2-inches tall, have 33-or 34-inch sleeves in your shirts and plan to do a lot of prone shooting. The target-rifle business taught me that riflemen do much better with minimum-length buttstocks than those even a trifle long. Though I never saw the Air Force Marksmanship Unit in action, whose top-position shooting men worked themselves down to 9- and 10-inch pulls, it worked out that four out of five men needed 13¼-inch pull, the odd man usually needing less!

The hunter particularly should pay attention to butt length. Too many try to rifle in their shirt-sleeves, in warm weather with their muscles free and loose. With a ½ inch of clothing or for the cold-weather hunt, they can't move as easily and end up catching the buttplate under their armpit as the buck trots into the trees.

Men with very short arms, boys with small hands and women with both can have much trouble with standard stock designs found on over-the-counter arms. Just a stock-shortening may fix up the man, but the boy and woman probably need this plus a raised comb or cheekpiece and a smaller, closer pistol grip. I have never seen a "boy's rifle" or "boy's shotgun" that appeared to be designed by anyone who had ever seen a boy. Apparently the thought is to take a couple inches off each end and that's it.

It is no great problem to design a rifle for a boy eight to twelve years old—lightweight rifles, rimfire and varmint center-fire calibers are available, and for the latter, semi-inletted stocks in all price ranges. For a .22 rimfire sporter, buy an extra factory stock, or make one from a blank of lightweight wood. Take off the new stock and hang it on the wall—he'll grow to fit it in a few years. Shape the semi-inletted blank, or wood (get a low-priced target type if possible—they have wood to allow shaping a small, close pistol grip and higher-than-normal comb) and make a three-quarter-size stock for the boy. And don't forget to lighten the trigger pull. His fingers aren't nearly as strong as yours.

For the small lady, it may be possible to shape a sporter stock to fit from a semifinished target- or varmint-style stock made for the action in the same manner. If not, and you want to turn out a decent job yourself, sacrifice the existing factory stock on the gun. Ignore the length—but if it's already shortened, glue a piece of wood on to lengthen it to normal pull. Cut off the fore-end tip 1 inch, and glue on a 2-inch straight piece, shaped to the fore-end cross section and left square on the end. Scrape the finish off the cheekpiece or comb area and off the pistol grip. Then mix stiff fiberglass and build up the cheekpiece or comb area and the grip curve forward. Put on layer after layer of resin until you can reshape and smooth out the surfaces, bottom of the grip, etc., and obtain the stock contours you need with a hacksaw and files.

This stock is now a pattern, to be sent to one of the stockmaking firms for duplication. The carving and wood may cost $50 on up, depending on what grade wood you want, but you'll get back ninety-percent or better finished stock to your own prescription. The extra length at each end is required for the machine's holding centers to be driven into—you'll make the tip and butt length to suit the lady. Or else.

Target stocks are in many ways easier than sporters to work with, as fit and function are the main objectives. Nobody cares if it's pretty or shiny, just that it's reasonably presentable. The "varmint" stock is a sporterized prone target type, retaining the larger grip, cheekpiece and fore-end characteristics of the target designs to more-or-less extent in order to retain the holding and aiming comfort and efficiency, but otherwise reduced in dimensions and well finished. They can and are made in all degrees of appearance and design between target and sporter, thus presenting the gun owner with an opportunity to really take off on his own in design modification.

The conventional commercial target stock is primarily the prone type, which can be laboriously used for position shooting as well. However, it is really only one of four types, each with subdivisions. The true prone stock is custom or semicustom, usually distinguished by a large, close grip and a very high comb or cheekpiece, often so high that the top must be grooved for bolt operation and a section be detachable to permit the bolt to be removed from the rifle. It is shaped for perfect comfort in holding a rifle steady in the prone position only and is very often completely unusable in any other position. Shaped to grip, hold and support the head for long periods of time, it may look little like a conventional stock of any other type. My own prone design someone named the "canoe-paddle!" Asked how I came up with it, I told the truth: I inletted a rifle into a large blank, and then cut off all the wood I wasn't supporting, vice versa or that wasn't supporting the rifle. That's design by the cut-and-try method. Such special prone-position stocks have butts so high at the heel that under recoil they only move back a little. When used on magnum long-range rifles, the heavy barrels, overall weight and big stocks minimize recoil considerably.

Factory target rifles such as the Winchester 52 and 70 and Remington 40-X come with conventional general-use stocks of essentially prone design, although they're usable for position work. Winchester, incidentally, now makes the pull length on their M70 target rifle 13¼ inches. None of these factory target stocks have cheekpieces. Necessarily made for a universal average-man fit, they can't fit everyone, of course. Simple alterations on length and comb height may be needed, and epoxy-bedding is a must.

The free rifle or international-competition stock, with its adjustable buttplates, hand supports on the grip and palm rest for shooting standing, is the most functional of all types in that the shooter assumes his comfortable prone, standing or kneeling position and adjusts the rifle so the sights are on the target. All he does is steady the arm and try to get the ultralight trigger off when centered. Buttplates shorten and lengthen, move up and down, etc., so that a well-designed free rifle will adjust to suit the physique of the shooter. The Russian-made Strela .22 has elevation and windage adjustment on the front sight as well as rear—the rear can use apertures in a high or low position, as well as normal micrometer adjustment—the butt can be lengthened and otherwise adjusted. The rifleman can be fat or thin, short or tall, and the rifle adjusted to fit.

Free-rifle stocks customarily have a thumb rest on the side of the grip and also a hole through the grip for the thumb, moderately high, and straight cheekpieces so the eye will be in line with the sights whether the head is held forward as in a prone position, or back for standing. The pistol grips are usually altered by the shooter for his most comfortable holding; some have an adjustable shelf on the side to support the weight of the hand. Palm rests are attachable fore-end grips or handles for the left hand (in the case of a right-handed shooter) to support the rifle in standing position without strain on the arm muscles. These can be and are of all shapes, sizes and materials, representing individual choice and design. There are countless variations in design of such stocks and accessories, all trying to make fit and comfort in shooting a little better.

U. S. riflemen, that is, the .22-caliber competitors, have evolved another target class: the "position" rifle, originally used mostly for four-position—prone, sitting, standing and kneeling—indoor gallery shooting, but now widely used outdoors as well. These may be conventional target types with adjustable hook and prone buttplates that are interchangeable and removable, with palm rests added, and perhaps the butt and grip remodeled for more comfort in the standing position; or semi-free-rifle types, having the thumbhole stocks and all or some of the accessories and features of the free rifle, but most often lacking the expensive, refined light-pull trigger systems, which are not permitted in all the position competitions. To one interested in beginning position shooting, the sky is the limit on experimenting with stock design.

The last stock design to mention is for the offhand target rifle, seldom used today, although a National Single-Shot Rifle Association is growing slowly. The offhand rifle, fired only in standing postion, is a descendant of the pioneer's long rifle by way of the German scheutzen target game, which flourished in the U. S. until World War I. They feature long, heavy barrels that "hang" or hold well, supported by buttstocks with considerable drop, high cheekpieces and hook or deeply-curved buttplates.

These stocks offer much to the person interested in making stocks both functional and ornamental. Carving and checkering are utilized often, and shaping of the cheekpiece, grip, etc., can follow individual preferences. The rifles are most often single-shot falling-block designs, old or new, so only the short buttstock and separate fore-end need be considered. You can buy these in fancy wood for a fraction of what a one-piece bolt-rifle blank of the same grade will cost. Of course, there's no law against stocking a bolt gun with an offhand stock if you just like to work in wood!

This brings us full circle, for a sporter, or hunting rifle, really is an offhand rifle stocked for sporting use and easy transport.

14

Metalworking

Tools

Metalworking as applied to firearms ranges from the simplest alteration
to ultradifficult design modification in the field of invention, which in
the case of firearms is modification since literally every principle involved was originally developed years ago. The gun owner/home gunsmith, unless able to use and own or have access to a lathe and milling
machine—the most expensive tools needed—will limit himself to the
comparatively low-cost drill press and belt sander added to the bench
grinder and hand tools. These will suffice to do nearly all minor metal-
work aspired to, such as making flat parts, accessories, finishing up semifinished parts for muzzle-loading arms, etc. If he—you—can collect a
band sander as well, it can be a great help for polishing and shaping
rounded metal parts, from screw heads to revolver and shotgun frames
in preparation for blueing—and, in addition, make stock sanding almost
a pleasure! Where shop space is very limited, a band sander—also a disk
sander for that matter—can be mounted on portable stands, stored in
the shop and carried outside to be used. And so serve the very valuable
end of keeping wood, rubber and metal dust out of the shop.

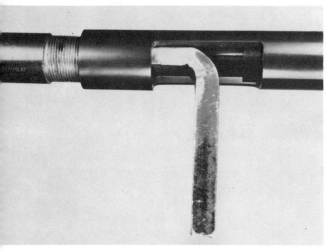

The "inside" wrench must be used on round receivers such as this Remington. The bent-over lip of the tool-steel bar must be filed to a close fit when pushed into the lug runways of the receiver. If it can move around, it can mar them.

A small, shaky drill press such as generally sold for do-it-yourself home shops isn't really the one to buy: these are primarily for wood and very light metal use. For the same amount of money, it is usually possible to get a used ½-inch/12-inch bench standard light industrial type with a 2½-inch or larger column. The designation means it will drill a ½-inch hole in steel, with the bit 12 inches from the column. The floor type, allowing long work to be drilled, as in the butt or fore-end tip of the stock, is perhaps more desirable, but it's scarcer and more expensive, and if the bench model is mounted on a corner of the bench or stand,the head can be swung out over the edge for such work. Holding the work, however, may require an ingenious setup.

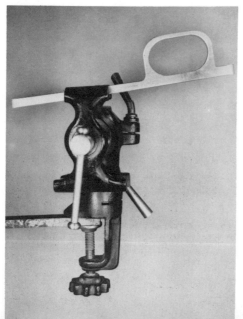

An all-angle vise that allows work to be held in almost any position is valuable when working on parts which have to be filed or hand-polished. Here the one-piece aluminum trigger guard for a single-shot rifle is in the vise.

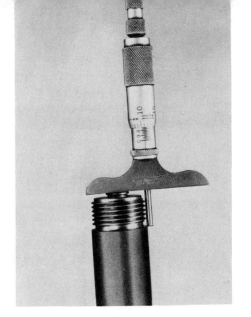

Preliminary headspace or fit of a pre-chambered barrel is checked by depth-micrometer, with gauge, or with new cartridge case in chamber and distance measured to shoulder on the barrel. This distance must be very close to that from front face of receiver to face of the bolt in closed position in the receiver measured by the micrometer.

The large belt sander, using 48-inch belts 6 inches wide, is primarily a wood-shop tool and has valuable but limited use for arms woodworking in shaping fore-ends, tips, ends of butts for pads, etc. However, it has even more use for shaping and polishing flat metal parts. Fine-grit belts, filled with wax or tallow, will polish any metal and give very nearly as true a flat surface as a surface grinder. Coarser belts will even chew away steel as nearly as fast as the grinding wheels on the bench grinder. Brass and aluminum can be shaped and finished in a fraction of the time required by other means.

These tools—drill press, sanders, bench grinder, along with the hand equipment and a propane torch—will allow production of replace-

The large belt sander does a lovely job cleaning up octagon barrels, though you need strong fingertips to bring them on and off the moving belt without canting faces. Photo shows a cleaned-up barrel and one not yet worked on.

These are the two most useful drilling vises, the adjustable-angle one at left and the flat job with sides ground square.

The square-sided vise holding a muzzle-loading barrel vertically through center hole in table. The piloted counterbore can clear out the bore hole to proper diameter for threading the top for the bolster or breech plug. The drill is just used to start the hole and make counter-boring easier. Long pilot on counterbore guarantees concentricity.

ment gun parts, springs, alteration and adaptation of various sights, scope mounts, etc., and well-done finishing of semifinished and rough-cast muzzle-loading gun parts of all types—even the complete manufacture of many. The drill press can become a multipurpose machine, there are books devoted to this one tool and its capabilities. However, the cost of special attachments is high and usually is not justified by an

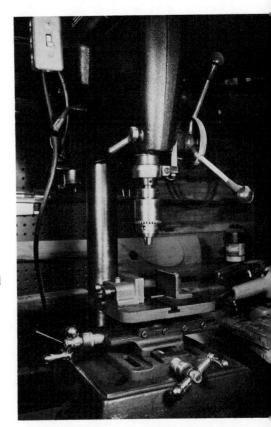

A milling attachment for drill press, useful for making small metal parts and tools. Drill must operate at fairly low rotational speed.

individual gun worker's needs for his own arms. For metal, the speed reduction attachments for light milling, the milling table and cutters will add up to 150 dollars or more, a high price for one or two jobs a year. The standard small drilling vise, several models of which are made by Palmgren, is an absolute necessity. Get the adjustable type which can be set and locked to hold the work from zero to ninety degrees to the drill bit.

Small Parts

The making of replacement small parts is on the increase, for original factory-made parts are unobtainable for many arms still in use and usable for many years to come. Round parts such as firing pins may be duplicated—if the correct diameter of steel drill rod is available—by hand shaping, holding in a drill-press chuck for final polishing, etc., or even made of any soft-steel round stock and then case- or surface-hardened by Kasenite or other similar product. These are carbonizing agents. A part made of soft steel is heated red hot then dipped in the powder which cooks onto and into it, forming a thick coating. After a minute, the part is then again heated by torch until red hot and then dropped into cold water. The surface is file-hard and wear-resistant, and the undersurface is malleable, making the part almost impossible to break. A dark face shield should be worn while doing such work, as the hardening agents burn with very bright flame during the second heating.

The drill press used for first operation on a rough casting for percussion-gun hammer, cutting the recess in nose so it can safely and properly hit the cap. Clamped in hardwood wedges, the irregular shape can be held for preliminary drilling, then the bottom of recess flattened with squared-off bit. (This hole looks off-center and it is, except that the "thick" side is due to a flared-out edge which has to be filed off, after which the hole will be in the middle).

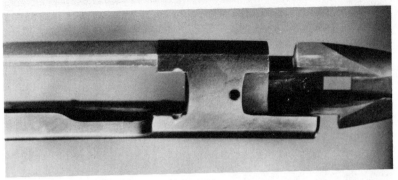

The clip-loading slot in M70 Winchester, for .30/06 use. Lay out with a simple aluminum pattern copied from a factory target model having the slots, and locate with screws in the existing holes in receiver. Layout coloring on the receiver permits the outlines of slot and recesses to be scribed, after which holes can be drilled to remove metal. The recesses of course are only to half depth and finished with flat-bottom bit to arrest the cartridge clip by its side extrusions, or detents.

Flat parts are laid out on flat stock of appropriate thickness that has been painted with layout dope—red or blue quick-drying paints made for the job. You could possibly mix your own with alcohol and coloring, or perhaps the remnant of an old lipstick. Outline the outside borders with center-punch marks so that you can drill small holes almost touching each other. Then the part-to-be can be broken out of the main piece of the stock and filed to shape. When the original part has one or more holes in it, use it for a drill jig and drill holes of the same size in the stock before layout. Then use the dope, put the old part on top of the metal bar or plate and use pins or drill bits to hold the two while marking the outline. Where straight lines are possible, a hacksaw would naturally be used for cutting to outlines.

Where a part has to replace a missing one so there is no pattern to go by, first try to borrow a similar firearm and study its parts. If that's not possible, find an old parts list showing the part. Someone you know is bound to have some old catalogs! While you may find a good illustration, it will have no dimensions: so, take some aluminum if possible, plastic if not, and start making dummies. The third one should either be the right size or tell you what the right size should be.

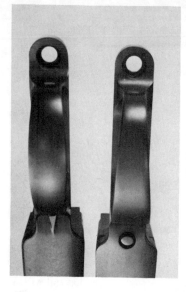

Trigger-guard remodeling is an easy and satisfying home job. At left is a commercial FN Mauser narrowed at both ends; at right, a military Mauser altered to the old "express" type, tapered from front to back. A bit of metal has been soldered to the release button, to protrude through hole and therefore allow removal of the floorplate by finger pressure alone.

A bolt fixture made by Ron DeWarf for engine-turning bolts, using standard nuts, bolts, bits of aluminum bar stock and threaded rod. Only the part entering rear of bolt requires use of a lathe, all others can be made by saw, file, and drill press.

The arbor or collet used in drill press to hold the Brightboy (rubber-bonded abrasive) rod producing the turning marking.

Work for advanced amateur gunsmith: firing pin lightened by grooving, and cocking piece altered to speed-lock Mauser action. Close-up of cocking piece shows how top must be cut back in order to allow a normal military or replacement scope-use safety to function in locking the firing-pin assembly.

Very often gun parts need not be duplicated perfectly as to shape. Shapes may have been dictated by milling setups or multiple-part holding fixtures to facilitate production in the factory. In fact, replacement parts can often be made that are far superior to the originals. I have always worked on the reasoning that when a part broke at an obviously weak point it was ridiculous to make a duplicate with the same obviously weak point. If it was at all possible to increase dimensions and so gain strength, I did it. So, check receiver-clearance cuts and functioning movements of adjoining parts to see if your replacement cannot be made better than the one that broke. Make firing-pin tips to fit their holes in frames, receivers and bolt faces and try them by hand without springs to make sure they cannot bind or stick. The body diameters of round pins and thickness of flat pins must be an easy slide fit, not sloppy. If they're too thin, they'll bind and eventually break.

Refinishing

Much metalworking for the individual comes in connection with refinishing, usually reblueing of arms. While I cannot recommend that anyone should go as far as to set up a complete hot-blue facility because of its complete inconvenience 99.9 percent of the time, I do recommend that one do his own preparation. This, the cleaning, polishing,

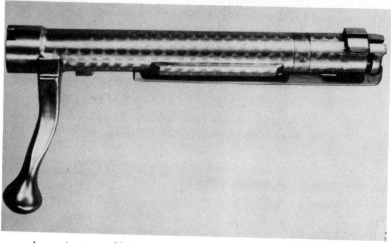

An engine-turned bolt, as good in appearance as any commercial job.

possible reshaping and alteration, are all time-consuming, and cause the high cost of commercial refinishing. And they are almost completely responsible for the appearance after finishing. You, the gun owner, can afford to spend many odd hours in hand-polishing and keep flat surfaces flat and edges sharp, where a professional too often leans the arm against a buffing wheel and polishes it bright in minutes—and rounds off edges, "saucers" pin and screw holes (making little hollows or saucers at their entrance and egress holes), and in general makes the frame or receiver appear as though a metal-eating giant had used it for an all-day sucker.

The band sander will polish rounded surfaces such as the tops of pump-action receivers, rifle receivers, revolver-grip back and front straps as well as almost all of the revolver frame excepting the flat sides and side-plate cuts. The belt sander with fine-grit waxed belts will clean up flat-sided receivers and parts, leaving only the final polishing for handwork with worn cloth and paper over file or smooth hardwood block. The hand grinder with rubber-grit "points" will clean out small hollows—cylinder flutes, in and around trigger-guard loops, etc., ready for final hand polishing by worn cloth over small dowels or wooden wedges. A greasily-smooth finish can be obtained quite rapidly. Wiped clean and inspected closely in strong light it will be a surface of minute scratches. Don't worry about buffing them out. If all these microscopic marks run the same way, when blued the finish will be beautiful! This is really the secret of good bluing. This may be disputed by those who can only approve a heavily-buffed mirror polish before blueing, and its resulting high shine afterward, but believe me, the hand-polish finish as described will look better longer.

Alterations to metal are of course done before final polishing: changing the contours of receiver tops, tangs on rifles and shotguns, grip shapes on handguns, trigger-guard remodeling, etc. In fact these should be the first jobs done in a refinishing program—after complete disassembly, of course! Next, strip the parts in a fifty–fifty water–muriatic acid solution, which will wash off the old blue. No large amount of acid is required—a small wide-mouthed jaw holding a pint is sufficient. Small parts can be dipped on wire hooks; larger have ends immersed and acid brought over exposed areas by a small cotton-cloth swab wired on a dowel. Thirty seconds is usually enough time in acid. Dip or wash off parts in plain water, rub with wet fine steel wool to get stubborn spots clean and do over if needed. The naked steel will be gray, rust will be eaten out of pits—and what you thought was a nice smooth surface doesn't look so smooth now. Refer to the above, "if all the marks run the same way, it'll look good."

Acid-cleaned steel is ready to rust instantly. Therefore, use long tweezers or make up swabs holding wads of fine (4/0) steel wool, and af-

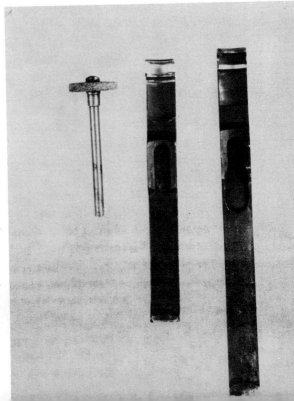

Part substitution: Pre-1964 Winchester Model 70 extractors are very expensive and probably will not be available many more years; 1903 Springfield extractors were made by millions and can be had for a few cents. Use of a hand grinder with stone ⅝" or so in diameter to widen groove between extractor lip and bolt-location lip easily fits the '03 extractor to the old M70 bolt, as illustrated. The shorter extractor is entirely satisfactorily in functioning.

ter drying the metal—insides of frames, primarily—use the wool, with oil on it, to scrub the nooks and crannies. Wash in solvent, dry, then oil inside areas, and you won't have to worry about rust while doing the outside polishing.

Long magazine tubes should have any bad burrs or longitudinal scratches cleared by light filing or sharp abrasive cloth over file, and then polished on the band sander. If you don't have a band sander, a grooved sanding block backing cloth or paper will do. In any case, a final hand job to run all polishing marks lengthwise must be done.

The same applies to barrels, though the acid cleaning is more important than with the tubes. Plug the muzzle so it may be placed in the acid container while the solution is applied all over the barrel by swab. Do not try to remove dents with a file or sander, however. This will create a depression or ring around the barrel which will show up after re-blueing. Appearance will be better if the dent is left in, and the overall surface of the barrel is polished.

Very occasionally a plated handgun will require refinishing. The only way to go is to completely disassemble, put wires on all plated parts and take them to a commercial plating firm. Every town of size has a company that refinishes auto bumpers. Have them deplate the parts, a simple reverse of plating, done electrically. Now you can polish and clean up nicks, etc., and make components ready for replating or reblueing. If the former, the auto outfit may be willing to plate with cadmium or chromium. If so, make sure they are familiar with plating small objects, know enough to protect threaded holes, etc. Should silver or gold finish be wanted, look up one of the gunsmiths advertising for such work and send it to him. For finishing blue, there's no problem. The secret is in the deplating: it is literally impossible to polish off old plating completely by hand or machine.

For any real blueing, I can only advise sending prepared parts, oiled against rust, to a man or firm doing blueing commercially. Since all he has to do is degrease and blue, he won't charge much. Should you be determined to do it all yourself, get a hot-blue outfit from Bob Brownell or Christy Gun Works and follow their directions. Tanks and heating units should be in a room of their own, or outside where the wind can blow away corrosive fumes.

I know of no easy-use cold blue that will give a decent finish to an entire arm today; however, many firms are furnishing the touch-up types and working better ones so we may have a breakthrough any time, and a first-class finish be available to all.

The muzzle-loading man can have a great time making up complete arms with such equipment. The big belt sander makes short work of polishing the flats on octagon barrels, for instance. Except for a forge, he has more and better tools than the pioneer gunsmiths who made complete guns. And, if he has progressed to this stage of equipment and work, he can go all the way and do the finish. Earlier I cautioned against trying to mix browning solutions, and the beginning amateur gunsmith should not. However, there is one which will give a good brown finish, equal to that on the finest antique rifles, on modern steel. Mix the following:

four-ounces sweet spirits of nitre
four ounces alcohol—grain or sugar
one-quarter-ounce mercuric chloride (110 grains on powder scale).

Shake it up, and it's ready to use. Use a small cotton-cloth swab to lay it on the metal, which must be thoroughly degreased first. It will dry rapidly. Allow metal twelve hours, then apply a second coat. Continue coats twice a day for a week, but after the first three, before applying the next, use the 4/0 steel wool to rub metal, lengthwise on barrel flats. Should you rub too hard and remove the beginning brown, further coats of the solution will restore the thin spots and corners. With time and patience, a very good brown can be achieved. Mercuric chloride is extremely poisonous and should be handled with great care. In the solution it can be handled with just ordinary care—at least I've had the solution on my fingers without damage to them, though I always washed them immediately in one of the cleaning solvents and then in water.

Raw Materials

General small metals working jobs such as making replacement pins, threading holes or screws, etc., are only difficult in that it is often hard to come by the raw material. Good steel is needed and probably in a decimal diameter just a little off a standard fractional size that might be more readily obtainable. One source is the use of small bolts (not "stove" bolts, obtainable at any hardware store), purchasing a long type not threaded all the way and utilizing the unthreaded shank for your material. Allen-head bolts are nearly always heat-treated and very strong, and may have to be annealed (heated and allowed to cool slowly) before work can be done on their steel.

Small pins, even shotgun firing pins, and screws shaped for threading can be made with use of a chuck attachment on the end of a bench-grinder shaft. These chucks cost only a dollar or two, and can be attached to any electric motor shaft. They are made for ½- and ⅝-inch shafts. The round stock can only be held by one end, and can be shaped by holding files against it, polished by cloth under the files, etc.

In the matter of cutting threads try to obtain a true cutting oil—made for the purpose, sold by industrial-supply firms under various trade names applying to threading and reaming. The common pipe-threading oil isn't as good, though it's far better than motor oil, etc. These cutting aids really do help. Dies and taps cut clean threads, last longer, and break seldom since they stay sharp.

Flat steel for parts making is always a problem in that even if you wish to go first-class and use tool steel, nobody will have your size in stock, and you'll have to wait for it. It's known as ground flat stock, and it comes in 18-inch lengths of all thicknesses and widths, including fractional dimensions. The wrapper will have heat-treating information: whether it is oil or water hardening, etc. The same dimensions can be had in ordinary cold-rolled steel, but the length is 12 feet. When you need only a couple of square inches this is a little redundant. Hit the

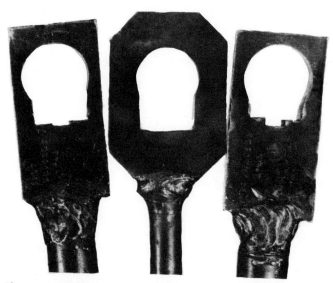

If you must do barrel work, you may have to make one of these receiver wrenches: Enfield (1917), M70 Winchester, and Mauser large-ring. The last type should be used on forged receivers.

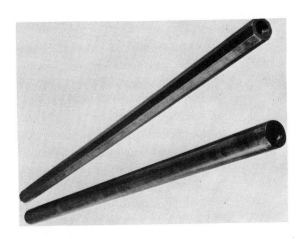

Barrel blanks for the lathe owner. Such straight, unfinished blanks are sold at low prices compared to turned, contoured and polished barrels, and the man with a lathe and the time can do all this himself.

nearest welding shops and machine shops, tell them your requirements and ask to root around in the scrap boxes. You'll probably go home loaded down, with their compliments.

The man who has or has the use of a lathe and knows how to operate it naturally has no problems in fixing up small bolts, screws, pins, etc. And of course he can progress to barrel turning and shaping from blanks, fitting to actions by threading, and chambering if he has the reamers for the cartridge concerned. If he wants to do barrelwork, however, he'll also need a barrel vise, the special screw-down clamp-type made for the purpose, and, if he doesn't want to damage receivers, he'll have to make himself receiver wrenches. Standard vises and pipe wrenches just won't do the job right!

Rifle barrelwork is standard machine-shop threading practice as far as fitting to the receiver goes, but chambering is a bit more difficult, requiring not only experience in keeping reamers properly sharp and clean-cutting but practice in their use. However, investment in reamers and gauges can be saved. For the past several years custom barrelmakers have been furnishing finish-yourself barrels, already threaded for the receiver and chambered for the cartridge. Douglas, Wilson, Manley and others furnish a wide selection of lengths, weights and calibers, Wilson perhaps the most complete line. These barrels are threaded and chambered a little long so they may be headspaced to fit individual rifle actions. A lathe is required for final fitting, the barrel being shortened at the breech end, and if necessary, the shoulder ahead of the threads moved forward a few thousandths of inch at a time until, threaded into the receiver, the bolt will close on the correct gauges. Without gauges, use a new unfired cartridge case. The bolt should close on it freely, but not close when a 0.010-inch (or say, .006-inch) shim is placed between

263

the bolt face and the cartridge-case head. These barrels cannot be furnished with extractor cuts made, so when the rifle requires this, such as 1903 Springfield or an old-type Winchester 70, the cut location must be marked on the barrel breech or cone, the barrel removed and the cut made by file and hacksaw to duplicate that of the old factory barrel.

There is an alternative, not requiring use of lathe, but calling for a finishing chambering reamer. These makers will supply fully-threaded barrels with short chambers; the barrel is screwed in tight, and then the reamer with extension handle is used to deepen the chamber until the bolt will close on the cartridge case or gauge. Most finish reamers sold have a throating section on them so they cut a seat or clearance for the bullet in the rifling ahead of the chamber. Never use a cartridge for checking headspace, however. The throat may grab the bullet early, before the shoulder of the cartridge reaches the shoulder of the chamber. Keep on cutting until the bullet is clear and you may create considerable excess headspace. Use cases without bullets for checking.

15

Welding, Soldering and Brazing

The joining of metals by heat processes is not always understood by the layman, and as it is or can be utilized in much firearms work we should be familiar with it. Welding is actual fusing together—melting together—similar metals, as steel to steel, aluminum to aluminum, etc., by bringing contacting edges to liquid state so they run together. A rod of the same metal, or close to it in an alloy, is generally used to add molten metal to the joint and bring the area of weld to full surface dimensions. Welding may be by acetylene (carbide gas) combining with oxygen, both under pressure, uniting and burning at the touch tip. This is the common oxyacetylene type: Temperatures over 5000 degrees F are produced, twice as high as needed to melt iron and ordinary steels. Varied and advanced similar processes employ other gases, some noninflammable, in shielding the weld area from outer air during fusion to protect against contamination causing defective fusion in special alloys, etc. Thus one may read of nitrogen and hydrogen welding and wonder.

Electrowelding is by arc—metal to be joined is placed with edges touching and connected with one side of a powerful electric current, the other side being connected to an insulated rod holder or a clamp held by the welder. When the rod is brought in contact with the work an arc—a short circuit—is made, of such intensity that the metal melts at point of contact. Rods, technically electrodes, are made in countless alloys to suit the material to be welded and are usually coated with a hard flux which burns to clean the weld as it goes. Electrowelding has also advanced from this basic system, the most common improved type being known as Heliarc. This type of welding uses uncoated rods with helium under pressure to keep the normal atmosphere and its oxygen content away from the weld. Oxygen not only burns, but combines with everything else; that's not always desirable. Rust is simple oxidation of steel or iron, for example. Under high temperatures, oxygen combines with metal ingredients and impurities to form scale on the welded surface which must be removed. Excess metal must be welded in so that the scaled areas can be completely machined down without making the weld area too thin or undersize. With the Heliarc system, extreme heat is applied only to the edges of parts being joined, the elimination of oxygen prevents scaling almost completely and little metal above the surface of the joint need be added. This is by far the best system for any gun-welding jobs.

Now that I've said what welding is, I say don't bother with it. Welding is a skilled trade that requires knowledge of metals and techniques in the handling of equipment gained only by training and experience, and the equipment is expensive. A Heliarc installation costs as much as a new car. Yet, for fifty dollars you can obtain small electrowelding setups to run off house current and do small jobs. They're not good enough for gun work, so don't be tempted. Take any welding jobs to the welding shops.

Brazing and soldering are another story indeed. Small propane gas torches are produced just for the home shops, are easy to use and are very handy in many gun emergencies. They develop sufficient heat for brazing—melting brass, copper and silver—heating soldering irons (should be copper!) and using on small steel parts for annealing, hardening and tempering.

Brazing is joining metals, similar or different, by means of a layer of soft metal melted between them and sticking to both. It is also sometimes refered to as "hard soldering." The surfaces to be joined must be physically and chemically clean, the latter by means of a flux—either powder or liquid—applied to the metal before or during heating. Ordinary borax is the common flux for common brass work, the brass rod being heated a little and dipped in powdered borax, which cooks onto it to form a coating. Both are then melted onto the joint to be brazed.

Silver solders are silver–copper alloys, are white or gray, have refined paste fluxes easy to use and are in general most useful for gun applications. Types are made with melting points as low as 800 degrees, but most run 1100 degrees or more. A silver-soldered joint is very strong. Many broken gun parts can be repaired with the process, although the necessary heat used will draw carbon from the steel and leave a case-hardened or hardened carbon-steel part soft.

It is seldom that broken parts, or small assemblies to be put together, can be clamped so that rods, wires or sheet solder can be applied during heating. In most cases the separate pieces will be cleaned, edges fluxed, and a small piece of the solder laid on the joint. Then all are heated until the solder melts and runs down between the pieces. When a sleeve or two cylindrical parts are to be joined, all contacting surfaces are fluxed, run together, with a little V groove at the visible junction. Small segments of silver solder or brass wire are laid into the V groove, and the assembly is heated until the solder runs down between all surfaces. Solder-on shotgun-choke bases, as per the Cutts Compensator type, are installed in this manner: the barrel is held vertical in the vise, solder laid in the groove between the barrel and choke base at the muzzle and melted down by a torch applying heat around the base—not directly on the solder.

The sweat-joint system is a little difficult to do with the hard solders, but in many instances it may be the only way. Say a lug on the shotgun barrel for the magazine tube or other fitting breaks loose and needs to be reattached. The original brazing job failed because of insufficient heat or an unclean surface. If considerable brass or silver remains from the first try, the job is easy: just clean with solvents then with a wisp of cloth in the tweezers, dipped in muriatic acid, being careful not to run any on the blue adjoining. Clamp the part in place, contacting surfaces fluxed and heat with torch until a bright line at the edge indicates that the solder has melted. Where you must add metal, the job can be a trifle difficult. Clean the part, clamp it, flux, heat it and any bar of metal, old screwdriver, etc. at same time. When hot, apply solder which will form a ball, and use the hot metal tip of bar or screwdriver to spread it around. You want a thin coating of metal. Then proceed with the clamping and attachment to barrel or other part, tightening clamping if possible at the moment the solder is completely fluid.

The most widely-used silver solder is probably Easy-Flo 45, a brand carried by welding-supply firms. Sil-Flo is another. Paste or semi-liquid fluxes are furnished and can be thinned with water. The $^1/_{16}$-inch diameter wire solder is the most useful form for the gun shop.

Not being affected by any of the corrosive blueing solutions, silver solder was used by many gunsmiths for attachment of front sight ramps when every hunting rifle had to have a ramp front sight. I always hated the job, not because of possible damage to the rifle barrel though heating it, but because it was hard to get ramps on straight. Straight for the shooter, that is! I put it on with squares, levels, straightedges so that it's perfect. But hand it to the customer and he takes one look and says "it points left a bit; please make it straight up and down." So I used band ramps with lock screws that could be turned to suit. Only now, there are no more band ramps on the market. And making a ramp sight base with a band to fit the specific barrel calls for considerable labor.

Therefore, a sweat-on ramp may be called for when a ramp is wanted, and the screw-attaching ones are not wanted. If a good clamping arrangement is worked out, it is possible to omit the plating with solder of one or both surfaces and use a narrow strip of ribbon silver solder between cleaned, fluxed and clamped parts, and then heat and increase clamp pressure. Whenever possible on barrel jobs of any type, use one of the special low-melting-point solders made for use with Prest-O-Lite or other propane torches—these will not work when heated by acetylene torches.

Write to ARC Products Manufacturing Division, Chemetron Corporation, 840 N. Michigan Ave., Chicago, Ill. 60611, for their All-State manual and catalog, listing all sorts of such products—430- and 509-degree silver-bearing solders, etc.

Interiors of barrels should be protected against possible scale and surface roughing that might result from excessive heat. This is not difficult since it is only necessary to make up a mixture of lampblack (carbon black) flour, salt and water and coat the inside of the barrel under the areas to be heated. Use one part black, two parts salt, one and a half flour and enough water to make a thin paste. It will prevent scaling and surface-burning of steels right up to cherry-red heats—1600 degrees—which should never be reached on any part of any gun barrel. Dry and hardened remnants of this scale-preventative must be scoured out of bores as soon as the metal is cool.

Common soft-soldering with lead–tin alloys is the same as brazing in concept. Joints are not nearly so strong, of course, and the solders are subject to attack by many corrosive agents. They will literally dissolve in any of the normal hot-blueing solutions that use caustic soda—lye—and nitrate. However, there are many useful shop applications for soft-soldering on tools, temporary fixtures and jigs, etc. Or to join a broken part so it may be used as a pattern to make a replacement. In this particular connection paste solders are very useful. These are pastes of powdered solder and flux. Just coat broken edges with the stuff and heat to form a joint.

All sorts of low-melting-point solders are made, to flow at varying temperatures from 400 to 600 degrees F, and presumably some with bismuth to melt at even lower temperatures, which I've never been able to find. The fluxes are rosin or acid. The rosin types are suited for soft metals—the common rosin-core wire solder is best used for copper-wire electrical connections, not gun-shop work. Acid flux is much the better, and can be purchased in small containers or made up. It is really zinc chloride, made by dissolving zinc in muriatic acid. Salvage a bit of zinc from an old battery and make your own. Buy acid brushes—tin-handled natural bristle—from welding-supply or hardware stores.

Soldering coppers, usually called irons, can be simple small types to be heated by torch or stove, or an electric heating-unit type. Since the lead solders can't stand the heat of direct torch flame, they are usually applied by the iron or copper being heated until the solder will melt and adhere to it for transport to the material to be soldered, the idea being that the iron will also heat the material sufficiently for the soldering to take place. Preheating by the torch will be necessary on large metal masses. Both iron and work are to be fluxed.

Double-barreled shotguns were once put together with soft solders, and probably nearly all the side-by-side doubles still made are so joined. On an old gun, either the top or bottom rib may come unsoldered, usually for a couple of inches at the muzzle. Resoldering can be trying, but is not really difficult. Clean under the spread ribs with steel wool swabs and hot water, allow to dry and then carefully acid-flux the solder remaining on the underedges of the rib and barrel, being careful not to touch the exposed blued areas as the flux will remove the blue. There should be enough original solder left to make a hold if reheated. If it looks pretty sparse, put in some paste solder or shavings from wire solder. For heating, I use copper or brass rods, ½-inch diameter and square, on the ribs, clamp the whole together with wire wound tightly around the barrels and rods and then heat these rods with a torch.

The torch can be used to do heat-blueing on screw heads, receiver tangs or any part where steel strength cannot be affected by heating. The part is just heated slowly until it turns blue—600 to 800 degrees F. Today most such jobs are done by the cold touch-up blues, but the heat-blueing may be better for some applications. It is usually a light, almost transparent true blue, ideal for matching screws and small parts on old guns, which may have had the original finish done just the same way.

The parts are heated, then wiped with a patch saturated in whatever oil or mixture you want to try. I remember one of mine was linseed oil and Hoppe's No. 9! Experiment and you can come up with minor jobs of color case-hardening.

In using heat in any form while working, take precautions. Have a container—pan—of water handy, with a saturated cloth in it, never work without a face shield and never without ventilation. A little burning acid may clear your sinus nicely, but too much isn't good for you. A couple of bricks and cheap clamps will do for holding the work, but they stay hot much longer than the work does, and since it is difficult to work with gloves on, you simply must train yourself to handle everything with long tweezers and pliers.

I have mentioned tweezers often, and should make it clear that these are working tools, not what your wife uses on her eyebrows. You can buy large types made for general bench use, or make them yourself. Take a worn-out cheap hacksaw blade; break and grind the teeth off completely—these usually have only one hardened edge. Heat with a torch in the middle until red and then bend around anything ⅜ to ½ inch in diameter. After bending, shape tips as you prefer—pointed, square, rounded, make tip or parallel contact, etc. If there is not enough spring to them, again heat the bend until red, dip in oil and immediately burn the oil off. This should give enough of a spring-temper to make them effective.

There are dangers in using heat and acid mixtures, of course, but compared to being at a service station heavy with gasoline vapors amid people lighting cigarettes and grinding on electric starters, even a welding shop seems pretty safe.

16

Modernizing
Military Arms

For forty-five years, beginning in 1920 and really ending in the mid-1960's, remodeling and rebuilding surplus military rifles and to a small degree, military handguns, was the main industry of the home gunsmith. This is still with us to some extent since large stocks of all types of foreign surplus arms dating back to the 1880's have been imported into the U. S. and are yet on sale. However, the practice has dropped, primarily I believe because the American gun owner has become familiar with the most modern sporting arms and affluent enough to afford them. He wants a light, streamlined rifle, with a fast lock time and a good trigger.

Remaking an old Mauser or Springfield to compare with a 700 Remington can be done only with the expenditure of extra money, as well as time, for professional gunsmithing such as altering bolt handles, for complete trigger systems, speed-locking parts, etc. By the time the arm has been stocked, the owner may have as much invested as he would in a new commercial sporter. The economy motive which activated remodeling in the past is now largely absent. Today, the man contemplating such a job is either principally interested in either providing himself with a handicraft project or wants to experiment with a type or

271

caliber of rifle perhaps not commercially available at all, or one with stock or barrel dimension features he cannot obtain except by his own labor.

Personally, I was never enthusiastic about restocking, bolt-altering and perhaps rebarreling military actions into usable sporting rifles, though I did a lot of the work. It always seems like buying an old army jeep and then trying to make a sports car out of it. This is not to say the guns aren't good: most are thoroughly safe and reliable, but the amount of time and labor required to bring them to top grade seems excessive.

Where time and labor are recreation, modernizing is thoroughly worthwhile, so go to it. The barrel question has already been answered—replacement barrels, threaded and chambered, are available now and no doubt will be for many years to come.

In the matter of calibers, some thought must be given to choice of cartridge case. The military-rifle actions were designed long ago to handle long, tapered cases and pointed bullets. Many modern cartridges have little taper and may be comparatively short and fat. Round-nosed soft-pointed bullets may be desired by the brush hunter—you like the 6mm? In the Mauser and Springfield, the .243 cartridge will not feed reliably unless the magazine box is blocked in the rear to shorten, the underrails of the receiver cut to accommodate the cartridge shoulder and a short follower and follower spring installed. However, the 6mm Remington will feed well in unaltered arms. The .308 cartridge has basically the same problems as the .243, and reliable feeding can be hard to attain. The .270 and .30/06 are a bit long for Mauser 8mm magazine boxes. However, these can be filed thinner at the ends, inside, and made to accommodate standard overall hunting-cartridge lengths. Either will feed perfectly with original followers and springs.

Cleanup of rough military finishes on exteriors of receivers and guards is not difficult except on the very hard WW II 1903 rifles, A-3 and A-4. The hand grinder and power sanding tools must be used. Removal of the old, unwanted original barrel may be the most difficult job. It can be rusted in, although this is not common, or it has been screwed into the receiver very tightly. The use of a thread-loosening agent—"Liquid Wrench," etc.—for days before attempting barrel removal may be necessary. A barrel vise and receiver wrench may be absolutely necessary, but in some cases the job can be done without them. Rifle barrels do not, or should not, have tight threading; that is, the thread of the barrel should not be a tight fit in the threaded receiver. The tightness of the fitting comes from the shoulder of the barrel pressing against the front of the receiver in the case of all actions excepting the Mauser, which

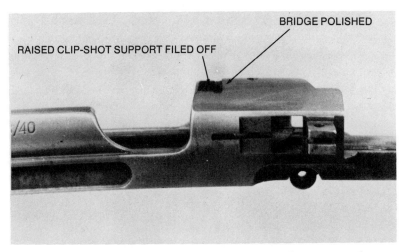

RAISED CLIP-SHOT SUPPORT FILED OFF

BRIDGE POLISHED

/40

Filing off raised clip-slot support and polishing bridge improves the appearance of old military receivers.

has an inner ring in the receiver against which the edges of the barrel may be bottomed with pressure. The ideal Mauser breeching has both the rear end of the barrel and the shoulder ahead of the thread's bearing.

If this end pressure of the barrel against the receiver can be relieved, it is usually possible to unscrew the barrel without much effort. Cut off the old one 6 inches or so ahead of the receiver, and chuck it in a lathe so that a parting (cutoff) tool can be brought into the barrel just ahead of the receiver and cut a groove around $1/16$-inch deep, working the tool back until there is only a paper-thin wall left against the receiver. This can be pried away with a knife or chisel. Shoulder pressure

Numrich Arms' cock-on-opening speedlock firing assembly for the M1917 surplus rifle.

against the receiver is now gone, and by clamping the barrel stub in an ordinary vise and using a thin hardwood board through the magazine opening in the receiver for a wrench, you have a fifty–fifty chance of unscrewing it. This relief-cutting may not do much for the Mauser happening to bottom at the breech, although cutting the shoulder clear will allow oil to reach the threads. This may help. In extreme cases, the barrel can be cut off at the shoulder groove, then the receiver placed on a 0.700-inch diameter mandrel you'll have to turn to fit, and set up in a lathe with the front end of the receiver in a steady rest—practically all

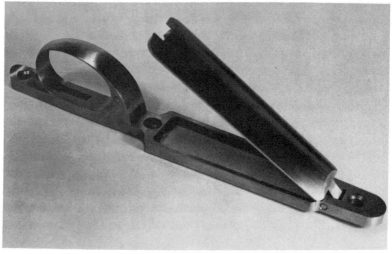

A beautifully made trigger guard assembly by Ed Blackburn, a California metalsmith. Nicely made accessories such as this add tremendously to the value and appearance of a custom rifle.

receivers have a short cylindrical section at very front—and the stub of barrel bored out. It will break loose before the boring tool can reach the receiver threads.

The remodeling of trigger guards to better appearance should always be done. It doesn't take a great deal of work, and adds a great deal to appearance. Receivers may have clip-slot bridges improved or eliminated, tangs cleaned of minor dents, etc. Bolt stops can be streamlined, have ends checkered and all such changes made. Drilling and tapping for scope or sight bases in the receiver should be done just before the finishing polishing work. It is easier to handle just a receiver than a barreled action. When a replacement stock is being handfitted to the barreled receiver, do this also before the final metal polishing, and save having to rework scratched places.

Sights should be mounted, and everything checked out—cheekpiece height on stock, bolt slot in stock, etc.—before the final cleanup for finishing. Should a receiver sight be used, in mounting be sure to locate it centered or forward in the receiver-bridge sidewall to eliminate interference with the bolt handle. On all or practically all military rifles

A Mauser trigger-guard bow that has been completely reshaped and reworked. Notice that the original flat-sided military guard has been ground and filed to graceful contours.

except Krag and Mannlicher types, the sight is mounted on the right-hand side of bridge, and the base can be positioned too far to the rear. There may be hard surfaces to drill and tap.

Many older rifles, particularly Mausers, have a case or surface hardening which will allow center punching easily, yet resist drilling. For such jobs, make the deepest center-punch mark possible, then tape a washer or bit of metal with a $^3/_{16}$-inch hole in it and use the tip of a small stone in a handgrinder to grind away the surface around the punch mark, taking care not to remove it, renewing if necessary. Now your drill should be able to do its work.

This is a detail of a Mauser action which has had the original safety replaced by one which is similar to, and operates exactly like, the Winchester Model 70 safety. This is good looking, convenient, and can be used with a scope. Work of this kind requires some good gunsmithing.

Should your Mauser receiver seem a little easy to drill, it should be heat-treated. The Erfurt small-ring ones are nearly always soft. These are very nice actions, and, heat-treated, are quite satisfactory for even the .270 Winchester cartridge, which is about as high-pressured a cartridge as you can find without going overboard into the wildcat field. The heat-treating is a carburizing or nitriding process leaving the surface very tough if not completely hard. It must be done by someone with experience, preferably one of the gun firms advertising for such work. The receiver can warp if not handled correctly. All drilling, tapping and remodeling of the receiver should be done before sending it for treatment. It will come back discolored but smooth and can easily be polished bright, but it won't drill or file very easily!

A word of explanation may be in order: most of the obsolete Mausers were made for the 7 by 57mm or 7.92 by 57mm (usually called 8mm) cartridges. These are or were loaded to medium pressures originally; then it was found that the 8mm had an extremely fast pressure

Here is a skeleton-type grip cap. The center of the metal cap has been cut out so that the checkered wood shows through. This is a fine custom feature and is found only on the best of custom guns.

This trigger guard was made by Clayton Nelson. It replaces the original Model 70 trigger guard. It has a push-button type floorplate release and is very streamlined and graceful.

drop. Heavy bullets and heavy loadings could be fired without requiring ultrastrong actions. So a receiver capable of faultless service with 8mm ammunition loaded to impressive ballistics can set back—fail to hold headspace as bolt lugs are forced back into receiver metal—when rebarreled to .270, .220 Swift, .30/06, etc. With the 8mm, pressure goes down the barrel fast; with the others, it slows down enough to drive the bolt back into the receiver a little harder. And the more taper to the case, the more bolt thrust against the receiver's locking-lug recesses.

Where a magazine has to be blocked so it will better handle cartridges shorter than the box was made for, the best method is to make a straight up-and-down block to fit inside at the back end, sawed and filed from a piece of aluminum, or even from very hard wood. To hold it in place, drill all the way through box and block together, and put in a pin, filing the ends flat and flush with the outside walls of the magazine box.

In the case of a few commercial rifles using long boxes blocked for short cartridges, mainly the old M70 Winchester type, you can improve them with a homemade block. The factory for some unknown reason slanted back their steel blocking plate at bottom, making the effective length longer than at the top and giving the follower room to slide and pivot. Replacement with a uniform straight block 0.425 to 0.450-inch thick aids feeding from the magazine and just about eliminates all magazine jams.

A detail of a Model 70 Winchester tang which has been reshaped. By reshaping and reducing the outline of the tang it is much more graceful and it looks better in a custom stock such as shown here.

277

Bullet-point protectors are a good idea for the heavy-recoil rifle such as the .270 and larger calibers. When a rifle fires, inertia of the cartridges in the magazine causes them to contact the front of the box hard enough to batter and flatten exposed lead bullet tips. Bullet-point protectors are simply thin (not over $1/16$-inch thick) strips of steel or brass soldered to the inside walls of the box vertically, located where the necks of cases lay when in the magazine. They have a slightly rounded rear edge that the shoulder of the cartridge will contact should it try to move straight ahead.

Bolt-lowering, or alteration for telescopic-sight use, should not be attempted. Send the bolt to one of the specialists doing such work. They do it very well indeed, and at low cost. The amateur gunsmith simply

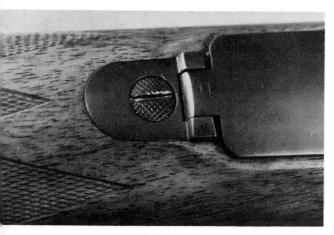

A nice little custom touch, and one easy to do, is checkering the action screws as here.

cannot justify the cost of welding equipment, holding fixtures, etc., needed for such work. He'll have enough to do as it is: even grinding the slot in the receiver tang for the lowered bolt handle is not to be taken lightly. Do this strictly cut-and-try: as the notch is deepened, use the bolt assembled except for the firing-pin spring, and grind and file until you can just push the firing pin completely forward into the "fired" position. Lipstick can be used on the root of the bolt handle to show high points as you work—it marks metal as well as wood. With the notch at perfect depth, you can just barely feel a trace of movement in the handle when you open the assembled bolt against mainspring pressure. If the notch is too deep, it moves up until the cocking cams are contacted, etc., and in firing, the bolt is turned down a bit too far so that some of the spring's energy is lost straightening it up in the firing cycle.

A bolt handle that jumps very visibly when the rifle is dry-fired has a notch too deep. While this can, of course, be controlled by the depth of the handle's relief-cut in the stock, use correct metal fitting where possible.

The remodeling of military handguns usually is limited to cleanup of exterior for good refinishing, installation of adjustable target sights and replacement of poor plastic or wooden stocks with better fitting (and looking) ones. Rebarreling is often impossible because of original design—for example, the numerous Webleys. However many surplus revolvers have been sold which have had cylinders rechambered to take more available ammunition or more popular calibers: 38 Smith & Wesson to .38 Special, .455 Webley to .45 anything, etc. During WW II Smith & Wesson made vast numbers of 4-inch barreled revolvers for British forces and others, chambered for the .38 S & W cartridge, then the official British revolver caliber. Popularly known as the "Victory" model, thousands of these have come back as surplus. To promote sales, importers have run .38 Special reamers into chambers so this longer and more powerful cartridge can be fired. However, while longer, the .38 Special isn't as large in diameter, so the cartridges fit pretty sloppily, the back ends of these chambers being suited to the .38 S & W case. The guns are safe with any factory-loaded cartridge the cylinder will accept, but stay with the original S & W. It's quite adequate for self-defense and informal target work.

The U. S. .45 pistol, Model 1911, is remodeled for target use by smoothing and tightening the action, replacing of service sights and adding a new barrel, link and bushing to obtain the tight locked-for-firing fitting of the barrel required for best accuracy. Kits of these parts often are advertised in shooting magazines just for the gun owner to utilize in his own remodeling and match-conditioning efforts.

There are just too many obsolete military arms extant to try to describe specific operations possible on all, so I can really deal only with generalities. The original home-modernizing on the bolt rifles consisted of cutting barrels and stocks to sporter lengths, attaching good metallic sights, rounding off fore-end tips, putting on a comfortable buttplate or pad, and, if the owner could work in wood, fitting wood blocks to the military buttstock to provide a pistol grip and higher comb and/or cheekpiece. From here to completely modernized jobs only utilizing the receiver and bolt of the original arm, the choice is wide open.

Military autoloaders are also with us, from the U. S. M-1 Carbine up to 7mm, 8mm and .30/06 infantry assault rifles. Even where they're legal to use in hunting, state laws usually require a magazine altered to

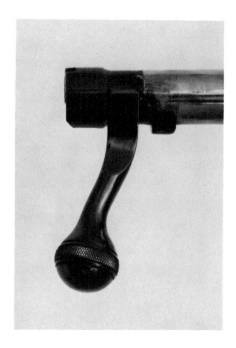

Military bolt handle altered for *low scope use.* Actually, it was replaced, as this is a separate handle made commercially just for the purpose of being welded to such bolts. There are professionals who specialize in doing this and advertise for the work; send your bolt to them.

hold no more than five cartridges. With foreign arms using box magazines, it is only necessary to make a wood block to fit inside the follower spring to limit capacity, exactly as is done with pump and autoshotguns to limit them to the capacity of two shells in the magazine. The M-1 Garand rifle must have the eight-round clip altered by annealing halfway up, making a vertical cut with a fine-tooth hacksaw and then bending the front ends freed by this cut up to only allow the clip to take four cartridges in top.

In reality, very little can be done to remodel this type of firearm beyond replacing sights or attaching telescopic sight mounts and altering the stock or restocking to gain a suitable butt. Mechanical alterations, even much work on the trigger pull, may interfere with satisfactory functioning. Attractive stocks are available for the little carbines, as well as scope mounts, but the owner can do little on the metal beyond refinishing the exterior. Changes of barrels to obtain more desirable calibers, etc., are solely for gunsmiths specializing in such work and guaranteeing results.

Complete and careful refinishing of the unaltered arm, giving it a good blue and fine stock finish will make it an attractive addition to the collection and a pleasure to handle and use, without trying for major changes.

17

The Semi-custom Rifle

A custom rifle is one made up to an individual's specifications, the same as a tailored suit. By professionals, such work is necessarily priced quite highly. A favorably comparing rifle can be obtained by the individual through use of component parts being sold for his and the gunsmith's use—so long as he wants a bolt-action type!

In actions alone, commercial and military Mauser types, medium and long Sako (Finnish) and BSA (British) are available; they may be had with factory or custom barrels fitted, in every caliber conceivable, either white or blued. U. S. firms—Winchester, Remington and Savage—sell their actions only with barrels fitted and finished in the standard range of calibers. So the metalwork can be no work at all. The wide choice of calibers, barrel lengths and weights will allow meeting "custom" requirements unless a specific wildcat cartridge is in mind. In this case, the gunsmith who originated or specializes in that cartridge and its barreling will be happy to sell a barreled-action assembly rechambered for his brainchild.

Stocks range from the twenty-five-dollar Sile sporters to be refinished, etc., by the rifle owner (now made for all the abovementioned

This is a custom stocked Winchester Highwall. Work was done by Hal Hartley, a master who specializes in maple. This wood is curly maple.

actions except the Winchester and Remington) to the deluxe handmade truly custom stock from a top stockmaker, with the completely finished Fajen and Bishops in between. Bishop can furnish many different styles, grades of wood and make to measurement with checkering, etc. The rifle is sent to them, and the stock is an individual fitting job. Or the stock can be ordered in finished state for bedding at home.

Since these actions come with scope and sight mounting holes and low bolts for scope use, a man doesn't need much beyond screwdrivers to put a first-class rifle together!

Where a little barrel-fitting work is possible, the action alone can be started with and then a special-cartridge varmint or target barrel obtained from Wilson or other maker that lists the calibers and dimensions desired. And Bishop and Fajen provide a wide choice of stocks for such rifles.

The choice of actions may be confusing. A little general information should help to explain the variety. The Fabrique Nationale Mauser action can be had normal or as a solid-bottom single-shot type, with or without adjustable triggers. They are not blued or even polished and are made by Fabrique Nationale in Belgium. Their barreled actions are beautifully blued and well finished in all respects.

A beautiful custom Model 70 Winchester restocked in beautiful wood by master stockmaker Dale Goens.

This handsome sporter is a Ruger No. 1 Single Shot rifle stocked in French walnut by Dale Goens.

The "Santa Barbara" Mauser action, lower in cost, also comes in white, with barreled actions polished and blued. These are true commercial actions, similar to the Fabrique Nationale action in having no clip slots, a solid left receiver wall, a low bolt handle and scope safety, and an adjustable trigger system. Made in the Spanish national armory, the steel and its heat treatment are very good; however, the machinework is not perfect and for good, smooth functioning, bolt runways, locking lugs and their recesses should be polished by hand. Light alloy or steel trigger guards can be had—always get the steel.

The Mark X Mauser action, imported by Firearms International, is made in the Yugoslav national armory and is extremely good in all respects: finish inside and out, operation, quality of steel and heat treatment. The adjustable trigger assembly is entirely of steel, with large, strong pins, the side safety is positive, and the housing does not take up so much of the undertang area so as to make good bedding difficult. Actions come polished and blued, as well as the barreled-action assemblies.

All of these commercial-Mauser actions come with hinged-floorplate guards, low bolt handles, side- or tang-type scope safeties and are drilled and tapped for scope and sight bases. Being based on the 1898 military Mauser action, the thread for the barrel is the same so that bar-

A Sako restocked in French walnut and nicely checkered with special custom pattern by Mike Conner.

rels for the '98 fit. Stocks made for the military type are not suitable: these new actions do not have the thumb cut in the left receiver wall so the stock walls should not be notched here, and the military trigger guard has a longer front tang than the hinged-plate commercial ones. Stocks inletted for the '98 guards have a ⅛ inch or so gap at the front when a commercial guard is used. Rear scope-mount bases for the military rifle have relief for the raised clip-slot lips, nonexistent on the commercial actions, for which a different base is made. All three of the actions use the same model mounts and sights.

Another Winchester Model 70 stocked in magnificent exhibition grade French walnut by Dale Goens. Notice the beautiful checkering pattern.

This Model 70 Winchester was restocked by ace stockmaker Leonard Brownell with Monte Carlo comb.

The firing-pin action on these commercial actions is the same as in the military ones—long fall, heavy pin. Where a milling machine is available, V slots can be milled lengthwise to lighten pins, and the sear face of cocking piece milled back to shorten the fall. With the Mark X, the safety functions without any change when this is done, but with some of the other trigger assemblies, some work may be needed to insure safety with the cocking piece locating farther forward in the cocked position than its original position. A lighter but safe trigger pull can usually be achieved by replacing the trigger-return spring with a weaker one and use of the engagement adjusting screw.

For other actions: the BSA is a modern, streamlined type, has a cocking indicator on its closed sleeve, low bolt, hinged plate, etc. The trigger, while adjustable to some extent, cannot be brought to less than a three-pound pull. The bolt stop is incorporated into the trigger assembly so that no other trigger system can be substituted. (Timney and Canjar triggers can be put on the Mausers.) Actions and barreled actions come blued. The .270 and .30/06 BSAs that I have tested have proved very accurate—minute-of-angle at 200 yards. And despite what you may read in enthusiastic write-ups, 2 inches at 200 yards with hunting bullets is not to be expected every day with every hunting rifle.

This Model 70, which belongs to Jim Carmichel, was stocked in French walnut by Clayton Nelson.

This is an unusual touch in that it is an ordinary Winchester Model 92 fitted with a semi-octagon barrel, and a full-length fore-end. This is top-notch work by well known stockmaker Nate Bishop.

The Sako actions and rifles are beautifully polished and blued; their finish is superior to all others except possibly the Mark X. The L-57 medium-length action is ideal for .22/250, .243, etc., cartridge lengths, and being small and light, it makes for ideal small-scale rifles for women's use. The adjustable trigger system is very good. This, too, has the hinged-floorplate guard for safe unloading without working all of the cartridges in and out of the chamber. The only weak point of the Sako is the extractor: it breaks. Obtain and carry a spare.

The Savage 110-L may not be as pretty as some actions, but it fills the need of the left-hander quite well. The unorthodox sear system

This Mauser is beautifully stocked and checkered by a newcomer to the
stockmaking ranks, Duane Wiebe. Pay particular attention to the unusual trigger-guard treatment and the semi-octagon ribbed barrel. This
is first-class work. Wiebe started his career as a part-time amateur.

works well, the trigger isn't bad and no great engineering is needed to
fix up a guard with the ordinary double-set triggers made for Mauser
use. The stamped floorplate isn't very attractive, but you can make up a
better one. The rifles shoot well, function reliably and don't break parts.

For the Remington and Winchester, Fajen, Bishop and custom-
stock men are sources of stocks. Timney, Canjar, and for Remington,
the fine Kenyon triggers can be used if the factory types aren't to your
liking.

All in all, a pretty fine individualized rifle can be assembled with
the components available, with such a semicustom type costing from
one-third to one-half that of a true custom job. And with little or even
no tool or equipment investment required, even the man with no shop
at all can have one.

18

Lock, Stock and Barrel

As always, when reviewing what one has written, things come to mind that should have been included somewhere. In a book of this kind, directed to readers who are perhaps not inclined to go all the way into setting up a complete workshop to service their own firearms, it is not really in order to write a complete, all-inclusive book on how to do every conceivable job on every firearm a reader might own. Such a book would have to be 7 inches thick and sell for fifty dollars a copy, and ninety-five percent of it would be worthless to ninety-five percent of its readers. Any man desiring further information on specific facets of gun work—stockmaking, blueing or browning metal, checkering, etc.— can find books devoted solely to each field. There are books covering all general gunsmithing techniques used by professionals—I wrote a 700-page epic of this sort myself a quarter of a century back that is now in its fourth or fifth printing, indicating that even if all the professionals bought three copies each, all would not be accounted for. So some non-pros are interested somewhat seriously.

"Lock, stock and barrel" now means a complete, thorough job on anything, the saying, of course, coming from the pioneer gunsmiths who literally made complete guns, the locks, the stocks and the barrels. And thus working in design, mechanics, woodworking and machineworking. Modern arms work still encompasses all of these fields, and I have attempted to touch them all lightly and give usable information so far as it goes. Most gunsmith operations I always consider twenty-five-percent equipment, twenty-five-percent skill and experience and fifty-percent intelligent forethought.

So, think around all the angles of what you want to do. Make lists of materials needed, figure out the undertaking step by step and put the steps in order. Draw diagrams, make a dummy or mock-up of the finished product, and then let a week pass while you just look at these and think about possible ways to do it better or easier.

In shop supplies, powder solvents, metal-fouling removers, etc., modern technology brings out new products almost every month. Follow the advertisements and new-product write-ups in gun and home-mechanics magazines and look over the items in hardware and industrial-supply stores. Every now and then you'll find something that is exactly what you've been needing.

The Chemetron Corporation, 840 N. Michigan Ave., Chicago, Ill. 60611, has solders that will work on practically anything from stainless steel to aluminum, inclusive, and at such low heats that steel will barely discolor.

There are more varieties of Lock-Tites than I know about to hold screws in threads tightly or not quite so tightly for blind holes and through holes, even for unthreaded tube joints. For cold-joining, epoxy cements exist that are claimed to have the strength of brazing. Ordinary "plastic steel" sold everywhere in tubes and small containers can often be used. That in can or jar with a separate hardener liquid where you mix what you need when you need it is best. I have used this to attach replacement ramrod thimbles on collector's-item muzzle-loaders where heat and/or soldering flux could damage the original delicate brown finish of the barrel and rib. I've also used it to attach scope-mount bases to the receiver of a match air rifle—drilling and threading the $1/_{32}$-inch thick steel was out of the question and soldering would have been difficult. (The Feinwerkbau's recoil shook the cheap air-rifle scope out of adjustment in a hurry, but the mount remained firmly in place.)

When disassembling arms, not only be certain that the screwdriver tip fits the screw slot exactly, but be sure to turn the screw in the correct direction: every now and then you may run into a screw with left-handed thread, opposite to normal. These usually hold a moving part whose movement might tend to loosen a right-hand thread. Therefore, if a screw does not appear rusted in or otherwise tight from natural reasons and yet firmly resists unwinding, try it the other way. Concerning rifle-barrel removal, I believe only the European-made Krags have a left-hand thread, all others being right.

The split pin has baffled many first-time disassemblers. These are found in older shotguns and rifles and a few modern ones, resemble screws, but turning gets no results. They must simply be driven out with drift punch. Close inspection will show the slot to be much deeper than that of a screw. These are designed to hold their places by a slight spring tension, the split end being spread a trifle. The ejector pin in the 1903 Springfield is a good example of the split pin.

Roll pins were widely used by Germany in WW II small arms and have been adopted by some U. S. manufacturers to hold nonmoving components together. These are spring-tempered incompletely-closed steel tubes that have an open slot. They are made larger than the hole they are to enter. Springing in on themselves, they may be driven into place and are, of course, very tight and hold their position well. Removal requires that a flat-end punch just under the hole diameter be very carefully placed on the pin end for the first hammer blow to avoid damaging the arm. While they often may be reused once, they may be loose after a second removal and so need replacement. As roll pins are much used in die and fixture assembly, any industrial-supply house can furnish them. Too-long ones are easily cut to length on the edge of a grinding wheel, end shaped and blued with touch-up. When buying a new roll pin, take the old one along, or the part with the hole, to obtain the correct diameter—just a little too big to push in.

Small files may have tips bent into short curves for use in restricted-movement areas by coating with antiscale mixture and heated red, bending between bits of brass, reheating and quenching in water or light oil. Large files require oxyacetylene-torch heat. It's cheaper than buying the bent file tools, known as rifflers. Scrapers and special wood chisels, little hook-cutters, etc., can be made in this way as well.

The black-powder shooter who equips himself with a bit of a shop soon finds that the ordinary petroleum-based solvent he buys at the gas station will clean percussion and flint guns faster and with less bother than water. Using two small containers of solvent on the bench, one for cleaning with brushes, the other for rinsing, and air from a compressor or vacuum cleaner to dry and then spread the protecting oil, home cleaning can be an easy short-time chore. This is not my innovation—in a gunsmith's book published in 1883 the author enthuses that no longer will water have to be used in cleaning, as benzine can be had from any drugstore and do a fine job of removing fouling and then evaporating to leave the metal clean. Benzine is a refined white-gasoline-type solvent formerly used to clean clothing, hats, etc., and is very, very inflammable. Don't consider using it, although you can obtain it almost anywhere as "lighter fluid"—fuel for sparking-type cigarette lighters. The standard cleaning solvent as sold by larger service stations is not volatile enough to worry about, and it does the job. While it will cut greases and oils and dry readily when not too badly contaminated with them, it really doesn't burn very well. When I started to use it in the shop in large, open pans I tested it by throwing lighted matches into it; it put them out. Naturally, it can be *made* to burn, but it isn't sensitive to sparks; its vapor won't ignite or explode from static electricity or flame so it is safe to use.

A shop expanded to contain a drill press, belt and band sanders and a small torch offers the opportunity to make tools and do work on many things. Knife-making is a current fad among sportsmen; custom knifemakers turn out expensive types, both finished and semifinished, and rough blades, hilts, handles and pommels can be purchased. It is possible to finish up rough components using only sanders and drill and temper small- and medium-sized blades with a light torch for heat.

Maintaining one's arms and equipment properly can be a necessary service not otherwise readily obtained. It can be absorbing handiwork reaching hobby level or a self-satisfying accomplishment. If you're a serious gun owner, there really isn't any excuse not to do at least some of your gunsmithing at home.

Glossary

Here is a short list of definitions of words pertaining to firearms. Concerning gun parts for a specific arm, try always to consult a factory parts list for that model, or a similar arm made by the same manufacturer. Quite often firms will use their own terminology. For instance, the swinging part holding the cylinder in side-swing revolvers as made by Colt and Smith & Wesson: one calls it a "crane," the other a "yoke."

Action   Operating mechanism—the working parts of an arm exclusive of stock and barrel parts. Used sometimes to describe as to type of arm, such as a ".270 sporter on a Mauser action."

Actuating   -rod, -slide, etc. Applies to a movable part that unlocks a bolt or breechblock. It may be manually operated, or moved by gas or recoil in autoloading arms.

Anvil   Any metal block used to hammer or punch work against. In a Boxer (American-type) primer, the steel stamping against which the firing pin forces the primer cup and priming compound, causing it to explode. In Berdan (foreign) cartridge cases, the integral teat in the case primer pocket, serving the same purpose.

Assembly   Two or more gun parts joining together for use. May or may not be pinned or joined by screws or held in a housing.

Assembly pin Also known as "slave pin." A pin used to hold an assembly together temporarily so it may be inserted into a housing or frame, when the longer permanent pin may driven through, this pushing the assembly pin clear of the arm.

Ball Besides meaning anything spherical—can be standard-type military ammunition, bullet only or a complete cartridge, not special purpose such as a tracer or incendiary, generally applicable also to any nonexpanding bullet.

Ballistics Characteristics of bullets in flight, but also applied to complete cartridges for comparison purposes.

Black powder Gunpowder. The original, made of charcoal, sulphur and nitrate. Fast burning, low pressure, very inflammable. Color is grayish-black, comes in irregular granules. Called "black powder" to make positive distinction from the modern propellants, which can be the same color and, in some pistol and shotgun types, look something like it. These modern propellants are always labeled, "rifle powder," "pistol powder," etc., but the word, "black," is never printed on any modern container for these are high-pressure types which can and will blow up arms made for black-powder use.

Block Usually short for "breechblock," a sliding, rotating or camming block of steel moved into a locked position to hold a cartridge in a chamber for firing.

Bolt The operating part of a bolt-action rifle, sometimes applied to a cylindrical breech block, and, of course, its ordinary definition of a holding screw, such as stock-bolt.

Bore The hole through a barrel. Sometimes applied as descriptive, such as "smallbore," .410 bore, etc.

Bore diameter Just what it says for shotguns. For rifled arms, the diameter from the top of the land to the opposing top of the land, the minimum diameter.

Caliber Size. In firearms, roughly the bore diameter originally, but now often corrupted and confused with a trade name. Often linked with a cartridge-case identification. In English and American usage, caliber is figured to 0.001 inch, that is .30 Caliber is 0.300 inch. Proliferation of case sizes in the same caliber has led to variations: .30/30, .300 Savage, .30/40 US, .30/06, .300 H & H, .308 Winchester, .300 Winchester Magnum—all are .30 caliber, but all are different in case dimensions. .220 Swift, .222 Remington, .223 Remington, .22/250, .224 Weatherby, etc., are all .22 center-fires of the same bore diameters, but all are of different size cases.

Cap lock A percussion-cap arm or also, just the lock mechanism.

Cast-off Applies to the buttstock on a rifle or shotgun angled to the side away from the shooter's face, to make the arm come to sighting position readily. Cast-on is opposite.

Chamber Area or part of arm machined to accept cartridge or shell. In cylinder of revolvers, in barrel of all other types of arms.

Choke Reduced diameter, hollow, or constriction in shot barrels at or just behind the muzzle to control shot patterns. Or, separate attachment to muzzle for same purpose.

Clip Small metal rack to hold cartridges for quick reloading of magazine arms. Now corrupted to also mean replaceable pistol and rifle magazines themselves.

Ejector The part which ejects—throws out—a case or cartridge when a gun action is opened.

Engagement The meeting and holding of parts to perform some function in the operation of an arm. Trigger engagement, sear engagement, etc.

Extractor Extracts—pulls—the case or cartridge out of the chamber.

Firing pin Part that strikes the primer and fires the cartridge. Some rifles have separate firing-pin tips doing this, which are called "strikers."

Flintlock Firing mechanism employing a hammer clamping a bit of flint which when activated by a spring and trigger release strikes a steel plate, called a frizzen, and produces sparks which ignite loose fine gunpowder, to burn through a hole in the side of the barrel and fire the charge inside. Became obsolete in 1820's when the percussion cap was invented.

Follower The metal part ahead of a magazine spring which follows and pushes cartridges into an action in position to load into a chamber.

Frame The principal part-holding component of a firearm, somewhat synonymous to the "Receiver," but today applied almost entirely to handguns, where it is what you're left holding after you take off everything removable.

Gage Special gun part or tool used to check safety or working tolerances, such as headspace gage or test bolt. Generally, any comparison-check tool.

Gauge Shotgun bore measurement, originally based on number of round lead balls per pound a gun was made to use, 12 gauge, 12 balls to a pound, 16 gauge, 16 to pound, etc. Because of the invention of shotgun shells and other factors, barrel diameters have become smaller than this would indicate. Modern "12-gauge" lead balls will actually run fifteen or more to the pound. The .410 is not a gauge and is the "410 bore" being a .410 inch inside barrel diameter.

Grooves In a rifle barrel the spiral cuts which make "rifling" to make bullets spin in flight and so hold their course through gyroscopic principle.

Groove diameter Diameter of a barrel from the bottom of one groove across to another, as opposed to "bore" diameter. For example, .30 caliber, minimum allowable bore diameter is .3000 inch, groove diameter, .3080 inch.

293

Hair trigger   Early name for set trigger which could be adjusted to a very light pull. Corrupted to now mean any very light trigger-pull.

Hammer   In firearms a spring-driven part that when released by the trigger, moves to contact the firing pin, percussion cap or frizzen to cause the arm to fire. May arms have the firing pin integral or attached to it, as in many revolver hammers. May be external to be cocked by hand or concealed under the slide of a pistol or in the receiver of a rifle or shotgun. In early days it was called the "cock" because of fancied resemblance to a rooster's head. "Draw the cock" meant to pull it back against its spring to firing position, eventually shortened to just "cock" which we use today to describe the same movement.

Hand   The part in a revolver, activated by the hammer or trigger being moved, which rotates the cylinder.

Headspace   The space or distance between the face of the bolt or block or slide and a predetermined point at or in the chamber. For rimmed cases it can be just the back edge of the chamber at the end of a barrel, or the front edge of a recess cut in the chamber of a barrel or cylinder which will accept the rim. For rimless pistol cartridges, the front end of the chamber governs the headspace, and in bottle-necked rifle cartridges, the point is on the angle of the shoulder where the body of the case reduces to the neck. Belted cases are treated as thick-rimmed ones, and the headspace is from bolt face to recess in chamber accepting the belt.

Housing   A container part that houses two or more smaller parts. Occasionally used rather incorrectly in place of "assembly."

Inertia firing pin   A firing pin too short to reach the primer, but, held to the rear by a weak spring, will fly forward when struck by the hammer and of its own weight cause the arm to fire. Best example is the Colt U. S. Model 1911 ("government") .45 pistol.

Inertial lock   A part in some pump and autoloading arms that locks the breech closed until the gun is fired. Its weight is moved by recoil to allow the gun to be again operated or fired. May or may not have an external projection for manual release so action can be operated without ammunition.

Jewelling   Decorating polished surfaces such as bolts and followers with hand or machined markings. Also known as Damascening, and engine-turning.

Land–lands   Raised spiral tracks in a rifled barrel, actually made by cutting the grooves.

Lifter   The part in repeating arms, usually tubular-magazine types, which lifts a cartridge so it can be fed into a chamber by a bolt.

Lug   A protruding section of a part designed to fit a recess or cam on another and so engage for holding or restraining.

Lug-locking   Lug or lugs that engage the receiver or frame to lock a breech for safe firing.

Lug-safety An auxiliary lug provided for a safety factor should locking lugs fail. In Mauser action, the small lug on the bolt engaging recess in the bottom of the receiver under the bridge; in Springfield, the lug on the side of the bolt ahead of the right side-wall of the bridge; in Remington and Winchester, the root of the bolt handle engaging the slot in the receiver tang.

Magazine Assembly or space holding several cartridges. May be in the arm or a separate removable component.

Pistol Any handgun not a revolver, correct name of which is "Revolving pistol," according to Colonel Colt, maker of the original.

Pin punch Also called a "drift" or drift punch. A metal tool with tip a straight cylindrical section, used to drift, or drive out metal pins and so free parts.

Pin vise A small hand tool having a chuck on the end to hold small pins, etc.

Receiver Main part of a gun action which receives the remaining parts.

Receiver bridge On a bolt-action receiver, the rear covering section, behind loading port and magazine area.

Receiver ring The front section of a bolt-action receiver, containing barrel threads.

Receiver tang The part of the action at the back end which is inletted into the wood stock for holding screws, provide for safety and trigger attachment, etc.

Sear A part providing connection between trigger and firing pin, or hammer.

Set trigger A trigger mechanism capable of being "cocked" and "fired"— when set, or cocked, a strong spring is compressed that when released by very light pull on the trigger forces a part against a sear or sear part causing it to release the firing pin or hammer and the arm to fire.

Slide In autoloading pistols, the moving housing of barrel or frame. The sliding part or parts of pump-action rifles and shotguns. In metallic receiver sights, the movable part.

Stock-stocks The wood—or plastic—providing handling for a firearm. Section rear of the action is called the buttstock, forward of action, either forearm or fore-end. In handguns it is usually plural—stocks—meaning the wood, plastic or other material making the handle. These are also incorrectly sometimes called "grips."

Wildcat A nonstandard caliber cartridge, usually made by altering a standard in shape or capacity.

Zero Applies to sights. Zero is a starting sight setting, i.e., "200-yard zero" is the sight set to make arm hit correctly at 200 yards. "Zero setting" means sight is adjusted all the way down to bottom, whether actually set anywhere for distance, except for some military rifles and training, when it may mean a setting for 1000 inches, 25 yards or 25 meters.

Sources of Supply

Knowing where to obtain parts, tools, cleaning and shop materials is very important. There are always several dozen firms and individuals involved in this aspect of the firearms industry. However, they come and go rapidly for the most part, many not remaining in business for more than a year or two. Any arm-oriented book you may pick up will have pages of sources. Only half of them are manufacturers who sell only to the trade, not to individuals, and half of the remainder have gone out of business since the book was printed. So I will list far fewer, established businesses that I trust will be in business for several years to come. However, it is possible to keep fairly up-to-date on people in the supply and service department by means of gun magazines and papers. *Shotgun News* is a bi-monthly advertising paper devoted to firearms ads (Box 1147 Hastings, Neb. 68901). *Gun Week*, a weekly publication, P. O. Box 150, Sidney, Ohio, 45365, carries ads of parts suppliers, also. A few copies of each will make a worthwhile reference library.

Anyone interested in muzzle-loading arms should join the National Muzzle Loading Rifle Association, Box 67, Friendship, Ind. 47021, and receive their monthly magazine, *Muzzle Blasts*. This journal keeps up to the minute on parts, accessories and everything pertaining to black-powder shooting.

The *American Rifleman,* published by the National Rifle Association, will carry advertising of all major companies in the gun world, as well as much general information.

Should you feel the need of instruction books, there are a dozen or more "gunsmithing" ones on the market at present, widely advertised in sporting magazines. All are of some value, but the best are the thick ones!

General Suppliers

Modern Arms

U. S. manufacture, write factory for current parts list, giving model number and serial number of arm involved. Foreign Manufacture, if possible, contact firm importing the arm involved, who can supply or advise parts supplier.

Obsolete and Obsolescent Arms

Numrich Arms Corp., 201 Broadway, West Hurley, N.Y. 12491.

Sarco, Inc. 192 Central Ave. Stirling, N.J.

Service Armament Co., 689 Bergen Blvd., Ridgefield, N.J. 07657.

Bob's Gun Parts, Box 2332, Hot Springs, Ark. 71901. (Parts for Current and recent German & Italian revolvers & pistols.)

Shelley Braverman, Athens, N.Y. 12015

Dixie Gun Works, Inc. Union City, Tenn. 38261

Finished and Semifinished Gun Stocks

E. C. Bishop & Son, Inc. Box 7, Warsaw, Mo. 65355

Reinhart Fajen, Box 338, Warsaw, Mo. 65355

Pachmayr Gun Works, 1220 S. Grand Avenue, Los Angeles, Calif. 90015

Roberts Wood Products, 1400 Melody Road, Marysville, Ga. 95901

Sile Distributors, 7 Centre Market Place, New York, N.Y. 10013

General and Specialized Gunsmithing Tools and Supplies

Bob Brownell, Main & Third, Montezuma, Iowa 50171

B-Square Company, Box 11281, Ft. Worth, Texas 76110

C. R. Pedersen & Son, Ludington, Mich. 49431

Frank Mittermeier, Inc. P.O. Box 2, New York, N.Y. 10465

W. C. Wolff Company, Box 232, Ardmore, Pa. 19003 (Gun springs only)

Kasenite Co., Inc. 3 King St., Mahwah, N.J. 07430 (Surface hardening compounds.

Rifle Barrels (Threaded, chambered, modern calibers, require minimum equipment for fitting, not blued.)
Federal Firearms Co., Inc., Box 145, Oakdale, Pa. 15071
D. M. Manley, 295 Main St., Brookville, Pa. 15825
Wilson Arms Company, Box 364, Stony Creek, Branford, Conn. 06405

Specialized Barrel Work

Reboring and rerifling rifle barrels to larger caliber; also controlled-pattern shotgun barrels—Atkinson Gun Company, Box 512, Prescott, Ariz. 86301.
Hard-Chroming shotgun barrels, Marker Machine Co., Box 426, Charleston, Ill. 61920

Muzzle-loading Arms, Parts, and Equipment

Antique Gun Parts, Inc., 569 S. Braddock Ave., Pittsburgh, Pa. 15221. Original and reproduction parts for antique firearms.
Jesse Booher, 2751 Ridge Ave., Dayton, Ohio 45414. Castings for buttplates, trigger guards, etc.
Cherry Corners Gun Shop, Box 275, Lodi, Ohio 44254. Percussion locks, triggers, stocks, other rifle components.
Connecticut Valley Arms Co., Candle Hill Road, Higganum, Conn. 06441. Complete arms, kits, parts from kits, including barrels.
Dixie Gun Works, Inc., Union City, Tenn. 38261. All categories of supplies.
Douglas Barrels, Inc., 5504 Big Tyler Road, Charleston, W. Va. 25312. Makers of barrels.
Frontier Carving Shoppe, 102 N. 2nd St. Hughesville, Pa. 17737. Semifinished stocks and blanks for muzzle-loading arms. (Manufacturer)
Golden Age Arms Co., Box 82, Worthington, Ohio 43085. Barrels, stocks, books on Americana, leather, etc.
Russ Hamm, 2617 Oleander Blvd., Ft. Pierce, Florida 33450. Manufacturer of flint and percussion locks.
Jomar Imports, 156 Cuba Hill Road, Huntington, N.Y. 11743. English flints.
William Large, Rt. 1, Ironton, Ohio 45638. Custom barrelmaker.
Joseph W. Mellott, 334 Rockhill Road, Pittsburgh, Pa. 15243. Manufacturer of threaded rifle and shotgun barrels.
Les' Gun Shop, P.O. Box 511, Kalispell, Mont. 59901. Barrelmaker, all calibers.
Numrich Arms Corp., West Hurley, N.Y. 12491. Barrelmakers, breech-plugs, etc.
R.E.D. Machine Co., 3063 Capistrano Way, Grove City, Ohio 43123. Manufacturer of berylium copper nipples, also flash caps, nipple wrenches, etc.
Replica Arms of Tulsa, 2425 E. 15th St. Tulsa, Okla. 74104. Rifle kits, etc.
Dave Taylor, Box 1, Little Hocking, Ohio 45742. Custom barrelmaker.
The Flint Shop, Rt. 1, Box 116–A, Round Rock, Tex. 78664. Flints in all sizes.
The North Star Tool & Mfg. Co., 2401 Guermsey Dell Ave., Dayton, Ohio 45404. Manufacturer of set triggers for rifles.
Uintah Basin Flints, Box 343, Roosevelt, Utah 84066. Agate flints.
Yeck Antique Firearms Co., Dundee, Mich. 48131. General supplies.

Replica Arms
(Copies and reasonable facsimilies of old firearms)

Centennial Arms Corp., 3318 W. Devon Ave., Lincolnwood, Ill. 60645. Remington percussion revolvers, 1863 Zouave rifles; Colt revolvers including an 1860 New Model .44 Army made in Belgium. (Others listed made in Italy.) Flint pistols, rifles, etc.

Centry Arms, Inc. 3 Federal St., St. Albans, Vt. 05478. Spanish-made single-shot percussion and flint pistols, muskets, shotguns, etc.

Dixie Gun Works, Inc., Union City, Tenn. 38261. All types of replica arms.

Lyman Gunsight Co., Middlefield, Conn. 96455. Remington percussion revolvers.

Navy Arms Co., 689 Bergen Blvd., Ridgefield, N.Y. 07657. Kentucky model rifles, percussion and flint Kentucky pistols, muskets, revolving carbine, Colt and Remington replica revolvers, etc.

Numrich Arms. Corp., West Hurley, N.Y. 12491. Muzzle-loading arms of all types, kits, underhammer rifles and pistols.

Replica Arms, Inc., Marietta, Ohio. 45750. Copies of Colt and Remington pistols, (complete line), percussion and flint arms.

Thompson/Center Arms Co., Rochester, N.H. 03867. Plains-type flint and percussion rifles, locks, triggers, guards, etc.

Tables of Useful Information

Decimal Equivalents of Millimeters

mm.	Inch.	mm.	Inch.	mm.	Inch.	mm.	Inch.	mm.	Inch.
.01	.00039	.21	.00827	.41	.01614	.61	.02402	.81	.03189
.02	.00079	.22	.00866	.42	.01654	.62	.02441	.82	.03228
.03	.00118	.23	.00906	.43	.01693	.63	.02480	.83	.03268
.04	.00157	.24	.00945	.44	.01732	.64	.02520	.84	.03307
.05	.00197	.25	.00984	.45	.01772	.65	.02559	.85	.03346
.06	.00236	.26	.01024	.46	.01811	.66	.02598	.86	.03386
.07	.00276	.27	.01063	.47	.01850	.67	.02638	.87	.03425
.08	.00315	.28	.01102	.48	.01890	.68	.02677	.88	.03465
.09	.00354	.29	.01142	.49	.01929	.69	.02717	.89	.03504
.10	.00394	.30	.01181	.50	.01969	.70	.02756	.90	.03543
.11	.00433	.31	.01220	.51	.02008	.71	.02795	.91	.03583
.12	.00472	.32	.01260	.52	.02047	.72	.02835	.92	.03622
.13	.00512	.33	.01299	.53	.02087	.73	.02874	.93	.03661
.14	.00551	.34	.01339	.54	.02126	.74	.02913	.94	.03701
.15	.00591	.35	.01378	.55	.02165	.75	.02953	.95	.03740
.16	.00630	.36	.01417	.56	.02205	.76	.02992	.96	.03780
.17	.00669	.37	.01457	.57	.02244	.77	.03032	.97	.03819
.18	.00709	.38	.01496	.58	.02283	.78	.03071	.98	.03858
.19	.00748	.39	.01535	.59	.02323	.79	.03110	.99	.03898
.20	.00787	.40	.01575	.60	.02362	.80	.03150	1.00	.03937

mm.	Inch.	mm.	Inch.	mm.	Inch.	mm.	Inch.	mm.	Inch.
1	.03937	21	.82677	41	1.61417	61	2.40157	81	3.18897
2	.07874	22	.86614	42	1.65354	62	2.44094	82	3.22834
3	.11811	23	.90551	43	1.69291	63	2.48031	83	3.26771
4	.15748	24	.94488	44	1.73228	64	2.51968	84	3.30708
5	.19685	25	.98425	45	1.77165	65	2.55905	85	3.34645
6	.23622	26	1.02362	46	1.81102	66	2.59842	86	3.38582
7	.27559	27	1.06299	47	1.85039	67	2.63779	87	3.42519
8	.31496	28	1.10236	48	1.88976	68	2.67716	88	3.46456
9	.35433	29	1.14173	49	1.92913	69	2.71653	89	3.50393
10	.39370	30	1.18110	50	1.96850	70	2.75590	90	3.54330
11	.43307	31	1.22047	51	2.00787	71	2.79527	91	3.58267
12	.47244	32	1.25984	52	2.04724	72	2.83464	92	3.62204
13	.51181	33	1.29921	53	2.08661	73	2.87401	93	3.66141
14	.55118	34	1.33858	54	2.12598	74	2.91338	94	3.70078
15	.59055	35	1.37795	55	2.16535	75	2.95275	95	3.74015
16	.62992	36	1.41732	56	2.20472	76	2.99212	96	3.77952
17	.66929	37	1.45669	57	2.24409	77	3.03149	97	3.81889
18	.70866	38	.149606	58	2.28346	78	3.07086	98	3.85826
19	.74803	39	1.53543	59	2.32283	79	3.11023	99	3.89763
20	.78740	40	1.57480	60	2.36220	80	3.14960	100	3.93700

Decimal Equivalents
of 8th, 16ths, 32nds, 64ths of an inch

8ths	32nds	64ths	64ths
$^1/_8 = .125$	$^1/_{32} = .03125$	$^1/_{64} = .015625$	$^{33}/_{64} = .515625$
$^1/_4 = .250$	$^3/_{32} = .09375$	$^3/_{64} = .046875$	$^{35}/_{64} = .546875$
$^3/_8 = .375$	$^5/_{32} = .15625$	$^5/_{64} = .078125$	$^{37}/_{64} = .578125$
$^1/_2 = .500$	$^7/_{32} = .21875$	$^7/_{64} = .109375$	$^{39}/_{64} = .609375$
$^5/_8 = .625$	$^9/_{32} = .28125$	$^9/_{64} = .140625$	$^{41}/_{64} = .640625$
$^3/_4 = .750$	$^{11}/_{32} = .34375$	$^{11}/_{64} = .171875$	$^{43}/_{64} = .671875$
$^7/_8 = .875$	$^{13}/_{32} = .40625$	$^{13}/_{64} = .203125$	$^{45}/_{64} = .703125$
16ths	$^{15}/_{32} = .46875$	$^{15}/_{64} = .234370$	$^{47}/_{64} = .734375$
$^1/_{16} = .0625$	$^{17}/_{32} = .53125$	$^{17}/_{64} = .265625$	$^{49}/_{64} = .765625$
$^3/_{16} = .1875$	$^{19}/_{32} = .59375$	$^{19}/_{64} = .296875$	$^{51}/_{64} = .796875$
$^5/_{16} = .3125$	$^{21}/_{32} = .65625$	$^{21}/_{64} = .328125$	$^{53}/_{64} = .828125$
$^7/_{16} = .4375$	$^{23}/_{32} = .71875$	$^{23}/_{64} = .359375$	$^{55}/_{64} = .859375$
$^9/_{16} = .5625$	$^{25}/_{32} = .78125$	$^{25}/_{64} = .390625$	$^{57}/_{64} = .890625$
$^{11}/_{16} = .6875$	$^{27}/_{32} = .84375$	$^{27}/_{64} = .421875$	$^{59}/_{64} = .921875$
$^{13}/_{16} = .8125$	$^{29}/_{32} = .90625$	$^{29}/_{64} = .453125$	$^{61}/_{64} = .953125$
$^{15}/_{16} = .9375$	$^{31}/_{32} = .96875$	$^{31}/_{64} = .484375$	$^{63}/_{64} = .984375$

Decimal Equivalents of Letter Size Drills

Letter	Size of Drill in Inches	Letter	Size of Drill in Inches	Letter	Size of Drill in Inches	Letter	Size of Drill in Inches
A	.234	G	.261	M	.295	T	.358
B	.238	H	.266	N	.302	U	.368
C	.242	I	.272	O	.316	V	.377
D	.246	J	.277	P	.323	W	.386
E	.250	K	.281	Q	.332	X	.397
F	.257	L	.290	R	.339	Y	.404
				S	.348	Z	.413

Decimal Equivalents of Number Size Drills

No.	Size of Drill in Inches	No.	Size of Drill in Inches	No.	Size of Drill in Inches	No.	Size of Drill in Inches
1	.2280	21	.1590	41	.0960	61	.0390
2	.2210	22	.1570	42	.0935	62	.0380
3	.2130	23	.1540	43	.0890	63	.0370
4	.2090	24	.1520	44	.0860	64	.0360
5	.2055	25	.1495	45	.0820	65	.0350
6	.2040	26	.1470	46	.0810	66	.0330
7	.2010	27	.1440	47	.0785	67	.0320
8	.1990	28	.1405	48	.0760	68	.0310
9	.1960	29	.1360	49	.0730	69	.0292
10	.1935	30	.1285	50	.0700	70	.0280
11	.1910	31	.1200	51	.0670	71	.0260
12	.1890	32	.1160	52	.0635	72	.0250
13	.1850	33	.1130	53	.0595	73	.0240
14	.1820	34	.1110	54	.0550	74	.0225
15	.1800	35	.1100	55	.0520	75	.0210
16	.1770	36	.1065	56	.0465	76	.0200
17	.1730	37	.1040	57	.0430	77	.0180
18	.1695	38	.1015	58	.0420	78	.0160
19	.1660	39	.0995	59	.0410	79	.0145
20	.1610	40	.0980	60	.0400	80	.0135

Sizes of Tap Drills (Fractional)

Nominal Size of Tap in Inches	Threads Per Inch		Tap-Drill		Actual % Full Thread Tap-Drill Will Give
	NC	NF	Nominal Size	Decimal Equiv.	
$^1/_4$	20		#8	.1990	79
			#7	.2010	75
			$^{13}/_{64}''$	.2031	72
$^1/_4$		28	#3	.2130	80
			$^7/_{32}''$	.2187	67
$^5/_{16}$	18		F	.2570	77
			G	.2610	71
$^5/_{16}$		24	I	.2720	75
			J	.2770	66
$^3/_8$	16		$^5/_{16}''$	.3125	77
			O	.3160	73
$^3/_8$		24	Q	.3320	79
			R	.3390	67
$^7/_{16}$	14		U	.3680	75
			$^3/_8''$	.3750	67
$^7/_{16}$		20	W	.3860	79
			$^{25}/_{64}''$	.3906	72
			X	.3970	62
$^1/_2$	13		$^{27}/_{64}''$	.4219	78
			$^7/_{16}''$	.4375	62

Sizes of Tap Drills (Fractional)
(Continued)

Nominal Size of Tap in Inches	Threads Per Inch		Tap-Drill		Actual % Full Thread Tap-Drill Will Give
	NC	NF	Nominal Size	Decimal Equiv.	
$1/2$		20	$29/64''$	.4531	72
$9/16$	12		$31/64''$	.4844	72
$9/16$		18	$1/2''$	.5000	87
			$33/64''$	.5156	65
$5/8$	11		$17/32''$	.5312	79
			$35/64''$	.5469	66
$5/8$		18	$9/16''$	.5625	87
			$37/64''$	.5781	65
$3/4$	10		$41/64''$	.6406	84
			$21/32''$	.6562	72
$3/4$		16	$11/16''$	.6875	77
			$45/64''$	.7031	58
$7/8$	9		$49/64''$	.7656	76
			$25/32''$	.7812	65
$7/8$		14	$51/64''$	.7969	84
			$13/16''$	.8125	67
1	8		$7/8''$	.8750	77
			$57/64''$	.8906	67
1		14	$59/64''$	.9218	84
			$15/16''$	.9375	67

Machine Screw Sizes for Tap Drills

Nominal Size of Tap In Inches	Threads Per Inch		Tap-Drill		Actual % Full Thread Tap-Drill Will Give
	NC	NF	Nominal Size	Decimal Equiv.	
0		80	$3/64''$	.0469	81
1	64		#53	.0595	66
1		72	#53	.0595	75
2	56		#51	.0670	82
			#50	.0700	69
2		64	#50	.0700	79
			#49	.0730	64
3	48		$5/64''$	.0781	77
			#47	.0785	75
			#46	.0810	66
3		56	#46	.0810	78
4	40		#44	.0860	80
			#43	.0890	71
4		48	$3/32''$	.0937	68
5	40		#39	.0995	79
			#38	.1015	72
			#37	.1040	65
5		44	#37	.1040	71
			#36	.1065	63

Machine Screw Sizes for Tap Drills

(continued)

Nominal Size of Tap In Inches	Threads Per Inch		Tap-Drill		Actual % Full Thread Tap-Drill Will Give
	NC	NF	Nominal Size	Decimal Equiv.	
6	32		#36	.1065	78
			$7/64''$	.1094	70
			#33	.1130	62
6		40	#33	.1130	77
			#32	.1160	68
8	32		#29	.1360	69
8		36	#29	.1360	78
			$9/64''$	.1406	65
10	24		#26	.1470	79
			#24	.1520	70
10		32	$5/32''$	.1562	83
			#21	.1590	76
			#20	.1610	71
12	24		$11/64''$	.1719	82
			#17	.1730	79
			#16	.1770	72
			#15	.1800	67
12		28	#15	.1800	78
			$3/16''$	.1875	61

American National Special (N.S.) Screw Thread Pitches and Recommended Tap Drill Sizes

Sizes	Threads per Inch	Outside Diameter of Screw	Top Drill Sizes	Decimal Equivalent of Drill
1/4	24		4	0.2090
	27	0.250	3	.2130
	32		$7/32$	.2187
5/16	20		$17/64$	.2656
	27	.3125	J	.2770
	32		$9/32$	.2812
3/8	20	.375	$21/64$	.3281
	27		R	.3390
7/16	24	.4375	X	.3970
	27		Y	.4040
1/2	12		$27/64$	0.4219
	24	0.500	$29/64$	.4531
	27		$15/32$	.4687
9/16	27	.5625	$17/32$	.5312
5/8	12	.625	$35/64$	.5469
	27		$19/32$	.5937
3/4	12	.750	$43/64$	.7719
	27		$23/32$	.7187
7/8	12		$51/64$	.7969
	18	.875	$53/64$	.8281
	27		$27/32$	.8437
1	12	1.000	$59/64$	.9219
	27		$31/32$	.9687

Metric Drills and Decimal Equivalents

Diameter mm.	Diameter Inches	Diameter mm.	Diameter Inches	Diameter mm.	Diameter Inches
0.30	0.0118	1.75	0.0688	3.70	0.1456
0.35	0.0137	1.80	0.0708	3.75	0.1476
0.40	0.0157	1.85	0.0728	3.80	0.1496
0.45	0.0177	1.90	0.0748	3.90	0.1535
0.50	0.0196	1.95	0.0767	4.00	0.1574
0.55	0.0216	2.00	0.0787	4.10	0.1614
0.60	0.0236	2.05	0.0807	4.20	0.1653
0.65	0.0255	2.10	0.0826	4.25	0.1673
0.70	0.0275	2.15	0.0846	4.30	0.1692
0.75	0.0295	2.20	0.0866	4.40	0.1732
0.80	0.0314	2.25	0.0885	4.50	0.1771
0.85	0.0334	2.30	0.0905	4.60	0.1811
0.90	0.0354	2.35	0.0925	4.70	0.1850
0.95	0.0374	2.40	0.0944	4.75	0.1870
1.00	0.0393	2.45	0.0964	4.80	0.1889
1.05	0.0413	2.50	0.0984	4.90	0.1929
1.10	0.0433	2.60	0.1023	5.00	0.1968
1.15	0.0452	2.70	0.1063	5.10	0.2007
1.20	0.0472	2.75	0.1082	5.20	0.2047
1.25	0.0492	2.80	0.1102	5.25	0.2066
1.30	0.0511	2.90	0.1141	5.30	0.2086
1.35	0.0531	3.00	0.1181	5.40	0.2126
1.40	0.0551	3.10	0.1220	5.50	0.2165
1.45	0.0570	3.20	0.1259	5.60	0.2204
1.50	0.0590	3.25	0.1279	5.70	0.2244
1.55	0.0610	3.30	0.1299	5.75	0.2263
1.60	0.0629	3.40	0.1338	5.80	0.2283
1.65	0.0649	3.50	0.1378	5.90	0.2322
1.70	0.0669	3.60	0.1417	6.00	0.2362

(continued)

Diameter mm.	Diameter Inches	Diameter mm.	Diameter Inches	Diameter mm.	Diameter Inches
6.10	0.2401	7.50	0.2952	9.00	0.3453
6.20	0.2441	7.60	0.2992	9.10	0.3583
6.25	0.2460	7.70	0.3031	9.20	0.3622
6.30	0.2480	7.75	0.3051	9.25	0.3641
6.40	0.2519	7.80	0.3070	9.30	0.3661
6.50	0.2559	7.90	0.3110	9.40	0.3701
6.60	0.2598	8.00	0.3149	9.50	0.3740
6.70	0.2637	8.10	0.3228	9.60	0.3779
6.75	0.2657	8.20	0.3230	9.70	0.3818
6.80	0.2677	8.25	0.3248	9.75	0.3838
6.90	0.2716	8.30	0.3268	9.80	0.3858
7.00	0.2755	8.40	0.3307	10.00	0.3937
7.10	0.2795	8.50	0.3346	10.50	0.4133
7.20	0.2834	8.60	0.3385	11.00	0.4330
7.25	0.2854	8.70	0.3425	11.50	0.4527
7.30	0.2874	8.75	0.3444	12.00	0.4724
7.40	0.2913	8.80	0.3464	12.50	0.4921
		8.90	0.3504		

Cartridge Conversion
from Meters to Inches

Metric	Inches	Metric	Inches
4mm	.157480	7.7mm	.303149
4.3mm	.169291	7.8mm	.307086
4.5mm	.177165	7.9mm	.311023
5mm	.196850	7.91mm	.311416
5.5mm	.216535	7.92mm	.311809
5.6mm	.220470	8mm	.314960
6mm	.236220	8.15mm	.320855
6.35mm	.249999	9mm	.354330
6.5mm	.255905	9.1mm	.358267
7mm	.275590	9.3mm	.366141
7.5mm	.295275	9.5mm	.374015
7.56mm	.297637	10.35mm	.407479
7.6mm	.299212	10.75mm	.423227
7.62mm	.299998	11.15mm	.438965
7.63mm	.300093	11.2mm	.440940
7.65mm	.301180	11.25mm	.462201

Sectional Densities of Bullets
Popular weights in standard calibers.

Bullet	Sectional Density	Bullet	Sectional Density
22 CALIBER (.222″)		32 CALIBER (.321″)	
40 Gr.	.114	170 Gr.	.234
22 CALIBER (.223″)		8mm (.323″)	
45 Gr.	.128	150 Gr.	.206
22 CALIBER (.224″)		170 Gr.	.233
45 Gr.	.128	388 CALIBER (.338″)	
50 Gr.	.143	200 Gr.	.250
53 Gr.	.151	225 Gr.	.281
55 Gr.	.157	250 Gr.	.312
60 Gr.	.171	348 CALIBER (.348″)	
6mm (.243″)		200 Gr.	.236
70 Gr.	.169	35 CALIBER (.357″)	
75 Gr.	.181	165 Gr.	.247
87 Gr.	.210	168 Gr.	.253
100 Gr.	.241	170 Gr.	.257
25 CALIBER (.257″)		180 Gr.	.272
60 Gr.	.130	190 Gr.	.286
75 Gr.	.162	220 Gr.	.332
87 Gr.	.188	303 CALIBER (.312″)	
100 Gr.	.216	150 Gr.	.218
117 Gr.	.253	174 Gr.	.252
165 Gr.	.247	32 CALIBER (.321″)	
168 Gr.	.253	170 Gr.	.234
170 Gr.	.257	8mm (.323″)	
180 Gr.	.272	150 Gr.	.206
190 Gr.	.286	170 Gr.	.233
220 Gr.	.332	338 CALIBER (.338″)	
303 CALIBER (.312″)		200 Gr.	.250
150 Gr.	.218	225 Gr.	.281
174 Gr.	.252	250 Gr.	.312

Sectional Densities of Bullets (continued)

Bullet	Sectional Density	Bullet	Sectional Density
348 CALIBER (.348″)		44 CALIBER (.429″)	
200 Gr.	.236	240 Gr.	.186
35 CALIBER (.357″)		44 CALIBER (.430″)	
6.5mm (2.64″)		265 Gr.	.204
100 Gr.	.206	45 CALIBER (.452″)	
129 Gr.	.266	185 Gr.	.127
140 Gr.	.288	45 CALIBER (.454″)	
160 Gr.	.330	250 Gr.	.173
270 CALIBER (.277″)		45 CALIBER (.458″)	
100 Gr.	.186	300 Gr.	.206
130 Gr.	.242	350 Gr.	.243
150 Gr.	.279	500 Gr.	.347
7mm (.284″)		158 Gr.	.177
120 Gr.	.212	35 CALIBER (.358″)	
139 Gr.	.246	200 Gr.	.224
154 Gr.	.273	250 Gr.	.280
175 Gr.	.310	275 Gr.	.308
7.35mm (.300″)		375 CALIBER (.375″)	
128 Gr.	.202	270 Gr.	.275
30 CALIBER (.308″)		300 Gr.	.306
100 Gr.	.151	44 CALIBER (.429″)	
110 Gr.	.166	240 Gr.	.186
130 Gr.	.196		
150 Gr.	.227	44 CALIBER (.430″)	
158 Gr.	.177	265 Gr.	.204
35 CALIBER (.358″)		45 CALIBER (.452″)	
200 Gr.	.224	185 Gr.	.127
250 Gr.	.280	45 CALIBER (.454″)	
275 Gr.	.308	250 Gr.	.173
375 CALIBER (.375″)		45 CALIBER (.458″)	
270 Gr.	.275	300 Gr.	.206
300 Gr.	.306	350 Gr.	.243
		500 Gr.	.347

Capacities of Popular Cartridges

Capacities are measured to the base of a normally seated bullet in the instance of straight cases, and to the junction of neck and shoulder in bottle neck cases. Cubic capacity is determined by weighing amount of water case will hold, and calculating from that the volume in both cubic inches and cubic centimeters.

Case	Grains° Water	Cubic Inches	Cubic Cm.	Case	Grains° Water	Cubic Inches	Cubic Cm.
.22 Hornet (late)	11.4	.045	.739	.270 Winchester	62.9	.250	4.07
.22 K-Hornet	13.4	.053	.870	.280 Remington	61.9	.245	4.00
.218 Bee	14.8	.059	.960	.284 Winchester	62.4	.247	4.04
.222 Remington	23.8	.094	1.54	7mm Mauser	53.2	.211	3.45
.22 Rem. Mag.	28.8	.094	1.87	7mm Rem. Mag.	79.9	.317	5.17
.223 Remington	28.3	.112	1.84	.30 Carbine	15.0	.059	.972
.219 Wasp	27.0	.107	1.76	.30/30 Winchester	35.8	.142	2.32
.219 Zipper	33.0	.131	2.14	.30 Remington	37.0	.147	2.39
.224 Weatherby	35.8	.142	2.32	.300 Savage	46.3	.184	3.00
.225 Winchester	38.0	.151	2.46	.30/40 Krag	47.5	.188	3.08
.22/250 Remington	42.1	.167	2.73	.308 Winchester	49.8	.198	3.23
.220 Swift	44.6	.177	2.89	.30/06 Springfield	61.3	.242	3.98
.243 Winchester	50.6	.200	3.28	.300 H & H Mag.	80.0	.318	5.18
6mm Remington	51.5	.204	3.33	.308 Norma Mag.	81.2	.322	5.27
.25/20 Winchester	14.6	.058	.946	.300 Win. Mag.	83.6	.332	5.42
.25/35 Winchester	33.7	.134	2.18	.300 Weatherby	91.7	.364	5.91
.25 Remington	35.3	.140	2.28	.303 Savage	34.3	.136	2.22
.250 Savage	42.0	.166	2.72	.303 British	45.9	.182	2.97
257 Roberts	53.7	.213	3.46	7.65mm Arg.	52.4	.208	3.39
6.5mm Jap.	44.0	.174	2.85	.32/40	33.4	.132	2.16
6.5mm M-S	45.0	.179	2.91	.32 Win. Special	35.8	.142	2.32
6.5x55mm	51.9	.206	3.36	.32 Remington	37.0	.147	2.39
6.55mm Rem. Mag.	66.1	.260	4.27	8x57mm Mauser	53.6	.212	3.46
.264 Win. Mag.	79.8	.318	5.17	.338 Win. Mag.	78.6	.313	5.09

°The weight of water capacity given is simply a convenience of measurement—under no circumstances should this be interpreted as loading data or a charge recommendation for *any* powder. It is only a basis for comparison of case volume and bears no practical relationship to the amount of any particular powder that might constitute a safe load.

Capacities of Popular Cartridges (continued)

Case	Grains° Water	Cubic Inches	Cubic Cm.	Case	Grains° Water	Cubic Inches	Cubic Cm.
.348 Winchester	66.4	.263	4.30	.32 S & W Long	9.5	.037	.615
.358 Winchester	45.7	.182	2.96	.32/20 Winchester	15.3	.016	.992
.35 Remington	40.2	.159	2.60	.38 S & W	7.0	.028	.454
.350 Rem. Mag.	62.2	.246	4.03	.380 Auto	6.0	.024	.388
.375 H & H Mag.	85.7	.340	5.53	9mm Luger	8.7	.035	.562
.38/40 Winchester	33.8	.134	2.19	.38 Super Auto	10.7	.043	.691
.38/55	37.5	.149	2.43	.38 Special	11.7	.047	.758
.444 Marlin	54.0	.214	3.50	.357 Magnum	15.2	.060	.984
.45/70	48.7	.194	4.16	.41 Rem. Mag.	21.0	.083	1.36
.458 Winchester	68.0	.270	4.40	.44 S & W Russian	18.8	.075	1.22
				.44 S & W Special	20.5	.081	1.33
HANDGUNS				.44 Rem. Mag.	25.2	.100	1.63
.22 Remington Jet	16.9	.067	1.09	.44/40 Winchester	32.6	.129	2.11
.221 Rem. Fireball	20.8	.083	1.35	.45 Auto Rim	13.8	.053	.862
.256 Winchester	19.0	.075	1.23	.45 A.C.P.	13.9	.055	.900
.32 S & W	3.3	.012	.214	.45 Colt	30.3	.119	1.96

Computing Weight of Steel

Weight in Pounds of a Lineal Foot of Round, Square and Octagon Stock

Size in Inches	Round	Octagon	Square
$1/16$	.010	.011	.013
$1/8$	.042	.044	.053
$3/16$	.094	.099	.120
$1/4$	.168	.177	.214
$5/16$	.262	.277	.334
$3/8$	.378	.398	.481
$7/16$	.514	.542	.655
$1/2$	.671	.708	.855
$9/16$	.850	.896	1.082
$5/8$	1.049	1.107	1.336
$11/16$	1.270	1.339	1.616
$3/4$	1.511	1.594	1.924
$13/16$	1.773	1.870	2.258
$7/8$	2.056	2.169	2.618
$15/16$	2.361	2.490	3.006
1	2.686	2.833	3.420
$1\frac{1}{8}$	3.399	3.585	4.328
$1\frac{1}{4}$	4.197	4.427	5.344

Weights of Sheet Steel and Iron
U.S. Standard Gage

Gage Number	Approx. Thickness (Inches)	Pounds per Sq. Ft.		Gage Number	Approx. Thickness (Inches)	Pounds per Sq. Ft.	
		Steel	Iron			Steel	Iron
0000000	.5	20.4	20.	17	.05625	2.295	2.25
000000	.46875	19.125	18.75	18	.05	2.04	2.
00000	.4375	17.85	17.5	19	.04375	1.785	1.75
0000	.40625	16.575	16.25	20	.0375	1.53	1.5
000	.375	15.3	15.	21	.03438	1.403	1.375
00	.34375	14.025	13.75	22	.03125	1.275	1.25
0	.3125	12.75	12.5	23	.02813	1.148	1.125
1	.28125	11.475	11.25	24	.025	1.02	1.
2	.26563	10.838	10.625	25	.02188	.8925	.875
3	.25	10.2	10.	26	.01875	.765	.75
4	.23438	9.563	9.375	27	.10719	.7013	.6875
5	.21875	8.925	8.75	28	.01563	.6375	.625
6	.20313	8.288	8.125	29	.01406	.5738	.5625
7	.1875	7.65	7.5	30	.0125	.51	.5
8	.17188	7.013	6.875	31	.01094	.4463	.4375
9	.15625	6.375	6.25	32	.01016	.4144	.4063
10	.14063	5.738	5.625	33	.00938	.3825	.375
11	.125	5.1	5.	34	.00859	.3506	.3438
12	.10938	4.463	4.375	35	.00781	.3188	.3125
13	.09375	3.825	3.75	36	.00703	.2869	.2813
14	.07813	3.188	3.125	37	.00664	.2709	.2656
15	.07031	2.869	2.813	38	.00625	.255	.25
16	.0625	2.55	2.5				

Melting Points of Common Metals

Metal	° Fahr.	Metal	° Fahr.
Mercury	−38	Wrought Iron	2700—2750
Sulphur	236	Stainless Steel	2400—2700
Tin	450	Carbon Steel	2400—2750
Bismuth	520	Cast Iron	2100—2350
Cadmium	610	Cast Steel	2600—2750
Lead	621	Palladium	2820
Zinc	787	Zirconium	3090
Antimony	1166	Vanadium	3128
Magnesium	1204	Platinum	3191
Aluminum	1218	Molybdenum	4595
Silver	1761	Tantalum	5252
Gold	1945	Tungsten	6152
Copper	1981	Carbon	6332
Manganese	2300	Brass	1700—1850
Silicon	2588	Bronze	1675
Nickel	2646	Solder (50–50)	450
Cobalt	2696	Babbitt Metals	350—450
Chromium	2768	Zinc Die Casting Alloy	715—720
Pure Iron	2800		

Wire Nail Sizes

Size (d = penny)	Length (Inches)	Number per Pound
2-d	1	900
3-d	1¼	615
4-d	1½	322
5-d	1¾	250
6-d	2	200
7-d	2¼	154
8-d	2½	106
9-d	2¾	85
10-d	3	74
12-d	3¼	57
16-d	3½	46
20-d	4	29
30-d	4½	23
40-d	5	17
50-d	5½	13 +
60-d	6	10 +

English and Metric Pitches

COMMON ENGLISH PITCHES			COMMON METRIC PITCHES		
Threads per Inch	Pitch		Pitch		Threads per Inch
	Inches	mm.	mm.	Inches	
4	0.2500	6.350	8.0	0.3150	3.2
4½	.2222	5.644	7.5	.2953	3.4
5	.2000	5.080	7.0	.2756	3.6
6	.1667	4.233	6.5	.2559	3.9
7	.1429	3.629	6.0	.2362	4.2
7½	.1333	3.387	5.5	.2165	4.6
8	.1250	3.175	5.0	.1968	5.1
9	.1111	2.822	4.5	.1772	5.6
10	.1000	2.540	4.0	.1575	6.4
11	.0909	2.309	3.5	.1378	7.3
11½	.0870	2.209	3.0	.1181	8.5
12	.0833	2.117	2.5	.0984	10.2
13	.0769	1.954	2.0	.0787	12.7
14	.0714	1.814	1.75	.0689	14.5
16	.0625	1.588	1.50	.0591	16.9
18	.0556	1.411	1.25	.0492	20.3
20	.0500	1.270	1.00	.0394	25.4
24	.0417	1.058	.75	.0295	33.9
27	.0370	.941	.45	.0177	56.4
28	.0357	.907	.42	.0165	60.5
32	.0312	.794	.39	.0154	65.1
36	.0278	.706	.36	.0142	70.6
40	.0250	.635	.33	.0130	77
44	.0227	.577	.30	.0118	85
48	.0208	.529	.27	.0106	94
56	.0179	.454	.24	.0094	106
64	.0156	.397	.21	.0083	121
72	.0139	.353	.19	.0075	134
80	.0125	.318	.17	.0067	149
			.15	.0059	169
			.13	.0051	195
			.11	.0043	231

Diameter and Pitch of Metric Threads

Diameter of Screw mm.	Pitch mm.
3	0.5
4	0.75
5	0.75
6	1.0
7	1.0
8	1.0
8	1.25
9	1.0
9	1.25
10	1.5
11	1.5
12	1.5
12	1.75
14	2.0
16	2.0
18	2.5
20	2.5
22	2.5
22	3.0
24	3.0

Tapers
Various Diameters for Given Lengths

Length of Tapered Portion Inches	Taper per Foot-Inches					
	$1/16$	$3/32$	$1/8$	$1/4$	$3/8$	$1/2$
$1/32$	.0002	.0002	.0003	.0007	.0010	.0013
$1/16$	.0003	.0005	.0007	.0013	.0020	.0026
$1/8$	.0007	.0010	.0013	.0026	.0039	.0052
$3/16$	.0010	.0015	.0020	.0039	.0059	.0078
$1/4$	.0013	.0020	.0026	.0052	.0078	.0104
$5/16$	.0016	.0024	.0033	.0065	.0098	.0130
$3/8$	.0020	.0029	.0039	.0078	.0117	.0156
$7/16$	.0023	.0034	.0046	.0091	.0137	.0182
$1/2$	.0026	.0039	.0052	.0104	.0156	.0208
$9/16$	.0029	.0044	.0059	.0117	.0176	.0234
$5/8$	.0033	.0049	.0065	.0130	.0195	.0260
$11/16$	.0036	.0054	.0072	.0143	.0215	.0286
$3/4$	.0039	.0059	.0078	.0156	.0234	.0312
$13/16$	.0042	.0063	.0085	.0169	.0254	.0339
$7/8$	.0046	.0068	.0091	.0182	.0273	.0365
$15/16$	.0049	.0073	.0098	.0195	.0293	.0391
1	.0052	.0078	.0104	.0208	.0312	.0417
2	.0104	.0156	.0208	.0417	.0625	.0833
3	.0156	.0234	.0312	.0625	.0937	.1250
4	.0208	.0312	.0417	.0833	.1250	.1667

Length of Tapered Portion Inches	Taper per Foot-Inches					
	$1/16$	$3/32$	$1/8$	$1/4$	$3/8$	$1/2$
5	.0260	.0391	.0521	.1042	.1562	.2083
6	.0312	.0469	.0625	.1250	.1875	.2500
7	.0365	.0547	.0729	.1458	.2187	.2917
8	.0417	.0625	.0833	.1667	.2500	.3333
9	.0469	.0703	.0937	.1875	.2812	.3750
10	.0521	.0781	.1042	.2083	.3125	.4167
11	.0573	.0859	.1146	.2292	.3437	.4583
12	.0625	.0937	.1250	.2500	.3750	.5000
13	.0677	.1016	.1354	.2708	.4062	.5417
14	.0729	.1094	.1458	.2917	.4375	.5833
15	.0781	.1172	.1562	.3125	.4687	.6250
16	.0833	.1250	.1667	.3333	.5000	.6667
17	.0885	.1328	.1771	.3542	.5312	.7083
18	.0937	.1406	.1875	.3750	.5625	.7500
19	.0990	.1484	.1979	.3958	.5937	.7917
20	.1042	.1562	.2083	.4167	.6250	.8333
21	.1094	.1641	.2187	.4375	.6562	.8750
22	.1146	.1719	.2292	.4583	.6875	.9167
23	.1198	.1797	.2396	.4792	.7187	.9583
24	.1250	.1875	.2500	.5000	.7500	1.0000

Tap Sizes for Taper Pipe

Tap Size Inches	Threads per Inch NPT	Drill Size Inches
$\frac{1}{8}$	27	$\frac{11}{32}$
$\frac{1}{4}$	18	$\frac{7}{16}$
$\frac{3}{8}$	18	$\frac{37}{64}$
$\frac{1}{2}$	14	$\frac{23}{32}$
$\frac{3}{4}$	14	$\frac{59}{64}$
1	$11\frac{1}{2}$	$1\frac{5}{32}$
$1\frac{1}{4}$	$11\frac{1}{2}$	$1\frac{1}{2}$
$1\frac{1}{2}$	$11\frac{1}{2}$	$1\frac{47}{64}$
2	$11\frac{1}{2}$	$2\frac{7}{32}$
$2\frac{1}{2}$	8	$2\frac{5}{8}$
3	8	$3\frac{1}{4}$
$3\frac{1}{2}$	8	$3\frac{3}{4}$
4	8	$4\frac{1}{4}$

Weights and Measures

Following are tables of weights and measures that are frequently required in hand-loading problems that arise.

"Metric" and "U.S." Constants—Conversion Factors

Millimeters	x	.03937	Inches
"	x	25.4	"
Centimeters	x	.3937	"
"	x	2.54	"
Meters	x	39.37	" (Act of Congress)
"	x	3.281	Feet
"	x	1.094	Yard
Square mm.	x	.0155	Square Inches
" "	x	645.1	" "
Square cm.	x	.155	" "
" "	x	6.451	" "
Cubic cm.	x	16.383	Cubic Inches
" "	x	3.69	Fluid drachms
" "	x	29.57	Fluid ounces
Grams	x	15.4324	Grains (Act of Congress)
" (water)	x	29.57	Fluid ounces
Grams	x	28.35	Ounces avoirdupois
Kilograms	x	2.2046	Pounds
"	x	35.3	Ounces avoirdupois
Kilograms per sq. cm. (Atmosphere)	x	14.223	Pounds per sq. in.
Kilogrammeters	x	7.233	Foot-pounds

Measures of Weight

AVOIRDUPOIS OR COMMERCIAL WEIGHT

1 gross or long ton equals 2240 pounds.

1 net or short ton equals 2000 pounds.

1 pound equals 16 ounces equals 7000 grains.

1 ounce equals 16 drachms equals 437.5 grains.

The following measures for weight are now seldom used in the United States:

1 hundredweight equals 4 quarters equals 112 pounds (1 gross of long ton equals 20 hundredweights); 1 quarter equals 28 pounds; 1 stone equals 14 pounds; 1 quintal equals 100 pounds.

TROY WEIGHT, USED FOR WEIGHING GOLD AND SILVER

1 pound equals 12 ounces 5760 grains.

1 ounce equals 20 pennyweights equals 480 grains.

1 pennyweight equals 24 grains.

1 carat (used in weighing diamonds) equals 3.168 grains.

1 grain Troy equals 1 grain avoirdupois equals 1 grain apothecaries' weight.

APOTHECARIES' WEIGHT

1 pound equals 12 ounces equals 5760 grains.

1 ounce equals 8 drachms equals 480 grains.

1 drachm equals 3 scriples equals 60 grains.

1 scruple equals 20 grains.

Index

Barrels *(continued)*
  cleaning, 134–135
  lapping, 138–139
  revolvers, 104–105
  shotguns, 121
  supply sources, 299
  threading, 263
Basement storage, 2
Bedding:
  accurizing, 194–196
  bolt-action centerfire rifle stocks:
    barrel, 62–64
    glass, 60–61
    receiver, 55, 59
  lever-action rifles, 78
  M-1 Garand rifle, 198–200
Belt sander, 251, 261, 290
Bench grinder, 4, 37, 211–212, 251
Benzine, 289–290
Bishop, E. C., 214
Bisonite, 55, 194
Bits, drill, 35, 37, 49–50
Black-powder arms, *see* Muzzle-loading arms
Blow-back autoloader, 12
Blueing, 258–259, 269–270
Bolt action, 10–11
Bolt-action center-fire rifles, 51–74
  accurizing, 192–203
  adjusting or replacing dovetail
    sights, 52–53
  barrel bedding, 62–64
  bolt maintenance, 72–74
  cleaning, 18, 20, 22, 72–73
  glass bedding, 60–61
  inletting stock for trigger guard
    assembly, 54, 56–58
  receiver bedding, 55, 59
  safety in handling, *xii*
  trigger adjustment, 65–70
Bore, ammonia treatment, 16–19
Bore-sighting, 182–184
Brass hammers, 4
Brazing, 266–268

Break-open pistols, 111
Break-open revolvers, 102–103
Brothers, George, 216
Brownell, Bob, 260
Browning, of muzzle-loading arms,
  150–156, 261
Bullet-point protectors, 278

Cabinet scraper, 221
Cap-lock revolver, 130
Carbonizing agents, 254
Cartridges, dummy, 82, 83
Case-hardening, 99, 100
Checkering, 225–239
  cradle, 227, 229, 230
  twelve-step clinic, 232–236
Cheekpieces, 241
Chemegron Corporation, 288
Chisels, 38, 43–45
Christy Gun Works, 118, 260
Cleaning, 15–34
  ammonia bore treatment, 16–19
  autoloading arms, 22–27, 111
  barrels, 16–19, 27, 30–33, 80, 88,
    104–105, 134–135, 260
  bolt-action center-fire rifles, 18, 20,
    22, 72–73
  handguns, 15, 18, 27–31, 33,
    104–105, 134–135
  lever-action arms, 22–27
  pump-action arms, 22–27
  rimfire rifles, 88
  scope lenses, 173
  shotguns, 20, 31
  single-shot arms, 20
  solvents, 22–27, 289–290
CO_2 rifles and pistols, 161–163
Colt .45 military pistol, 14
Colt revolvers, 90–95, 101
Copper solders, 269

Disk sander, 249